D1560583

Quick & Easy

Christmas Bazaar Crafts

QUICK & EASY
Christmas Bazaar Crafts

JIM WILLIAMS

Rodale Press, Inc.
Emmaus, Pennsylvania

OUR MISSION

We publish books that empower people's lives.

RODALE  BOOKS

The author and editors who compiled this book have tried to make all of the contents as accurate and as correct as possible. Illustrations, photographs, and text have all been carefully checked and cross-checked. However, due to the variability of local conditions, craft materials, personal skill, and so on, neither the author nor Rodale Press assumes any responsibility for any injuries suffered or for damages or other losses incurred that result from the material presented herein. All instructions and illustrations should be carefully studied and clearly understood before beginning any project.

Printed in the United States of America on acid-free ∞, recycled ♻ paper, containing 15 percent post-consumer waste

QUICK AND EASY CHRISTMAS BAZAAR CRAFTS
EDITORIAL STAFF
EDITOR: Karen Bolesta
COVER AND BOOK DESIGNER: Marta Mitchell Strait
ILLUSTRATORS: Glenn Hughes, Nita Hughes, and Charles Metz
CHARTIST: Lisa Wiener
PHOTOGRAPHERS: Michael Watson and John Hamel (page 216)
PHOTO STYLIST: Jim Williams
STUDIO MANAGER: Mary Ellen Fanelli
COPY EDITOR: Ann Snyder
EDITORIAL ASSISTANCE: Stephanie Snyder
MANUFACTURING COORDINATOR: Jodi Schaffer

RODALE BOOKS
EDITORIAL DIRECTOR, HOME AND GARDEN: Margaret Lydic Balitas
SENIOR EDITOR, CRAFT BOOKS: Cheryl Winters Tetreau
ART DIRECTOR, HOME AND GARDEN: Michael Mandarano
COPY DIRECTOR, HOME AND GARDEN: Dolores Plikaitis
OFFICE MANAGER, HOME AND GARDEN: Karen Earl-Braymer
EDITOR-IN-CHIEF: William Gottlieb

If you have any questions or comments concerning this book, please write to:

Rodale Press, Inc.
Book Readers' Service
33 East Minor Street
Emmaus, PA 18098

Library of Congress Cataloging-in-Publication Data

Williams, Jim, date
Quick and easy Christmas bazaar crafts / Jim Williams.
p. cm.
ISBN 0-87596-691-8 (hardcover : alk. paper)
1. Christmas decorations. 2. Handicraft. I. Title.
TT900.C4W53 1995
745.594'12—dc20 95-13805

Distributed in the book trade by St. Martin's Press

2 4 6 8 10 9 7 5 3 1 hardcover

To the four women who have influenced my life:
my grandmother Dorothea, for many loving memories;
my mother, Betty, for her support and guidance;
my wife, Lynn, for her untold patience, love, and understanding;
my daughter, Talathy, for being a delightful and talented young lady whom I dearly cherish.

Contents

Get Ready for Christmas

Gifts from Heaven and Earth

Victorian Elegance

For Kids of All Ages

Bazaar Gifts with a Natural Touch

Successful Bazaar Secrets

Introduction

Jim with his wife, Lynn, and daughter, Talathy

Crafting Christmas Memories

The Christmas holidays have always been special to me. It's not the number of presents I received as a child or the lavish decorations and crafts we made each year that I remember, but the simple, and, I suppose, quite ordinary things that come to mind now as I sit down to write.

A Childhood Remembered

As a kid growing up in the fifties in upstate New York, I remember snowy white winters—ones where the lake-effect snow from Lake Ontario could dump two to three feet in one kerplop. This meant lots of shoveling and lots of outdoor fun.

I always enjoyed the annual trek to the nearby hillside farm to cut down our Christmas tree. Our family looked through rows of trees for that very special tree. The tree farmer, who also happened to be our dentist and father's good friend, would hitch up the pony to drag our tree back over the snow-covered fields and through hedgerows and fences to our car. Once home, we squeezed the tree through the front door to take its place of honor. Once the tree was standing in its chosen spot, it was ready for me to decorate, with help from my younger brothers.

A Budding Crafter

Early on, I had an affinity for making things, but two of my early crafted ornaments stand out in my mind. The first was a treetop angel, appropriately dubbed "Gloria." She was resplendent in her simple paper cone gown, Styrofoam head, and her tresses of silver tinsel hair, her crowning glory, so to speak. The second memorable project was a set of small drums crafted from cardboard tubes, scraps of felt, and some of my grandfather's old poker chips. The cardboard drums were a bit more involved than Gloria and required more planning and skill.

Special, too, was another simple Christmas tradition in which we took part. The church bazaar was a regular event that signaled the start of the holidays when I was younger. Upon entering the church basement, we knew we would find all sorts of holiday goodies, ornaments, and crafts. In fact, one of my very first purchases was a cardboard ice cream carton-turned-waste can with a Currier and Ives winter print. For some reason, that particular item appealed to me—perhaps it was the snowy scene and winter activity that reminded me of the Christmases I so loved.

A Career with Crafts

I went on to study art and to teach arts and crafts in high school for ten years. With my wife, Lynn, and daughter, Talathy, we began to establish our own Christmas traditions. I wanted to provide my daughter with very special Christmases each year—ones that would flood her memory bank with happy, creative times.

Each year the tree took on a different theme—dramatic red and silver, country blue with blue gingham bows, or all-white, dripping with pearls and lace. But there were always spaces for those special ornaments that Talathy had crafted, ornaments that I hold dear to my heart to this day. Her nursery school plaster handprint requires a sturdy branch each year and the adorable bride and groom ornaments she crafted from clothespins always find a proud spot at eye level. Add to that the clamshell men she made from shells gathered on trips to Cape Cod and a fat, crayoned cardinal that's surprisingly realistic.

My own crafting took on the form of needlepoint pillows and rugs, and, of course, a needlepoint Christmas stocking for Talathy that Santa still fills each year. In my own work, I was intrigued by the textures of stitches and colors of yarn, and strived to achieve intricate pieces that would span the gap between crafts and art. I began to sell my needlework pieces in galleries and my original designs to magazines and books.

Crafts became an even more integral part of my life when we moved to the Midwest, and I took an entry-level crafts editor position with Meredith Corporation. Here, my crafts design and photo-styling abilities blossomed with the various aspects of the job. In a short time, I found myself working on crafts and Christmas decorating for their major publication, *Better Homes and Gardens.* When I was fortunate enough to become their executive crafts and Christmas editor, Christmas was soon a year-round affair. When we weren't celebrating it with a 14-foot ornament-laden tree each year in our vaulted family room, I was producing one of the annual features for the magazine—designing, crafting, organizing, and directing photography in locations all over the country. In addition, I was planning and designing for the magazine's monthly features and for its popular "100 Ideas under $100" issue, a long-time source for crafters and bazaar participants.

Style, Imagination, and Warm, Lasting Memories

A move to New York City and the prospects of freelance crafts design for various publications has immersed me even further into the crafts world and Christmas. Producing this book and developing the crafts within it have given me an opportunity to further develop easy-to-make crafts that have a sense of style and heirloom quality that will attract the eye of crafters and craft lovers alike.

On these pages you'll find dozens of quick and easy crafts, as well as some slightly more time-consuming ones, that you can make for your own enjoyment as well as to offer at your bazaar for the enjoyment of others. You will also find tips for selling your craft creations at local bazaars and advice on starting a sale of your own for your favorite association, church group, or local charity.

Search through these fun-filled chapters for projects that you and your family can create together. There are plenty of easy ornaments, toys, wearables, and accessories for the home to provide hours of family pleasure and warm, lasting Christmas memories of your own.

HAPPY HOLIDAYS!

Jim Williams

JINGLE BELLS
arr. Lowell E. Shaw
Horn 1 in F
Fast
(mute)
muted
(open)
Ho
Ho

Get Ready for Christmas

Jump on the holiday bandwagon and get an early start crafting these Christmas toys, gifts, and trims for your bazaar or benefit. Each of the projects in this chapter will bring full-spirited holiday fun.

Favorite Yuletide Trims

These charming country stitcheries signal the season with traditional colors and themes. The perky Felt Cardinal, the Ho Ho Ho Ornament, and the Holly Wreath Ornament each beckon to be hung among fragrant pine boughs.

Felt Cardinal

Size

6 inches tall

What You Do

1. Enlarge the **Felt Cardinal Patterns** as directed in "Enlarging Patterns" on page 238.

2. From the felt, cut two bodies, two tails, and one gusset.

3. Using a ¼-inch seam allowance and referring to the **Body Diagram,** sew the bodies together, sewing from the large dot under the beak, around the top of the head, and down the back to the tail area. Also sew from the small dot at the derriere up to the tail area. Leave the straight edge of the tail open.

Body Diagram

4. Sew the gusset to one side of the body, matching the large and small dots and easing in any fullness. Leave the other side open for stuffing.

5. Turn the cardinal to the right side and stuff. Slip-stitch the gusset closed.

6. Using a 1/4-inch seam allowance, sew the tail pieces together, leaving an opening at the bottom. Turn the tail to the right side, but do not stuff it.

7. Slip the tail over the tail opening of the body, overlapping the edges by 1/2 inch; slip-stitch the tail in place.

8. Sew the seed bead eyes in place where indicated on the pattern, pulling the thread tightly to indent the eye area.

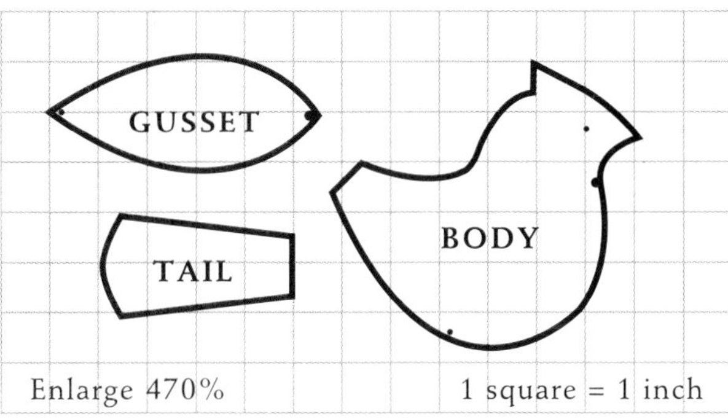

FELT CARDINAL PATTERNS

What You Need

Felt Cardinal

- 9 × 12-inch piece of red felt for the cardinal
- Matching sewing thread
- Polyester fiberfill
- 2 black seed beads for the eyes

Ho Ho Ho Ornament

- 10-inch square of 11-count white Aida
- One skein of embroidery floss for each color in the **Color Key**
- Size 22 or 24 tapestry needle
- 8-inch circle of fusible fleece
- 6-inch circle of cardboard for the base
- Hot glue gun and glue sticks
- 8-inch length of 1/4-inch-wide red satin ribbon for the hanger
- 3/4 yard of 1/2-inch-diameter red upholstery cord
- Cellophane tape
- 6-inch circle of red felt for the backing

Ho Ho Ho Ornament

Size

6 inches in diameter

What You Do

1. Zigzag the edges of the Aida to prevent raveling. Find the center of the Aida and mark it with a pin. Find the center of the **Ho Ho Ho Ornament Chart** on page 4 by connecting the arrows.

2. Matching the centers of the chart and the Aida, cross-stitch the design using three strands of floss.

3. Using two strands of floss, backstitch the flower stems with ultra dark pistachio green.

4. Wash and press the completed cross-stitch as directed in "Washing and Pressing" on page 241.

5. Trim the Aida to an 8-inch circle, centering the cross-stitch design. Clip the seam allowance all around the circle at 1 1/2-inch intervals, making each cut about 3/4 inch deep.

6. Glue the fleece to the cardboard circle base. With the right side out and the design centered, stretch the cross-stitch over the fleece-covered circle; glue the excess cloth to the back of the cardboard, overlapping the clipped edges as necessary to create a smooth finish.

7. Fold the ribbon hanger in half and glue it to the back of the covered circle.

8. Starting behind the ribbon, glue the cord around the edge of the ornament, securing the cord ends with cellophane tape.

9. Glue the felt backing in place.

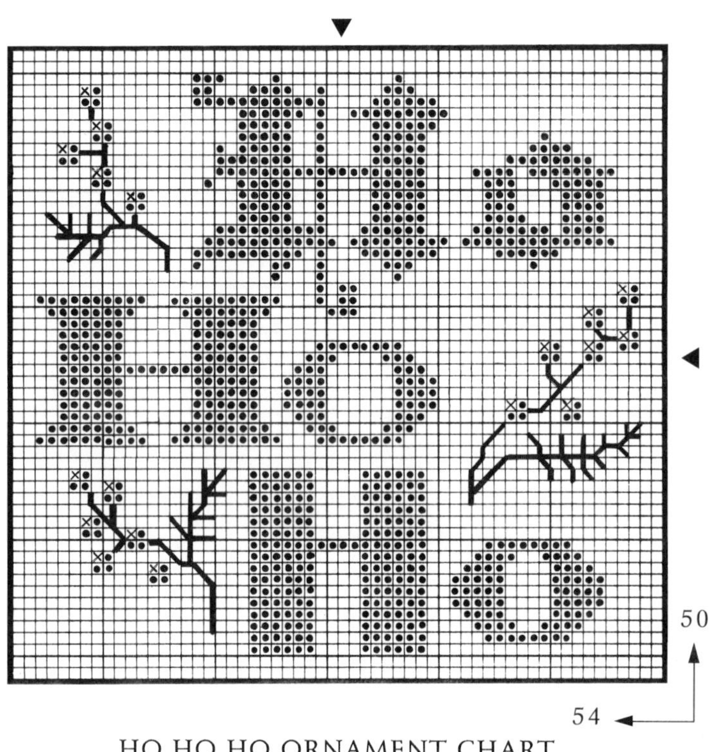

HO HO HO ORNAMENT CHART

HO HO HO ORNAMENT COLOR KEY

	DMC	Anchor	J. & P. Coats	Color
●	321	9046	3500	Christmas Red
×	986	246	6021	Ultra Dk. Pistachio Green

PROJECT POINTERS

The stunning Felt Cardinal on page 2 can be made into an ornament as well, eliminating a few sewing steps. Enlarge the ***Felt Cardinal Ornament Pattern*** *as directed in "Enlarging Patterns" on page 238. From red felt, cut two bodies and two wings using pinking shears. Place one wing on each body where indicated on the pattern, adding a dab of glue to the wrong side of the wing to secure it. Topstitch around each wing, using the sewing lines on the pattern as a guide. Sew one seed bead eye on each bird where indicated on the pattern. Fold a 6-inch length of red satin ribbon in half to form a loop and glue it to the wrong side of one bird. With wrong sides facing and using the sewing lines on the pattern as a guide, topstitch the birds together to create an ornament. No gusset, no stuffing, no fuss!*

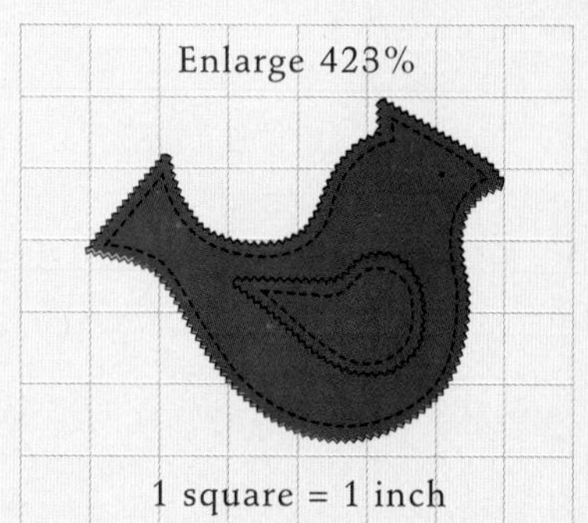

FELT CARDINAL ORNAMENT PATTERN

Holly Wreath Ornament

SIZE

6 inches in diameter

WHAT YOU NEED

HOLLY WREATH ORNAMENT

- 10-inch square of 11-count white Aida
- One skein of embroidery floss for each color in the **Color Key**
- Size 22 or 24 tapestry needle
- 6-inch circle of cardboard for the base
- Hot glue gun and glue sticks
- 8-inch length of ⅜-inch-wide red satin ribbon for the hanger
- ¾ yard of ½-inch-wide white rickrack for the edging
- 6-inch circle of red felt for the backing

WHAT YOU DO

1. Zigzag the edges of the Aida to prevent raveling. Find the center of the Aida and mark it with a pin. Find the center of the **Holly Wreath Ornament Chart** by connecting the arrows.

2. Matching the centers of the chart and the Aida, cross-stitch the design using three strands of floss.

3. Wash and press the completed cross-stitch as directed in "Washing and Pressing" on page 241.

4. Trim the Aida to an 8-inch circle, centering the cross-stitch wreath. Clip the seam allowance all around the circle at 1½-inch intervals, making each cut about ¾ inch deep.

5. With the right side out and the design centered, stretch the cross-stitch over the cardboard circle base; glue the excess cloth to the back of the cardboard, overlapping the clipped edges as necessary to create a smooth finish.

6. Fold the ribbon in half to form a loop and glue it to the back of the covered circle for a hanger.

7. Starting behind the ribbon, glue the rickrack to the back edge of the covered circle so half of the rickrack width extends beyond the edge of the circle.

8. Glue the felt backing in place.

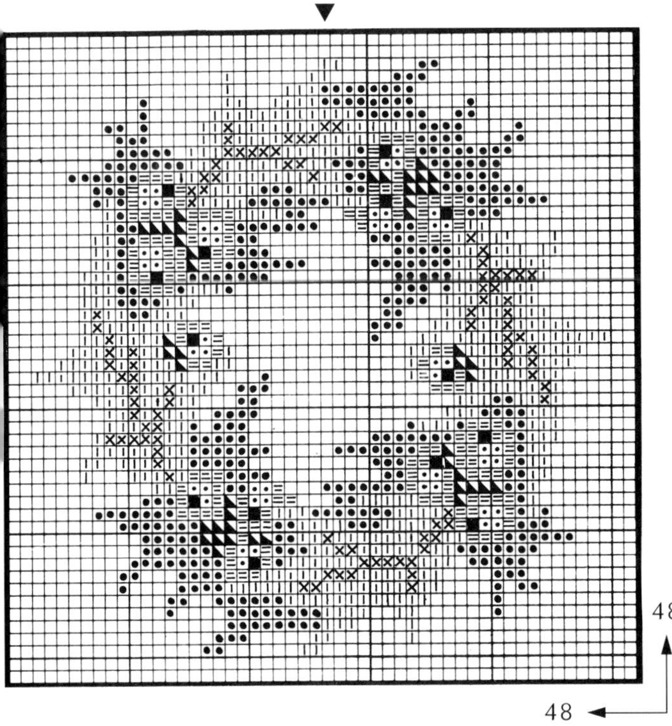

HOLLY WREATH ORNAMENT CHART

HOLLY WREATH ORNAMENT COLOR KEY

	DMC	Anchor	J. & P. Coats	Color
■	310	403	8403	Black
◣	347	1025	3013	Very Dk. Salmon
×	703	238	6238	Bright Chartreuse
=	891	35	3012	Very Dk. Carnation
ǀ	907	255	6001	Lt. Parrot Green
●	909	923	6228	Christmas Green
•	3706	33	3152	Lt. Carnation

Holiday Baby Bibs

The machine-appliquéd Snowman, Santa, and Christmas Tree bibs will deck little revelers in holiday style. Just in time for baby's first Christmas, these novelty bibs will catch the eye of gift-givers everywhere.

Snowman Bib

Size
8¾ × 14 inches

What You Need

Snowman Bib

- ⅜ yard of muslin for the bib
- ⅜ yard of light blue print fabric for the sky and tie
- 1 yard of fusible web
- ¼ yard of white-on-white print fabric for the snowman
- ¼ yard of cream print fabric for the snowbank
- Scrap of black solid fabric for the hat
- ⅜ yard of tear-away stabilizer
- Matching sewing thread
- One skein of orange embroidery floss for the carrot nose
- Sharp embroidery needle
- Nine ¼-inch-diameter black buttons for the "coal" eyes, mouth, and buttons

What You Do

1. Enlarge the **Snowman Bib Patterns** on page 8 as directed in "Enlarging Patterns" on page 238.

2. From the muslin, cut one bib for the base and one bib reverse for the backing. From the blue, cut one 1 × 36-inch bias strip for the tie, as directed in "Cutting Bias Strips" on page 238.

3. Following the manufacturer's directions, fuse the fusible web to the blue, the white, the cream, and the black. Trace the mirror image, or reverse, of each appliqué onto the paper side of the fusible web, then cut it out as follows: From the blue, cut one sky. From the white, cut one small snowball, one medium snowball, and one large snowball. From the cream, cut one left snowbank and one right snowbank. From the black, cut one left hat brim, one right hat brim, and one hat. Remove the paper backing from the appliqué pieces.

4. Referring to the **Appliqué Placement Diagram,** arrange the appliqués on the bib base, layering them as indicated by the dashed lines; omit the hat at this point. Fuse the appliqués in place, following the manufacturer's directions.

Appliqué Placement Diagram

5. Center and pin the tear-away stabilizer to the back of the appliquéd bib base. Using matching thread and a closely spaced zigzag stitch, machine appliqué all edges of the appliqués, including the outer bib edges. Machine appliqué the twig arms with black thread as indicated by the thin lines on the sky pattern. Carefully remove the stabilizer by tearing it away.

6. With right sides together and raw edges even, sew the appliquéd bib base to the muslin bib backing around the machine-appliquéd outer edge, leaving the neck edge open for turning. Clip the curves and trim the seam allowance. Turn the bib to the right side and press well.

7. Fold under ¼ inch along both long edges of the tie and press well. Open out one long edge. With the right sides together, center and pin the tie to the neck edge, aligning the opened-out edge of the tie with the raw neck edge. Using a ¼-inch seam allowance, sew the tie in place. Fold the tie to the back of the bib, then slip-stitch it in place along the neck edge. Topstitch the folded edges of the tie ends closed. Knot each tie end.

8. Fuse the hat in place, overlapping a small portion of the bias tie. Machine appliqué around the hat using black thread.

9. Referring to the **Embellishment Diagram** and using the embroidery needle, satin stitch the nose with orange floss. Sew on the "coal" buttons as follows: two for the eyes, four for the mouth, and three for the buttons down the front.

Embellishment Diagram

BIB AND BIB REVERSE
SMALL SNOWBALL
SKY
LARGE SNOWBALL
LEFT SNOWBANK
RIGHT SNOWBANK
MEDIUM SNOWBALL
HAT
LEFT HAT BRIM
RIGHT HAT BRIM

Enlarge 373%

1 square = 1 inch

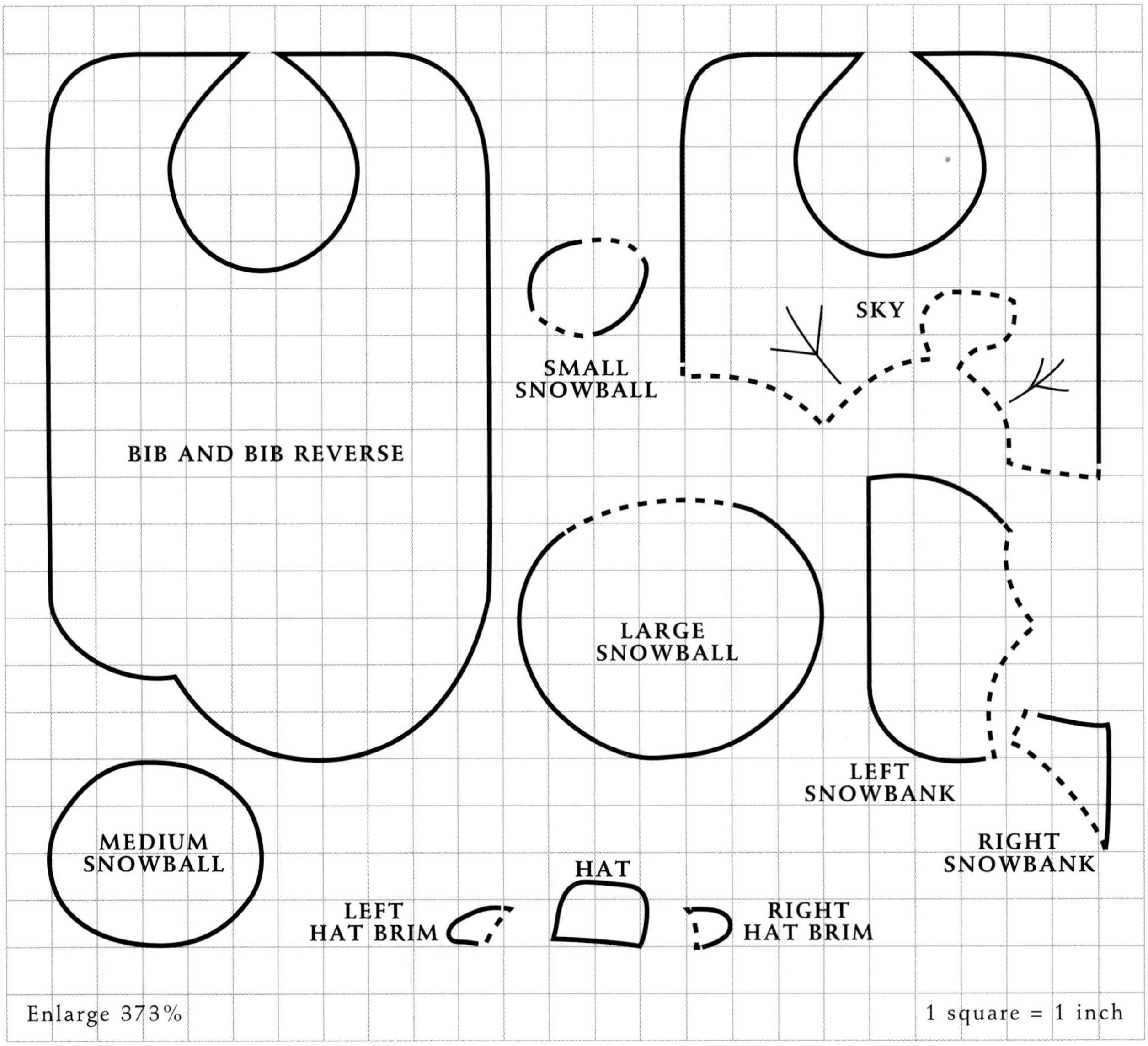

SNOWMAN BIB PATTERNS

Santa Bib

Size

$10\frac{1}{2} \times 15$ inches

What You Do

1. Enlarge the **Santa Bib Patterns** on page 10 as directed in "Enlarging Patterns" on page 238.

2. From the muslin, cut two bibs, one for the base and one for the backing. From the red, cut one left hat and one left hat reverse, and one right hat and one right hat reverse.

3. Following the manufacturer's directions, fuse the fusible web to the white, the pale pink, the pink, the green, and the ecru. Trace the mirror image, or reverse, of each appliqué onto the paper side of the fusible web, then cut it out as follows: From the white, cut one beard and one mustache. From the pale pink, cut one face. From the pink, cut one nose and one lip. From the green, cut two holly leaves. From the ecru, cut one hat brim. Remove the paper backing from the appliqués.

4. Referring to the **Appliqué Placement Diagram,** arrange the appliqués on the bib base, layering the appliqués as indicated by the dashed lines and omitting the upper holly leaf at this point. Fuse the appliqués in place, following the manufacturer's directions.

What You Need

Santa Bib

- $\frac{3}{8}$ yard of muslin for the bib
- $\frac{1}{4}$ yard of red solid fabric for the hat
- 1 yard of fusible web
- $\frac{1}{4}$ yard of woven white terry cloth for the beard and mustache
- Scraps of pale pink and pink solid fabrics for the face, nose, and lip
- Scrap of green print fabric for the holly
- 4×12-inch piece of black-on-ecru print fabric for the hat brim
- $\frac{1}{2}$ yard of tear-away stabilizer
- Matching sewing thread
- One skein of black embroidery floss for the eyes
- Sharp embroidery needle
- Three $\frac{1}{2}$-inch-diameter red shank buttons for the holly berries
- Velcro dot fastener
- 2-inch-diameter white pom-pom

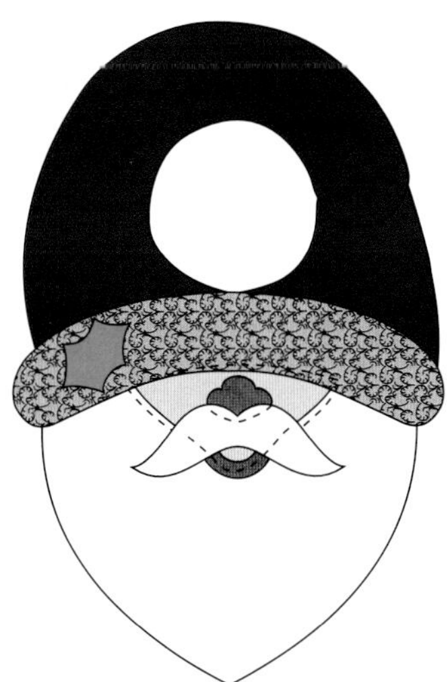

Appliqué Placement Diagram

5. Center and pin an 11-inch square of tear-away stabilizer to the back of the appliquéd bib base. Using matching thread and a closely spaced zigzag stitch, machine appliqué the edges of the appliqués, including the outer bib edges (except for the upper hat brim edge). Also machine appliqué the vein in the holly leaf as indicated on the pattern. Remove the stabilizer by tearing it away. Set the appliquéd bib base aside.

6. With right sides together and raw edges even, sew the left hats together, leaving the bottom edge open. Clip the curves and turn to the right side. Press. Repeat for the right hats.

7. With right sides together and raw edges even, sew the appliquéd bib base to the muslin bib backing around the machine-appliquéd outer edge, using a ¼-inch seam allowance; leave the entire top edge open for turning. Clip the curves and trim the seam allowance. Turn the bib to the right side and press.

8. Insert the hat pieces between the bib base and bib backing so the raw edges of the hat extend about ½ inch inside. Pin the hat pieces to the appliquéd bib only. Center and pin a 6 × 11-inch piece of tear-away stabilizer to the back of the hat brim and holly leaf. Keeping the bib backing loose, machine appliqué the upper hat brim edge.

9. Fuse the remaining holly leaf in place and machine appliqué around it. Also machine appliqué the vein in the holly leaf. Remove the stabilizer by tearing it away.

10. Slip-stitch the bib opening closed.

11. Referring to the **Embellishment Diagram** and using the embroidery needle, satin stitch the eyes with black floss. Sew the three buttons in place for the holly berries. Sew one part of the Velcro fastener to the inside of each neck overlap, then sew the pom-pom to the front of the overlap.

Embellishment Diagram

LEFT HAT AND LEFT HAT REVERSE

BIB

MUSTACHE

FACE

NOSE

HOLLY LEAF

LIP

BEARD

RIGHT HAT AND RIGHT HAT REVERSE

HAT BRIM

Enlarge 370%

1 square = 1 inch

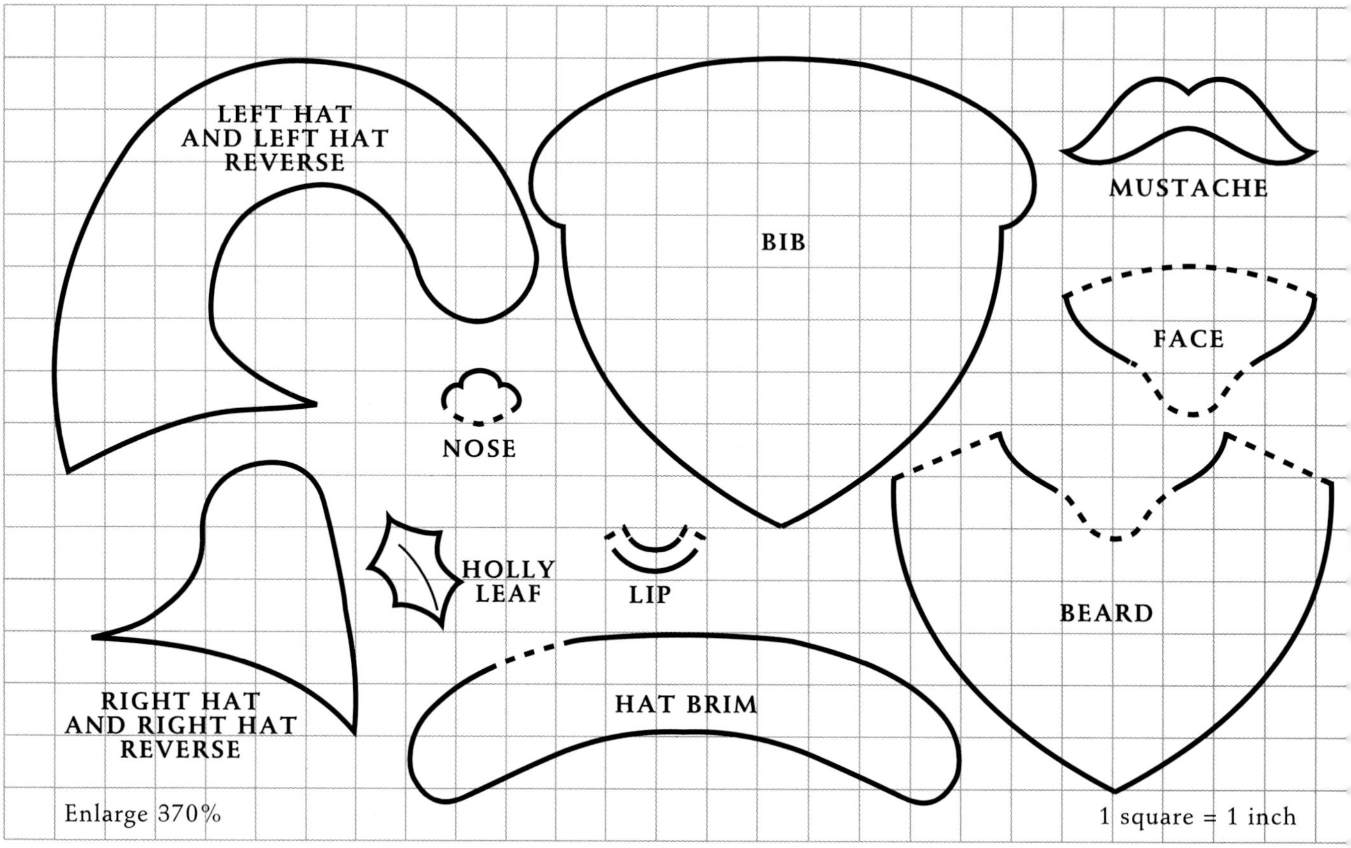

SANTA BIB PATTERNS

Christmas Tree Bib

SIZE

11 × 12 inches

WHAT YOU NEED

CHRISTMAS TREE BIB

- 14-inch square of woven green terry cloth for the bib base
- 14-inch square of green solid cotton fabric for the bib backing
- Scraps of brown, yellow, blue, white, and red solid fabrics
- 1/4 yard of fusible web
- 3/8 yard of tear-away stabilizer
- Matching sewing thread
- 1 yard of 3/8-inch-wide green bias tape for the tie

WHAT YOU DO

1. Enlarge the **Christmas Tree Bib Patterns** on page 12 as directed in "Enlarging Patterns" on page 238.

2. From the terry cloth, cut one bib for the base. From the green solid, cut one bib reverse for the backing. From the brown, cut one 1¼ × 1¾-inch strip for the trunk.

3. Following the manufacturer's directions, fuse the fusible web to the yellow, blue, white, and red scraps. Trace two Christmas ball appliqués onto the paper side of the fusible web of the yellow, blue, and white fabrics and three Christmas ball appliqués onto the red fabric. Then cut them out. Remove the paper backing from the appliqué pieces.

4. Referring to the **Appliqué Placement Diagram,** arrange the appliqués on the right side of the terry cloth tree. Fuse the appliqués in place, following the manufacturer's directions.

Appliqué Placement Diagram

5. Center and pin the tear-away stabilizer to the back of the appliquéd bib. Using matching thread and a closely spaced zigzag stitch, machine appliqué around each Christmas ball. Remove the stabilizer by tearing it away.

6. With right sides together, fold the trunk in half crosswise and sew along both long edges, using a ¼-inch seam allowance. Turn it to the right side and press. With raw edges aligned, pin the trunk to the appliquéd bib where indicated by the large dots on the pattern. Baste in place.

7. With right sides together and using a ¼-inch seam allowance, sew the appliquéd bib to the bib backing, leaving the neck edge open for turning. Clip the inside corners and trim the seam allowance. Turn the bib to the right side and press.

8. Open out the bias tape. With right sides together, center and pin the bias tape tie to the neck edge, aligning one long raw edge of the tie to the raw neck edge. Using a ¼-inch seam allowance, sew the tie in place. Fold the tie to the back of the bib, then slip-stitch it in place along the neck edge. Topstitch the folded edges of the tie ends closed. Knot each tie end.

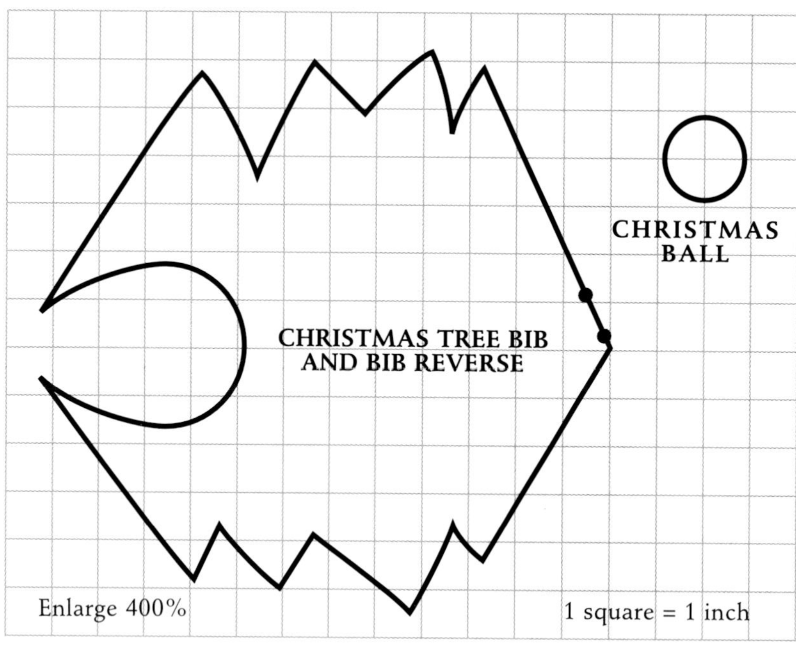

CHRISTMAS TREE BIB PATTERNS

Money-Saving Tip

You can save precious pennies if you reach into your scrap bag to make these cute holiday bibs. Use bits and snips of calico scraps for the snowman and his magical hat, Santa's face and decorative holly leaves, and the tree trunk and Christmas balls. You could back each bib with patterned remnants rather than a solid color fabric since remnants are less expensive per yard.

Save on the cost of "coal" buttons and use mismatched ones out of your button jar. Or embroider French knot buttons, eyes, and mouth using two strands of black tapestry wool. You may also want to consider using inexpensive tea towels instead of terry cloth for the Santa Bib and Christmas Tree Bib. Check your local discount stores for plain white and green towels; if you're lucky enough to get them on sale, you can save a bundle.

The light blue sky fabric on the Snowman Bib can be cut of white broadcloth, then spatter painted, saving you money on high-priced cotton prints. To spatter paint, lay the broadcloth on a plastic-covered flat surface. Dip a paintbrush into one of your chosen paint colors. Hold a sturdy dowel horizontally 12 to 24 inches above the fabric. Rap the handle of the paintbrush on the dowel to spatter the paint onto the fabric. Repeat the spattering technique for each color. Crafting expensive-looking fabric out of inexpensive plain broadcloths can reduce the cost of supplies for a high-volume bazaar crafter.

Festive Dots and Stripes

These fun-loving ornaments and the candy candlestick will bring a smile to all passersby. And, best of all, they are easy enough for kids to make. Get the children of your organization involved in the Christmas bazaar festivities by having them turn out jolly Polka-Dot Balls, fun Popcorn and Candy Cane Balls, and whimsical Candy Cane Candlesticks by the dozens.

Festive Dots and Stripes

WHAT YOU NEED

POLKA-DOT BALLS

- 2-inch-diameter red glass Christmas ball
- Two 2½-inch-diameter silver glass Christmas balls
- Squeezable tube paint in silver, black, and white

POPCORN AND CANDY CANE BALL

- 3-inch-diameter Styrofoam ball
- Off-white spray paint
- Two ¼-inch-diameter, 6-inch-long pointed dowels or two sharpened pencils
- Two ¼-inch-diameter, 6-inch-long candy canes
- 6-inch length of ¼-inch-wide red satin ribbon for the hanger
- Hot glue gun and glue sticks
- About 60 kernels of popped popcorn or enough to cover the ball

Polka-Dot Balls

SIZE

2 and 2½ inches in diameter

WHAT YOU DO

Note: Use silver paint for the red ball and black and white paint for the silver balls, or select any color combination of Christmas ball and paint. To prevent paint smears, paint the dots on the upper half of the ball first and let them dry thoroughly; after the paint has dried, complete the dot pattern on the lower half of each ball.

1. Holding the ball in your hand, and beginning at the top near the hanger, create a row of dots with the paint around the hanger and then halfway down the ball. For various effects, consider concentric circles of dots evenly spaced around the ball, clustering more dots at the top and bottom of the ball. Or randomly sprinkle dots all around the ball.

2. Hang the ball to dry.

Popcorn and Candy Cane Ball

SIZE

About 6 inches high

WHAT YOU DO

1. Working in a well-ventilated area, spray paint the ball with the off-white paint.

2. Using the dowels, pierce two holes in different directions through the ball, crossing the dowels in the center of the ball; see the **Dowel Diagram.** Remove the dowels, then insert the candy canes into the holes, turning the hooks until you have a pleasing arrangement.

Dowel Diagram

3. Poke a small hole in the top of the ball using the point of a pencil. Fold the ribbon in half and hot-glue the ends of the ribbon into the hole to form a loop for hanging.

4. Beginning at the hanger and working in rows, hot-glue the popcorn around the hanging loop and over the surface of the ball; fit each kernel as tightly as possible to cover the entire Styrofoam ball.

Candy Cane Candlestick

SIZE

6 inches high

WHAT YOU DO

1. Hot-glue a candy cane to the dowel so that the hook of the cane extends away from the dowel, leaving 1 inch of the straight end sticking above the dowel; see the **Candlestick Diagram.** The hooks of the candy canes will form the base of the candlestick, and the 1-inch end will form the candleholder.

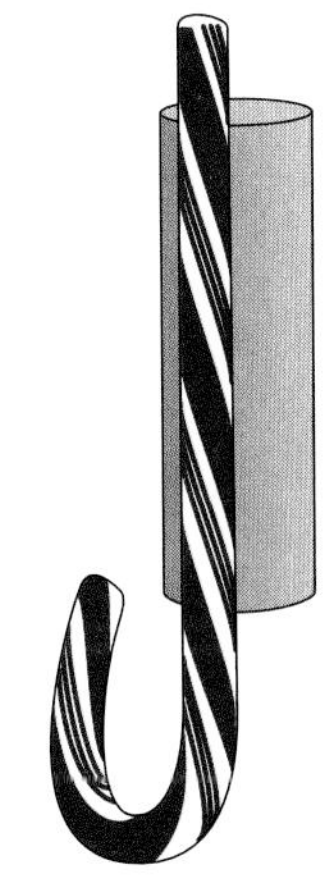

Candlestick Diagram

2. Glue another candy cane next to the first one in the same manner, taking care to align the curved base of the cane with the base of the previous candy cane. Continue adding canes around the dowel piece to complete the candlestick.

WHAT YOU NEED

CANDY CANE CANDLESTICK

- Twelve 1/4-inch-diameter, 6-inch-long candy canes
- 1-inch-diameter, 3-inch-long dowel
- Hot glue gun and glue sticks

PROJECT POINTERS

Candlesticks can be made in a wide variety of materials. Some of these materials, however, are flammable. The Candy Cane Candlesticks are designed to be a festive decoration. If you decide to light candles in them, don't leave them unattended since the flame will melt the candy canes and could cause a fire.

Make a tag for your customers that reads: "If you choose to light the candles you've placed in these candlesticks, extinguish the flame when the candle burns to within 4 inches of the candlestick." Then, attach the tag to the candlestick with a pretty ribbon.

If displaying candles in your booth, always sell them in pairs. Most of your customers use two candlesticks at a time and will need two candles, so take advantage of the opportunity to sell additional wares. By offering candles to go, shoppers get the convenience of an organized craftsperson and a quick stop. And you'll make the sales time shorter so you can assist other shoppers with purchases at your table.

A Cowboy Christmas

Lasso tradition and round up a cowboy theme for your bazaar booth with these western-style holiday crafts. Lighthearted and fun, the Nine-Patch Denim Pillow, Cowboy Boot Stocking, and Denim Pony Candy Cane Holder are sure to rustle up cowpokes and customers alike.

Nine-Patch Denim Pillow

Size

13½ inches square

What You Do

1. Cut nine 5-inch squares from the denim, incorporating seams and parts of pockets into most of the squares for interest. Cut a 15-inch square for the pillow back.

2. Using a ¼-inch seam allowance, sew the squares into three rows of three squares each, taking care to alternate fabric and seam directions in each row. Sew the three rows together to make a nine-patch square; see the **Assembly Diagram.**

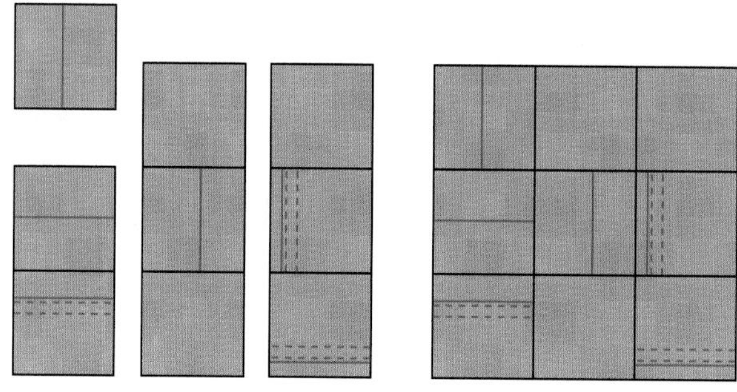

Assembly Diagram

3. Referring to the **Embroidery Diagram** for placement and the photograph for color suggestions, embroider over the seam lines of the pieced pillow top, using a combination of blanket stitches, featherstitches, herringbone stitches, long stitches, French knots, and couching stitches. Refer to "Stitch Details" on page 243.

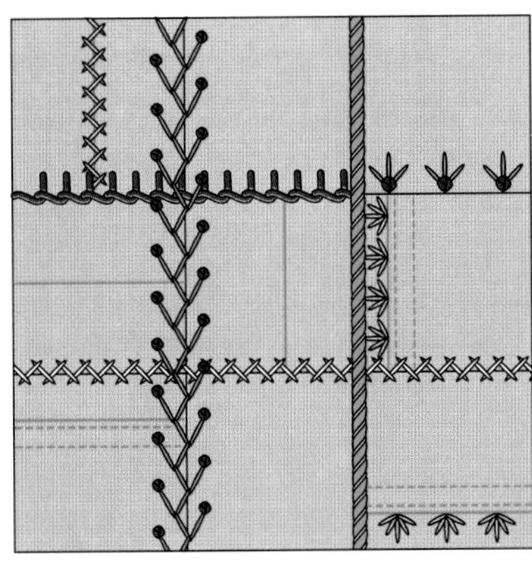

Embroidery Diagram

WHAT YOU NEED

NINE-PATCH DENIM PILLOW

- About ½ yard of worn denim or two denim pant legs
- Matching sewing thread
- About 4 yards each of red, green, gold, yellow, and white tapestry wool yarn
- Large-eye sharp tapestry needle
- 12-inch-square pillow form

4. Assemble the pillow as directed in "Assembling a Pillow" on page 240.

MONEY-SAVING TIP

Even if you're able to find previously worn jeans at a thrift shop for the Nine-Patch Denim Pillow, you may find yourself making a bigger financial investment than you care to, since jeans of any sort are expensive. Instead, consider making the nine-patch design out of bandannas. You could use one color for each of the squares or use two colors checkerboard-fashion. If your booth features the western look, stick with traditional blue or red bandannas. If you want a more Christmassy look, search out green or gold bandannas. Back the pillow with a full bandanna and leave off the embroidery to save money and time.

If you want a more intricate look than the nine-patch itself, consider making the pillow with five nine-patch blocks and four plain ones; see the ***Double Nine-Patch Diagram.*** *Display the pillows in a big wicker basket for a western feel or in a fabric-lined basket for a fancier look. If you have a well-worn ladder-back chair, stack the pillows on top of one another for a visually appealing display that echoes the rustic feel of the Old West.*

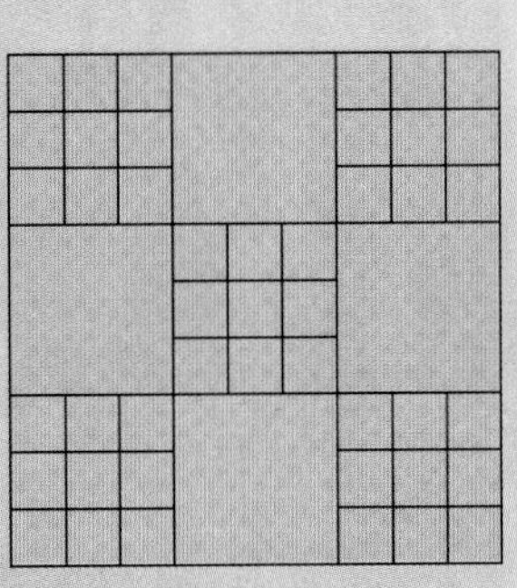

Double Nine-Patch Diagram

What You Need

Cowboy Boot Stocking

- Two 9 × 12-inch pieces of red felt for the boot
- Matching sewing thread
- 9 × 12-inch piece of black felt for the heel and calf
- 3 × 6-inch piece of white felt for the inlay
- Tacky glue
- 6-inch length of ⅝-inch-wide red grosgrain ribbon for the boot straps

Denim Pony Candy Cane Holder

- Two 5-inch squares of worn denim for the pony and ears
- Matching sewing thread
- 6-inch length of red fringe for the mane
- Hot glue gun and glue sticks
- Yellow embroidery floss
- ⅜-inch-diameter dark blue button for the eye
- ½ yard of ⅛-inch-wide cream satin ribbon for the bridle and reins

Cowboy Boot Stocking

Size

9½ inches long

What You Do

1. Enlarge the **Cowboy Boot Stocking Pattern** as directed in "Enlarging Patterns" on page 238.

2. Place the red felt pieces on top of each other. Trace around the entire boot, including the boot calf area and heel, but do not cut it out. Using a ⅛-inch seam allowance, sew around the boot, leaving the top edge open. Cut out the boot on the traced line, taking care to cut away all traced lines.

3. From the black, cut out one heel and one boot calf, cutting out the decorative inlay area on the calf. From the white, cut out an oval slightly larger than the decorative inlay.

4. Glue the oval to the back of the boot calf piece, centering it behind the decorative inlay area. Glue the boot calf and the heel to the boot.

5. Topstitch along the side edges of the boot calf, using a ⅛-inch seam allowance.

6. Cut the ribbon in half and fold each length in half. Glue the ends of one ribbon length to the center top of the boot front for boot straps, having one end on the outside of the boot and one end on the inside of the boot. Repeat for the boot back.

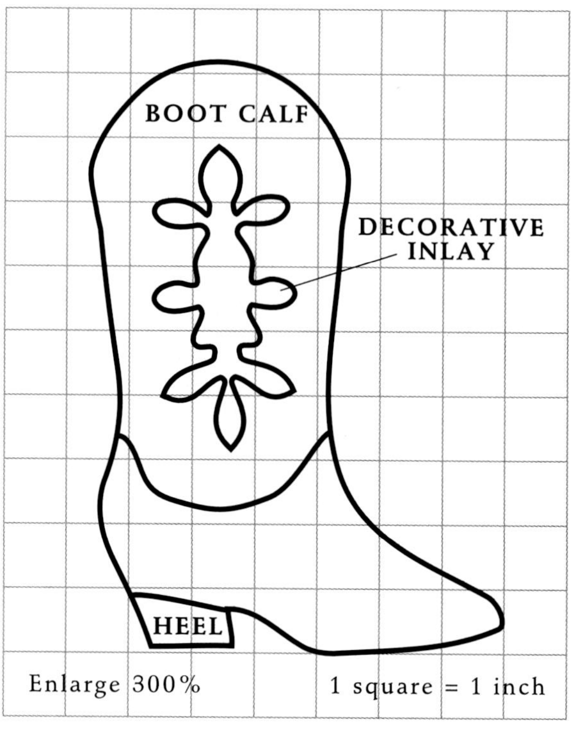

COWBOY BOOT STOCKING PATTERN

Denim Pony Candy Cane Holder

SIZE

5 inches high

WHAT YOU DO

1. Enlarge the **Denim Pony Patterns** as directed in "Enlarging Patterns" on page 238.

2. From the denim, cut out two pony front and back pieces and two ears.

3. With the right sides together, sew the pony front and back together, using a 1/4-inch seam allowance. Clip the curves, turn the pony to the right side, and press.

4. Glue the mane to the pony front, starting at the lower back edge and ending at the small dot indicated on the pattern.

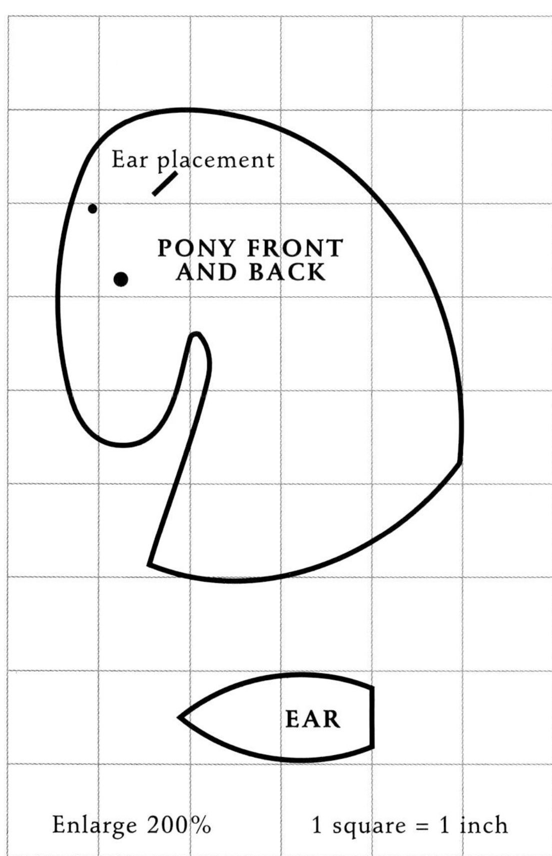

DENIM PONY PATTERNS

5. With wrong sides together, fold each ear in half lengthwise, then glue the lower end to the pony where indicated on the pattern. Once the glue has dried, open out the top end of the ear to give it a three-dimensional look. Fray the raw edges of the ear for a rustic look.

6. Using the embroidery floss, sew the button eye to the pony front where indicated by the large dot on the pattern.

7. From the ribbon, cut a 2-inch and a 4-inch piece. To make the bridle, glue the 2-inch piece of ribbon around the nose, the 4-inch piece around the head in front of the ears, and the remaining ribbon to the nose bridle for the reins, as shown in the **Bridle Diagram.**

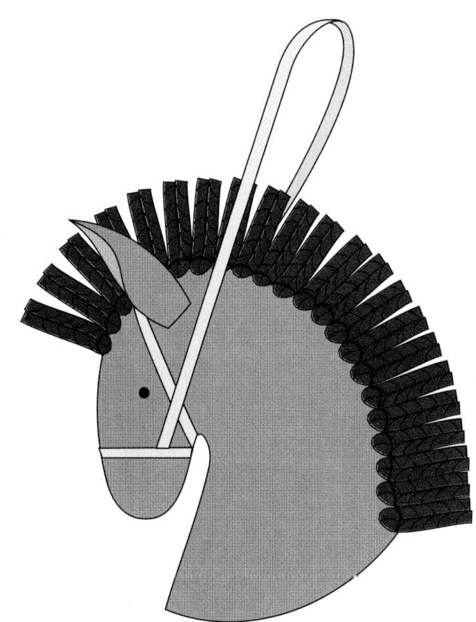

Bridle Diagram

8. Fray the neck edge of the pony for a rustic look.

Folk-Art Santa

Santas have been favorite collectibles for years, and they are still increasing in popularity. This country St. Nick is laden with tree, wreath, and sleigh bells. Sewn from raw linen with an easy-to-craft pecan face, he'll grace your Christmas booth while he awaits a home atop a fireplace mantle or as a tabletop centerpiece.

SIZE
16 inches tall

WHAT YOU NEED
- ½ yard of 44-inch-wide natural raw linen fabric for the body
- 5 × 14-inch piece of white felt for the cuffs and hat trim
- Scrap of red felt for the mittens
- Matching sewing thread
- Polyester fiberfill
- 2 cups of plastic pellets
- 2-inch-long pecan for the face
- Tacky glue
- Black puff paint with fine-tip applicator for the facial features
- Small sprig of silk berries and leaves for Santa's hat
- 4-inch-diameter twig wreath
- Nine ⅜-inch-diameter silver jingle bells for the sleigh bells
- ½ yard of ⅝-inch-wide red grosgrain ribbon for the sleigh bells
- 7-inch-high artificial Christmas tree

WHAT YOU DO
Note: All seam allowances are ¼ inch.

1. Enlarge the **Folk-Art Santa Patterns** as directed in "Enlarging Patterns" on page 238.

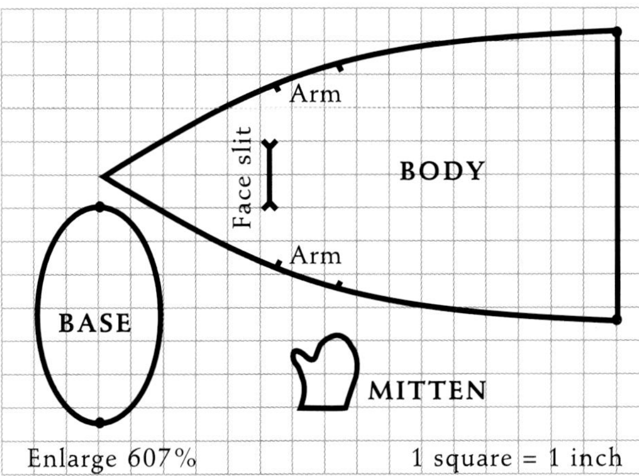

FOLK-ART SANTA PATTERNS

2. From the linen, cut two bodies, one base, and two 5 × 9-inch pieces for the arms. From the white felt, cut two 1½ × 6½-inch pieces for the cuffs and one 1½ × 13-inch strip for the hat trim. From the red felt, cut two mittens.

3. With right sides together, fold each arm in half to form a 2½ × 9-inch piece. Sew along one short edge and the long edge. Turn to the right side and stuff to within ½ inch of the open end, shaping and rounding the arm as you stuff. Flatten the open end of each arm, having the seam at the underarm edge, and press.

4. Baste the arms in place on one body where indicated by the marks on the pattern, having the arms pointing to the center of the body piece; see **Diagram 1.** With right sides together, sew the body pieces together, leaving the bottom edge open. Sew the base to the bottom of the body, matching the large dots and leaving an opening for turning. Clip the curves, then turn Santa to the right side. Stuff the top three-quarters of Santa firmly with fiberfill. Fill the remaining quarter of the body with plastic pellets to weight it, then slip-stitch the opening closed.

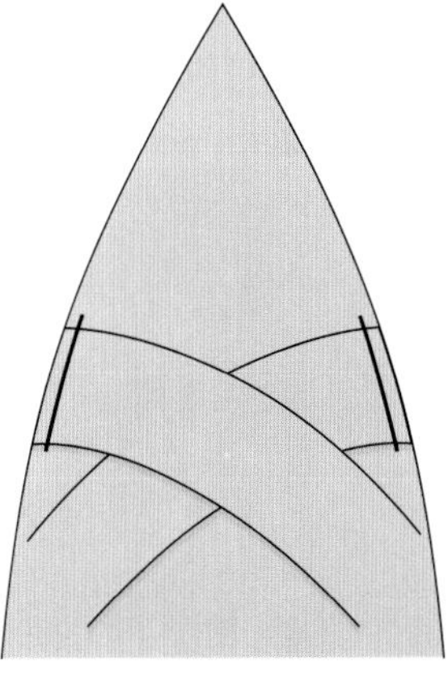

Diagram 1

5. For the face, make a $1\frac{1}{2}$-inch slit on the front of the body where indicated on the pattern. At the ends of the slit, make $\frac{1}{4}$-inch angled cuts away from the slit. Fold under the raw edges and glue the pecan in place, taking care to have the folded fabric edges adhere to the nut.

6. Glue small clumps of fiberfill around the pecan for the hair and beard; see **Diagram 2.**

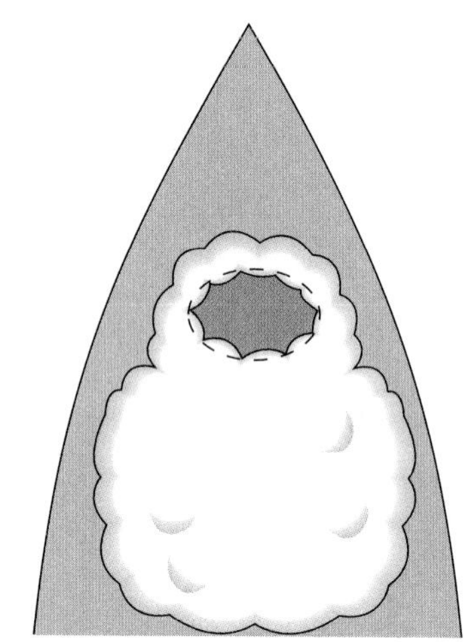

Diagram 2

7. With black puff paint, make dots for the eyes. Let dry thoroughly before proceeding.

8. Glue one mitten to the end of each arm. Glue one cuff to each arm, covering the upper edge of the mitten and overlapping the cuff ends. Glue the hat trim around the head, angling it down to a point in the back and overlapping the ends. Groom Santa's hair if necessary.

9. Glue the silk berries and leaves to the hat brim.

10. Slip the twig wreath onto Santa's right arm and hand tack the arms together at the cuff.

11. Sew the jingle bells to the ribbon length, spacing them about $1\frac{1}{2}$ inches apart and leaving about 3 inches free on each ribbon end. Clip the ribbon ends diagonally. Drape the ribbon over Santa's right arm and hand tack in place.

12. Nestle the artificial tree near Santa's left elbow; glue in place if desired.

PROJECT POINTERS

This charming Folk-Art Santa could be made in a variety of styles. For a more traditional look, cut the body and base out of jolly red wool. Add green woolen mittens and white wool cuffs and hat trim. Sew gold-tone or black buttons on Santa's "jacket" and his cuffs, then add a bouncy yarn pom-pom to his hat.

For a luxurious Victorian Santa, start with a regal velvet body and base, perhaps in a violet or royal blue color. Add paisley mittens and velvet cuffs and trim. If you're able to locate unspun white mohair, glue tufts of it around Santa's face for his hair and beard. Sew a silken tassel to the tip of his hat. To add even more elegance, use a narrow leather strap for the sleigh bells instead of ribbon. Lightly spray paint the silk holly with metallic silver or gold.

For a more rustic Santa, use rough-woven burlap for Santa's body. Tear homespun plaid strips for the cuffs and hat trim and hand tack them in place. Reach into your scrap basket for a pretty calico for the mittens. Or if you can knit, why not add a pair of hand-knit mittens with a casual rolled edge instead of ribbing? Use faux lamb's wool for the beard and a spray of preserved holly for the hat accent.

If the bazaar you plan to display your wares at is rather upscale, you'll need a project that really stands out in your booth. This Santa is easy enough for assembly line crafting, yet he offers limitless possibilities for uniqueness.

St. Nicholas Place Mat

This jolly old elf brings a touch of whimsy to the table during the holidays. Subtly printed fabrics and crisp machine appliqué give him his character, which will delight the kid in each and every one of us.

St. Nicholas Place Mat

What You Need

- ½ yard of muslin for the place mat
- 1¼ yards of fusible web
- ½ yard of white-on-white print fabric for the beard
- 4 × 10-inch piece of cream print fabric for the mustache
- 5 × 18-inch piece of black-on-ecru fabric for the hat brim and pom-pom
- 4 × 8-inch piece of red print fabric for the hat
- 6 × 10-inch piece of pale pink solid for the face and lower lip
- Scraps of pink and mauve solid fabrics for the cheeks, nose, and mouth
- ¾ yard of tear-away stabilizer
- Matching sewing thread
- One skein each of black and white embroidery floss
- Sharp embroidery needle

Size

14¼ × 19½ inches

What You Do

1. Enlarge the **St. Nicholas Place Mat Patterns** as directed in "Enlarging Patterns" on page 238.

2. From the muslin, cut one place mat for the base and one place mat reverse for the backing.

3. Following the manufacturer's directions, fuse the fusible web to the white, cream, ecru, and red prints and the pale pink, pink, and mauve solids. Trace the mirror image, or reverse, of each appliqué onto the paper side of the fusible web, then cut out as follows: From the white print, cut one beard. From the cream print, cut one mustache. From the ecru print, cut one hat brim and one pom-pom. From the red print, cut one hat. From the pale pink solid, cut one face and one lower lip. From the pink solid, cut one left cheek and one right cheek. From the mauve solid, cut one nose and one mouth. Remove the paper backing from the appliqués.

4. Referring to the **Appliqué Placement Diagram,** arrange the appliqués on the place mat base, layering the appliqués as indicated by the dashed lines. Fuse the appliqués in place, following the manufacturer's directions.

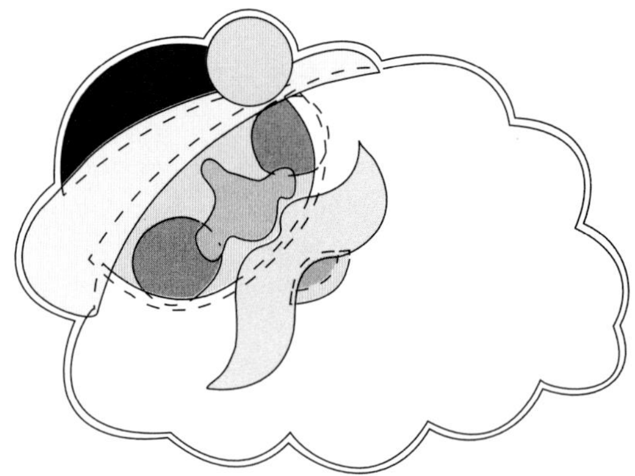

Appliqué Placement Diagram

5. Center and pin the tear-away stabilizer to the back of the appliquéd place mat base. Using matching thread and a closely spaced zigzag stitch, machine appliqué all edges of the appliqués, including the outer place mat edges.

6. Referring to the **Embroidery Diagram** for stitch placement and "Stitch Details" on page 243, work the eyebrows in outline stitch using two strands of black floss. Satin stitch the pupils with two strands of white floss and the irises with two strands of black floss. Remove the stabilizer by tearing it away.

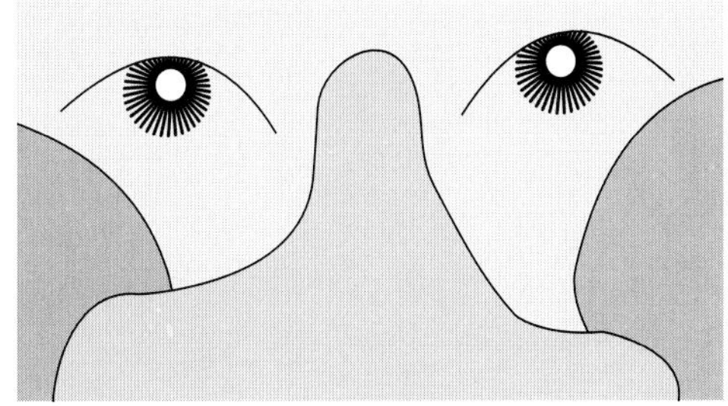

Embroidery Diagram

7. With right sides together and raw edges even, sew the appliquéd place mat base to the backing around the machine-appliquéd outer edge, leaving an opening for turning. Clip the curves and trim the seam allowance to reduce bulk. Turn the place mat to the right side and press well, taking care not to crush the embroidery stitches. Slip-stitch the opening closed.

Project Pointers

One of the hardest parts of sewing is choosing fabrics. Texture, or the illusion of it, plays a vital role in the success of your project. For the place mat, I chose a white-on-white print for St. Nicholas's beard. While the fabric itself is flat and untextured, the paisley print mimics the curls of a beard. Instead of using a furry or plush fabric, I chose a print that echoes the pile lines of a fur-type fabric for St. Nick's hat brim. When selecting fabric, remember that the flat, printed fabrics are just as effective as three-dimensional ones, but are much easier to sew.

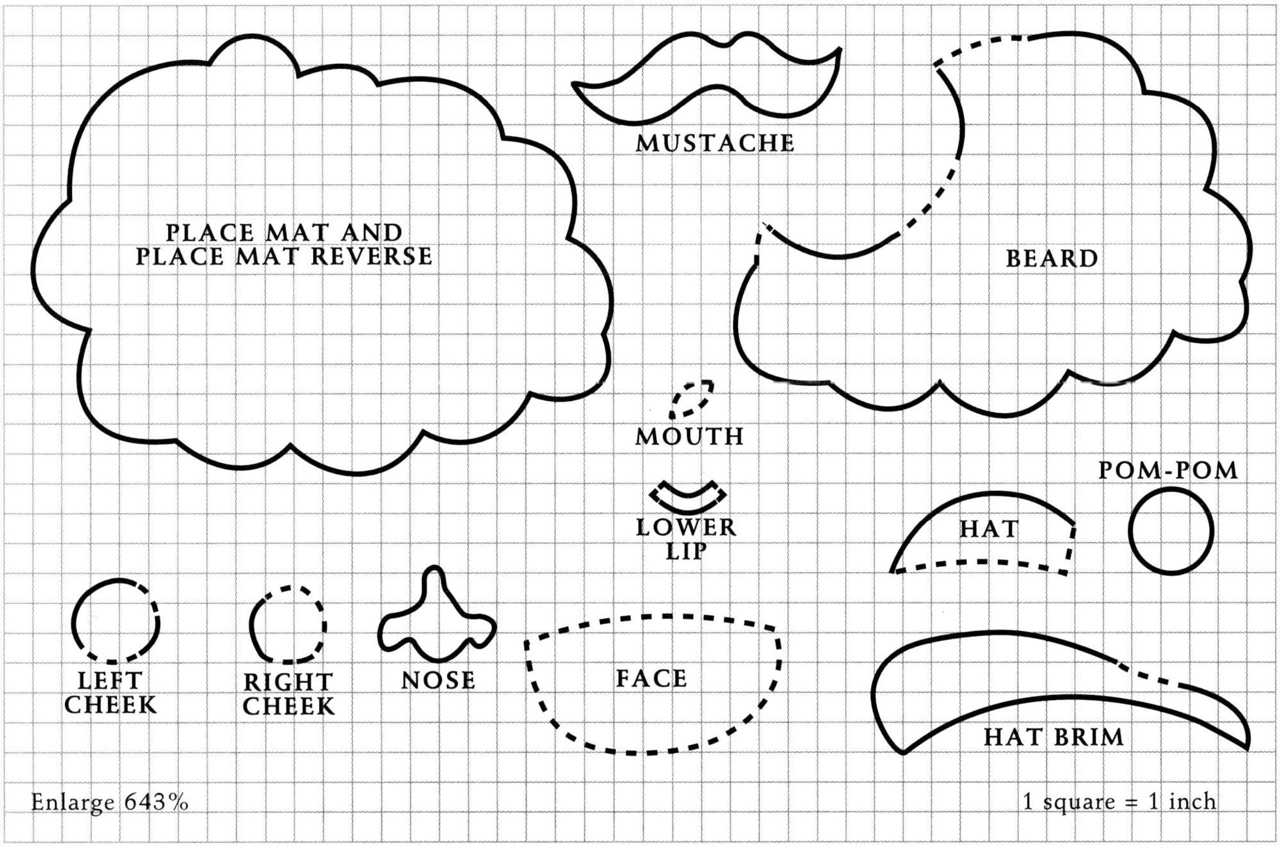

PLACE MAT AND PLACE MAT REVERSE
MUSTACHE
BEARD
MOUTH
POM-POM
LOWER LIP
HAT
LEFT CHEEK
RIGHT CHEEK
NOSE
FACE
HAT BRIM
Enlarge 643%
1 square = 1 inch

ST. NICHOLAS PLACE MAT PATTERNS

Gingerbread Man Ornaments

These fun-loving, spicy little characters will add a touch of glee to your holiday booth and tree. Bright rickrack serves as frosting, and seed beads substitute as raisins to create a hand-decorated look. As an added attraction, whip up a batch of gingerbread cookies in the same shape to sell along with the tree ornaments—who will be able to resist this confectionary combination?

Size

6 inches tall

What You Do

1. Enlarge the **Gingerbread Man Pattern** as directed in "Enlarging Patterns" on page 238.

2. Trace around the pattern on one square of each felt color; do not cut them out. Place the same-color squares on top of each other. Sew around the gingerbread man 1/8 inch inside of the marked lines. Cut out the gingerbread men on the lines, taking care to cut away all lines.

3. Cut and glue rickrack to the neck, arms, legs, and body for the frosting; refer to the **Embellishment Diagrams** for placement. Add puff paint eyes and buttons. For each mouth, bring a threaded needle from the back to the front of each gingerbread man, thread four beads, then insert the needle back into the man to create a curved smile; secure the thread. Blush the cheeks.

4. Cut the ribbon into three equal lengths. Fold each ribbon length in half to form a loop and glue one to the back of each ornament for a hanger.

Embellishment Diagrams

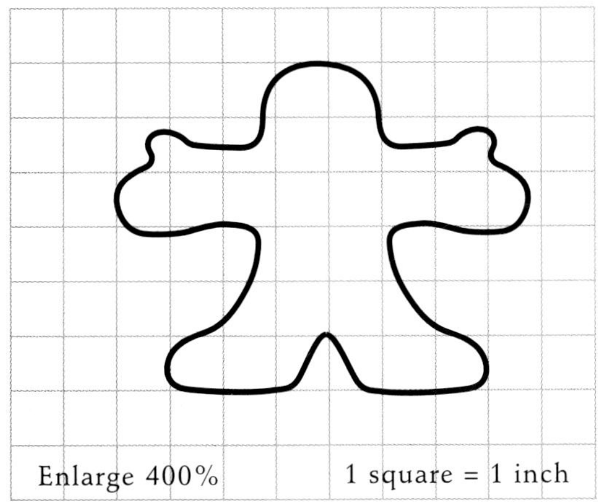

GINGERBREAD MAN PATTERN

What You Need

- Two 8-inch squares each of light tan, medium tan, and brown felt for the gingerbread men
- Matching sewing thread
- 5/8 yard of narrow-width white rickrack for the frosting
- 1/8 yard of wide-width white rickrack for the frosting
- 3/8 yard of medium-width green rickrack for the frosting
- Hot glue gun and glue sticks
- Red, black, and white puff paints with fine-tip applicator for the eyes and buttons
- Twelve 6 mm metallic gold bugle beads for the mouth
- Powder blusher for the cheeks
- 1/2 yard of 3/8-inch-wide red satin ribbon for the hangers

Project Pointers

Search out your grandmother's favorite gingerbread recipe and spend an afternoon making cookies to accompany the ornaments. Cut the pattern out of wax-coated cardboard. Roll out the dough, then cut around the pattern using the tip of a sharp knife. Use sprinkles, raisins, and silver dragées to decorate these delights, then bake according to the recipe's directions.

To package and sell your handmade treats, bundle four cookies together with a pretty plaid ribbon, lay them in a small basket, then attach a felt gingerbread man ornament to the basket handle and sell them as an ensemble. Or sell a cookie and an ornament as a set. You could also offer a free cookie to the customer if she purchases three or more ornaments.

Santa's Helper Hat

Take a cue from St. Nick himself and stitch up a selection of these whimsical toppers. Perfect for kids, teens, and fun-loving adults, these Santa-styled hats are crafted from specialty fabrics and plush fake fur.

Size

20-inch circumference for child's size small
22-inch circumference for child's size large
26-inch circumference for adult's size small
28-inch circumference for adult's size large

What You Do

1. Enlarge the **Santa's Helper Hat Patterns** as directed in "Enlarging Patterns" on page 238. To check the fit, loosely tape the side seam of the paper pattern together and try it on. There should be 2 to 4 inches of extra room to allow for the thickness of the fake fur. Make any necessary size adjustments to the pattern.

2. From the fabric, cut one hat. From the fake fur, cut one 5 × 20½-inch strip for the child's size small hat brim. For child's size large, cut a 5 × 22½-inch strip. For adult's size small, cut a 5 × 26½-inch strip and for adult's size large, cut a 5 × 28½-inch strip. Also cut five petals for the pom-pom.

3. With the right sides together, fold the hat in half lengthwise and sew the side seam, using a ¼-inch seam allowance; see **Diagram 1.** Do not turn the hat to the right side.

Diagram 1

4. With right sides together and using a ¼-inch seam allowance, sew the short ends of the hat brim strip together to form a continuous loop. Slip the hat brim loop over the hat, having the wrong side of the hat facing the right side of the hat brim strip. Matching the raw edges, sew the hat brim to the hat, using a ½-inch seam allowance; see **Diagram 2.** Use a pin to raise the fake fur nap from the seam.

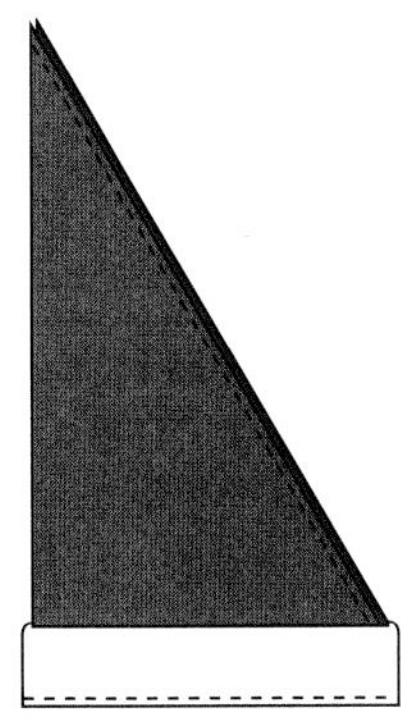

Diagram 2

5. Turn the hat right side out. Fold the brim to the outside, leaving about 1 inch of the brim inside the hat. Turn under ½ inch on the long raw edge of the outside brim, then slip-stitch it to the hat, easing in any excess.

6. To make the pom-pom, place the right sides of two pom-pom petals together. Sew along one edge, using a ¼-inch seam allowance; see **Diagram 3.** Continue adding petals in the same manner, then join the first petal to the fifth, leaving a 1½-inch opening in this seam for stuffing. Clip the curves and trim the excess fur. Turn the pom-pom to the right side and stuff very firmly. Slip-stitch the opening closed. Securely hand tack the pom-pom to the tip of the hat.

WHAT YOU NEED

- ¾ yard of desired color medium-weight wool or cotton fabric for the hat
- ¼ yard of cream fake fur for the brim and pom-pom
- Matching sewing thread
- Polyester fiberfill for the pom-pom

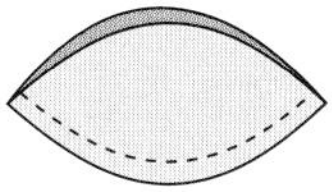

Diagram 3

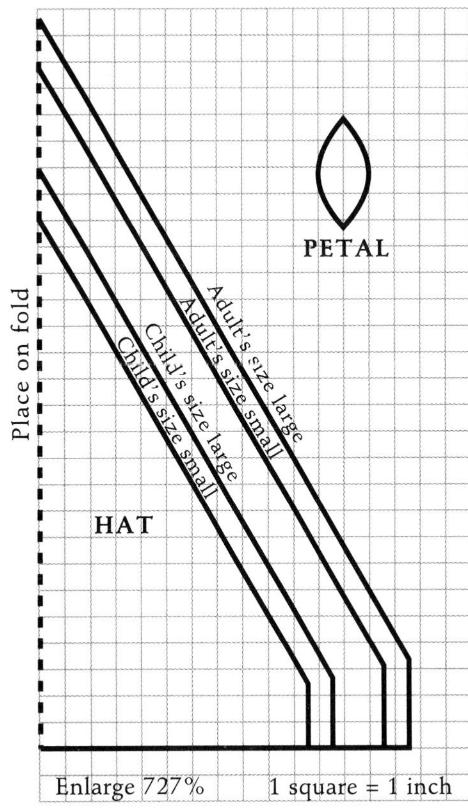

SANTA'S HELPER
HAT PATTERNS

Holiday Napkins

Personalize purchased napkins with simple embroidery touches and painted accents. The Christmas Ball, Featherstitch, and Button-Dotted napkins will make welcome Christmas gifts for holiday shoppers. The Napkin Ring Wreaths are painted wooden rings with bright dots for holly.

Christmas Ball Napkin

Size

Motif is 1½ × 1¾ inches

What You Do

1. Press the napkin and lay it out on a smooth, clean work surface.

2. Squeeze the fabric paint onto the saucer or palette, then thin it with water, if necessary, to create a smooth, creamy consistency. To paint the napkin border, load the brush with paint and run it along one napkin edge just outside the hem-stitching; take care to maintain a straight edge. Try to paint the edge in one coat since additional coats may stiffen the napkin excessively. Touch up spots if necessary. Wash the saucer and brush with soap and water before the paint dries. Allow the painted edge to dry thoroughly.

3. Repeat Step 2 for the remaining edges of the napkin.

4. Pin or baste the waste canvas to the lower right corner of the napkin, matching the corner edges.

5. Using a pin, mark the placement of the first stitch by measuring 2½ inches in from the right edge and 2¾ inches up from the bottom edge. Find the center of the **Christmas Ball Motif Chart** by connecting the arrows. Matching the center of the chart and the marked first stitch, cross-stitch the design using three strands of floss.

6. Using three strands of floss, backstitch the ornament hanger with pearl gray. Work the long-stitch branches and pine needles with three strands of dark parrot green; see "Stitch Details" on page 243.

7. Trim the waste canvas close to the stitching. Dampen the canvas with the plant mister, then allow the canvas sizing to soften for a few minutes. Using tweezers, carefully draw out the canvas threads one at a time. Press the completed napkin face down on a well-padded surface.

COLOR KEY

	DMC	Anchor	J. & P. Coats	Color
●	326	59	3401	Very Dk. Rose
/	335	38	3283	Rose
×	415	398	8398	Pearl Gray
	702	226	6239	Dk. Parrot Green

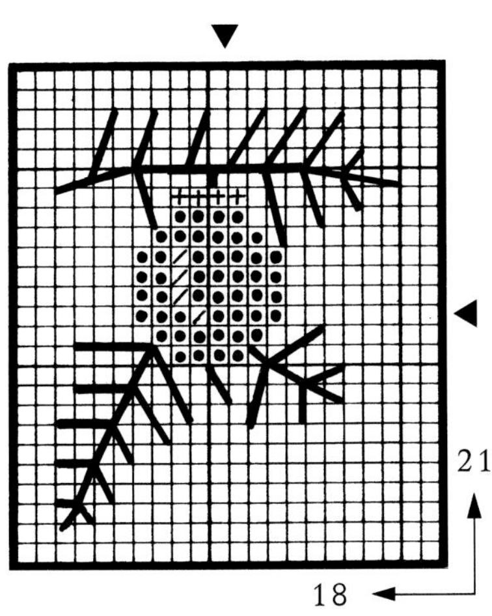

CHRISTMAS BALL MOTIF CHART

WHAT YOU NEED

CHRISTMAS BALL NAPKIN

- Linen napkin with 1-inch-wide hemstitched border
- Green fabric paint
- Saucer or palette
- 1-inch-wide sable or synthetic paintbrush
- 5-inch square of 14-count waste canvas
- One skein of embroidery floss for each color in the **Color Key**
- Sharp embroidery needle
- Plant mister
- Tweezers

FEATHERSTITCH NAPKIN

- Green striped or plain cotton napkin
- One skein of red embroidery floss
- Sharp embroidery needle

Featherstitch Napkin

SIZE

Each stitch is about ⅜ inch long

WHAT YOU DO

1. Press the napkin and lay it out on a smooth, clean work surface.

2. Cut an 18-inch length of embroidery floss. Using three strands of floss, work the featherstitch border around the napkin, about 1 inch in from the edge; see "Stitch Details" on page 243.

What You Need

Button-Dotted Napkin

- Red-and-green plaid cotton napkin
- One skein of embroidery floss to match the plaid
- Assorted sizes of antique bone or odd-lot white buttons, enough to place one button at each major intersection of the plaid
- Sharp embroidery needle

Napkin Ring Wreath

- Green acrylic paint
- Saucer or palette
- 2-inch-diameter wooden ring
- 1/4-inch-wide paintbrush
- Red puff paint with fine-tip applicator
- 6-inch length of 1/8-inch-diameter metallic red cord for the bow
- Hot glue gun and glue sticks

Napkin Ring Wreath

Size

2 inches in diameter

What You Do

1. Squeeze the green paint onto the saucer or palette, then paint the wooden ring with two coats of green paint; allow the paint to dry thoroughly between coats. Wash the saucer and brush with soap and water before the paint dries.

2. Using the red paint, make small dots for the holly berries; see the **Holly Berry Diagram.**

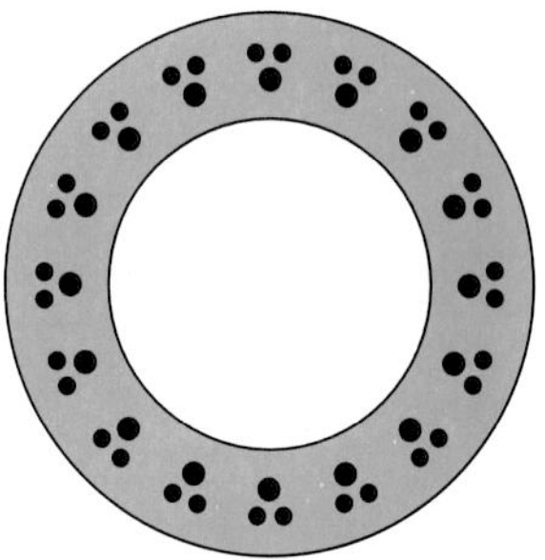

Holly Berry Diagram

3. Tie the cord in a bow, then glue it to the bottom of the wreath.

Button-Dotted Napkin

Size

Buttons are various sizes

What You Do

1. Press the napkin and lay it out on a smooth, clean work surface.

2. Using six strands of embroidery floss, insert the needle up through the center of one of the plaid intersections of the napkin. Thread on a button, then insert the needle back through the cloth to the wrong side. Knot the ends of the floss tightly and clip away the excess.

3. Repeat Step 2 at each intersection of the plaid.

Project Pointers

I recommend a sable brush, instead of a synthetic one, for painting the border on the Christmas Ball Napkin on page 30. Sable brushes are quite expensive but well worth the money if you plan to paint a number of napkins for your bazaar. These brushes hold more paint, give a crisper line, and clean up nicely. The natural "spring" and razor-sharp edges make the brush worth the money if you are crafting in multiples.

Christmas Carol Frames

These unique holiday bazaar items will leave your customers singing yuletide praises. The Jingle Bells and Collaged Sheet Music frames will gladden the hearts of those looking for special Christmas gifts or handcrafted frames for their favorite holiday photographs.

Jingle Bells Frame

Size

8½ × 11-inch frame with 4½ × 3-inch opening

What You Do

1. Mark the photograph opening on one piece of mat board; see **Diagram 1.** Using a ruler to ensure a straight cut, cut out the opening with the craft knife, changing blades as necessary.

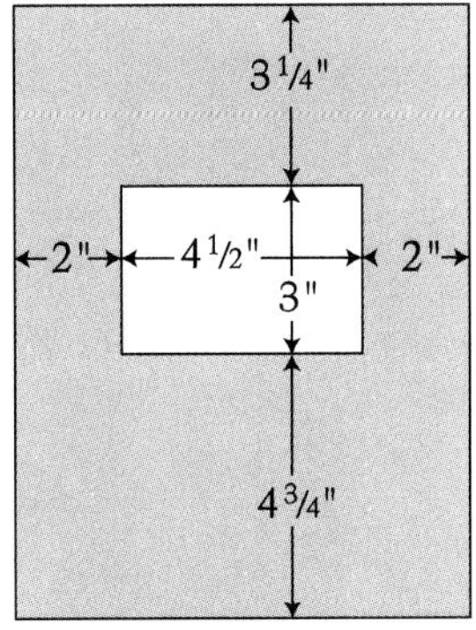

Diagram 1

2. Enlarge the **Jingle Bells Frame Stand Pattern** on page 35 as directed in "Enlarging Patterns" on page 238. From one mat board, cut one frame

What You Need

Jingle Bells Frame

- Three 8½ × 11-inch pieces of mat board for the frame front, back, and stand
- Craft knife with extra blades
- Four 8½ × 11-inch sheets of holiday sheet music for the frame back and stand
- White acrylic paint
- Saucer or palette
- Paintbrush
- Spray adhesive
- 8½ × 11-inch sheet of "Jingle Bells" sheet music for the frame front
- Hot glue gun and glue sticks
- ½ yard of red piping for the photograph opening
- 6-inch length of ¾-inch-wide red grosgrain ribbon for the support
- Three 1-inch-diameter gold jingle bells for the frame accent
- ¾ yard of ⅝-inch-wide gold-edged red satin ribbon for the frame accent

stand. From the holiday sheet music, cut two frame stands, extending the top edge 1 inch for the flap.

3. Squeeze the paint onto the saucer or palette; then using the brush, paint the edges of the mat boards and frame stand since the sheet music will not cover the edges. After painting the edges, wash the saucer and brush with soap and water before the paint dries.

4. Using the spray adhesive, spray the back of the "Jingle Bells" sheet music and place it on the mat board with the photograph opening, aligning all edges. Once the adhesive is dry, cut out the photograph opening in the sheet music. Using hot glue, glue the piping to the edge of the photograph opening, beginning and ending the piping in the lower right corner. Glue the piping selvage smoothly to the wrong side of the mat board. Set the frame front aside.

5. Using the spray adhesive, cover the front and back of the frame stand with the holiday sheet music, keeping the flaps at the top free. Using the two remaining sheets of music, cover the right and wrong sides of the remaining 8½ × 11-inch mat board for the frame back. Allow each covered piece to dry thoroughly.

6. Using spray adhesive, glue the flaps together, then bend them to the wrong side of the frame stand. Center and glue the flap to the frame back, aligning the lower edges of the frame and frame stand. Using hot glue, glue about ¾ inch of grosgrain ribbon end to the frame stand and ¾ inch of the other end to the frame back for the support. See **Diagram 2.** Let the glue dry thoroughly. This forms the assembled frame back.

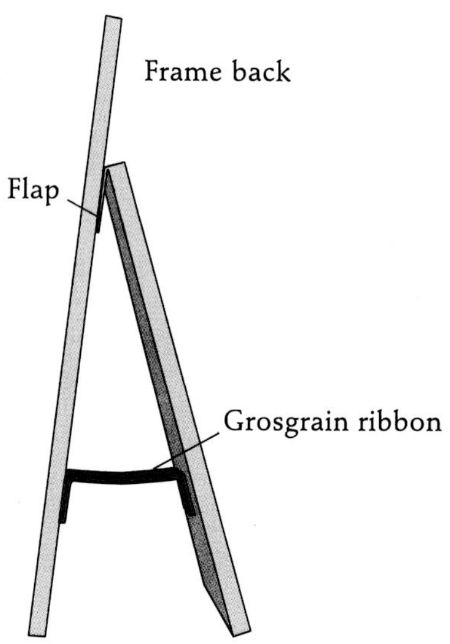

Diagram 2

7. To assemble the frame, hot-glue the wrong side of the frame front to the front of the frame back, leaving the bottom edge open so that photographs may be inserted in the frame; do not allow the glue to spread into the window. Press the perimeter of the frame under heavy books to seal, allowing the glue to dry thoroughly.

8. For the frame accent, thread the bells onto the satin ribbon and knot them in place in the center of the ribbon. Tie the ribbon into a bow and hot-glue it to the lower right corner of the opening to cover the cut edges of the piping. Twirl the ribbon ends and hot-glue them to the sheet music, as shown in the photograph on page 33.

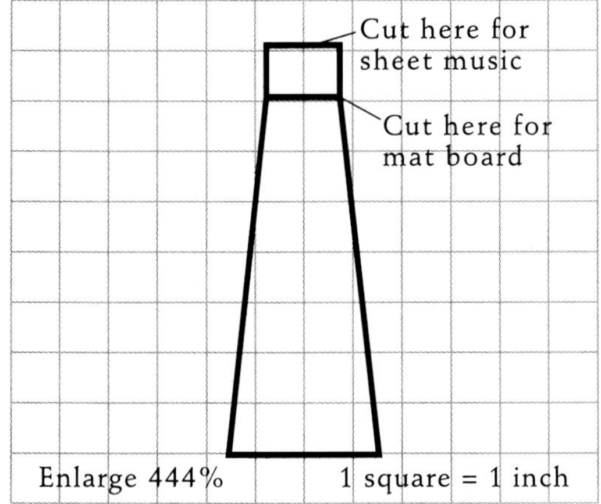

JINGLE BELLS FRAME STAND PATTERN

Collaged Sheet Music Frame

Size

4½ × 6-inch frame with 3 × 4½-inch opening

What You Do

1. Remove the glass, hardware, and cardboard backings from the frames. Work with one frame at a time.

2. Cut the sheet music into medium-size pieces, about 8 × 8 inches. Using the spray adhesive, spray the wrong side of the sheet music and position each piece on the frame, angling and overlapping for effect. Fold the edges of the sheet music over the sides of the frame and around to the back, trimming away any excess. Allow the adhesive to dry thoroughly.

What You Need

Collaged Sheet Music Frame

- Unfinished wooden double frame with hinge hardware, with each frame measuring 4½ × 6 inches
- 2 to 3 sheets of holiday sheet music for the frame covering
- Spray adhesive
- Sharp, pointed scissors
- Hot glue gun and glue sticks

3. Using sharp, pointed scissors, make a small slit in the center of the sheet music that covers the photograph opening, then make mitered cuts to each corner of the opening; see the **Photograph Opening Diagram.** For best results, the cuts must be precise and go directly into the center of each corner. Fold the sheet music flaps to the wrong side of the frame and glue them in place. You may find it necessary to add a drop of hot glue at each corner.

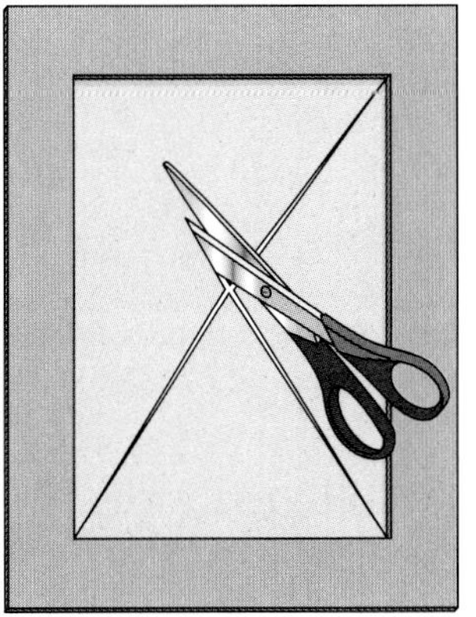

Photograph Opening Diagram

4. Reassemble the frames.

Holiday Sentiment Pillows

Spread some holiday cheer throughout your booth. Small pillows make great decorative accents in a room, and even smaller ones are just right to tuck into a tree or hang from a doorknob as an unusual ornament. The Faux Redwork Ornament and the cross-stitched Noel Pillow will shout "Season's Greetings" to all who pass by.

Faux Redwork Ornament

Size

5 × 6¼ inches

What You Do

1. Center the white fabric on top of the **Full-Size Painting Pattern.** Trace the design with the puff paint. Allow it to dry thoroughly.

2. Fold the ribbon in half to form a hanging loop. Place the raw ends of the hanger at the center top of the ornament front and baste in place.

3. With right sides facing and using a ¼-inch seam allowance, sew the ornament front and back together, leaving an opening for turning. Clip the corners, then turn and press lightly from the back side only. Stuff the ornament with fiberfill and slip-stitch it closed.

4. Beginning between the ends of the ribbon hanger, slip-stitch the upholstery cord around the ornament, covering the seam edge. End the cord between the ribbon hanger ends at the start, slip-stitching the ends together. Sew the appliqué to the base of the ribbon hanger.

What You Need

Faux Redwork Ornament

- 4¾ × 6-inch piece of white fabric for the ornament front
- Red puff paint with fine-tip applicator
- 8-inch length of ⅜-inch-wide red satin ribbon for the hanger
- Matching sewing thread
- 4¾ × 6-inch piece of red print fabric for the ornament back
- Polyester fiberfill
- ⅝ yard of ⅜-inch-diameter green upholstery cord for the trim
- 2-inch-wide lace appliqué for the hanger accent

FULL-SIZE PAINTING PATTERN

What You Need

Noel Pillow

- 11 × 15-inch piece of 11-count white Aida
- One skein of embroidery floss for each color in the **Color Key**
- Size 22 or 24 tapestry needle
- 5/8 yard of red plaid taffeta for the ruffle and pillow back
- Matching sewing thread
- 3/8 yard of bleached muslin for the covered pillow form
- Polyester fiberfill

Noel Pillow

Size

10 × 14 inches, including ruffle

What You Do

1. Zigzag the edges of the Aida to prevent raveling. Find the center of the Aida and mark it with a pin. Find the center of the **Noel Pillow Chart** by connecting the arrows.

2. Matching the centers of the chart and the Aida and using three strands of floss, begin stitching at the center point, working outward until the entire design is complete.

3. Wash and press the completed cross-stitch pillow top as directed in "Washing and Pressing" on page 241.

4. With the design centered, trim the Aida to 9 × 13 inches.

5. From the taffeta, cut two 5 × 42-inch strips for the ruffle and one 9 × 13-inch piece for the pillow back.

6. With right sides together and the raw edges even, sew the short ends of the two ruffle strips together to form one continuous ruffle; see **Diagram 1.**

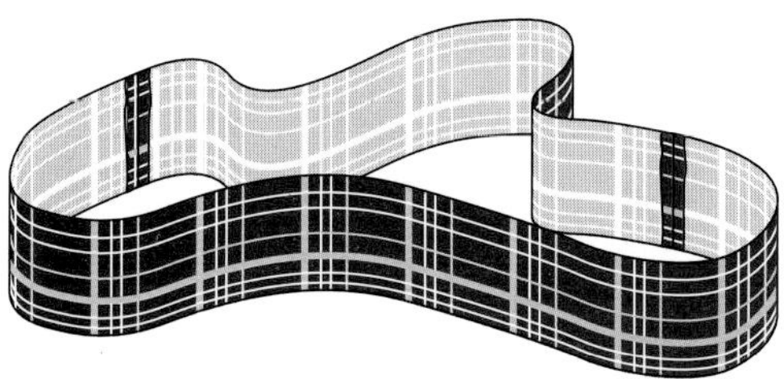

Diagram 1

7. Press the seams open. Turn right side out, fold the loop in half lengthwise, and press. Sew a line of gathering stitches 3/8 inch from the raw edges through both layers of the ruffle. Fold the ruffle in half to find the midpoints and place a pin at these points. Then match the midpoints of the ruffle and mark the quarterpoints with pins; see **Diagram 2.**

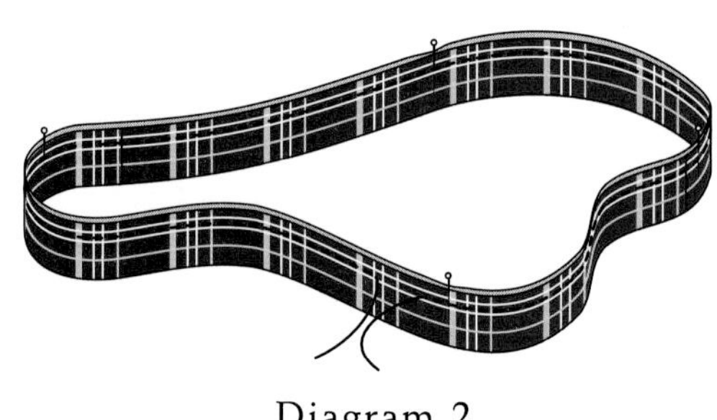

Diagram 2

8. Sew the ruffle to the pillow top as directed in "Attaching Ruffles" on page 240.

9. Make one 8 × 12-inch covered pillow form as directed in "Covered Pillow Forms" on page 240.

10. Assemble the pillow, using a 1/2-inch seam allowance as directed in "Assembling a Pillow" on page 240.

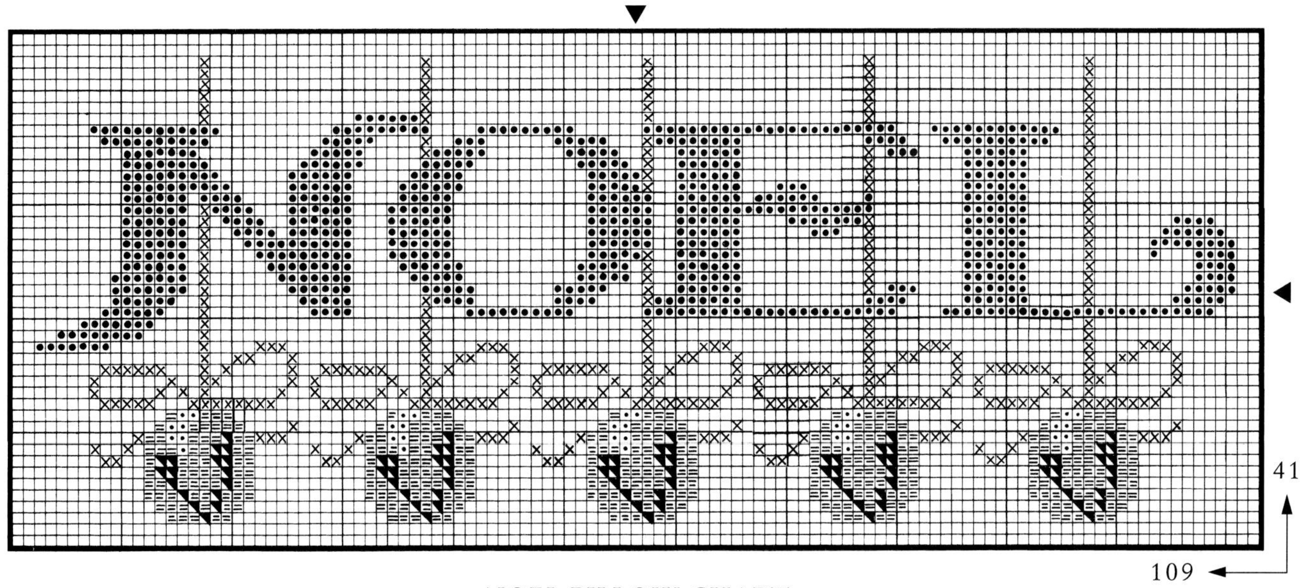

NOEL PILLOW CHART

COLOR KEY

	DMC	Anchor	J. & P. Coats	Color
◥	310	403	8403	Black
×	349	13	2335	Nasturtium
●	700	228	6227	Bright Christmas Green
•	725	305	2294	Topaz
=	729	890	2875	Med. Old Gold

PROJECT POINTERS

True redwork, often referred to as Turkey work, was popular in the early part of this century. Redwork is named for the brilliant red thread (imported from Turkey) used in the needlework designs from that period. Redwork embroidery features basic outline stitches and backstitches, and is usually worked on pillowcases and bed linens.

To create the Merry Christmas design on page 37 in quick-to-stitch redwork, simply transfer the lettering and border to a piece of tightly woven white cotton, using a transfer paper such as Saral. Follow the manufacturer's directions to transfer the design. Referring to "Stitch Details" on page 243, work the design with small outline stitches and the dots with French knots. Finish the ornament with a white backing, red cord, and a red ribbon hanger for an heirloom-quality craft.

Rudolph the Reindeer Puppet

Whose child could resist this perky hand puppet for playtime? Complete with a red button nose and a jingle bell collar, he's just waiting for the chance to lead Santa's sleigh and wish you a happy holiday season.

Size

20 inches tall

What You Do

1. Enlarge the **Rudolph the Reindeer Puppet Patterns** on page 42 as directed in "Enlarging Patterns" on page 238.

2. From the wool, cut two bodies, heads, and ears. From the evenweave, cut two inner ears. From the black felt, cut two hooves. From the brown felt, cut four 7 × 9-inch pieces for the antlers.

3. With right sides facing and the points facing in, sew one hoof to each "arm," using a ¼-inch seam allowance; see **Diagram 1.**

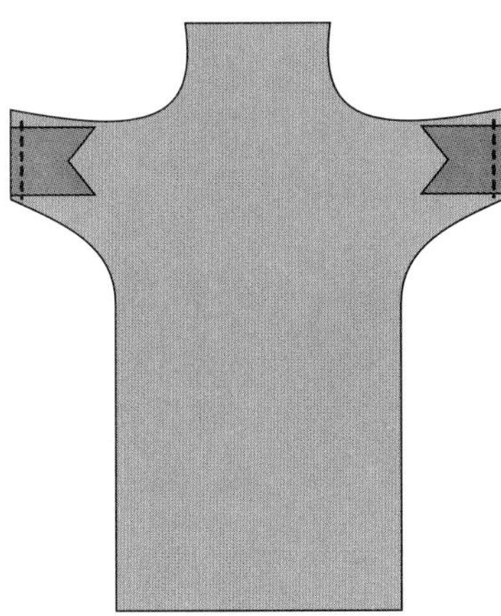

Diagram 1

4. With the right sides together, sew the bodies together, taking care not to catch the hooves in the seams; leave the neck and bottom edges open for turning. See **Diagram 2.** Clip the curves, trim the seam allowances, and turn to the right side. Turn under ¼ inch around the lower edge and slip-stitch the hem in place. Set the body aside.

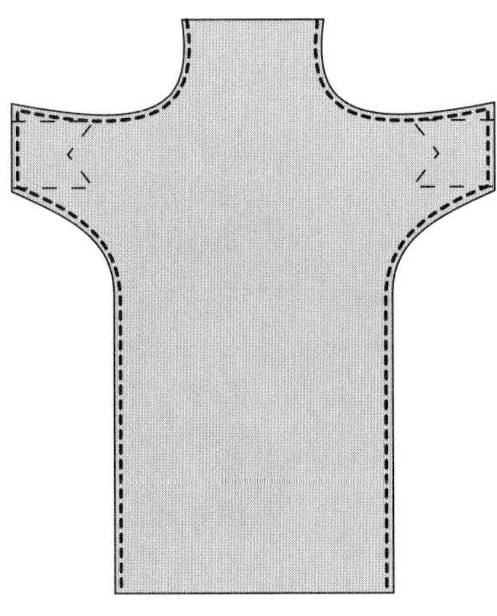

Diagram 2

5. With the right sides together, sew the heads together, leaving the neck edge open. Clip the curves, trim the seam allowances, and turn to the right side. Stuff the head firmly with fiberfill, then insert the cardboard tube about halfway into the neck opening. Glue the tube in place, using a minimal amount of glue.

6. Insert the other half of the cardboard tube into the neck opening of the body. Overlap the raw edges of the neck opening, then securely slip-stitch them to each other.

7. With the right sides together, sew one ear and one inner ear together, leaving the straight edge open. Clip the curves, trim the seam allowances, and turn to the right side. Turn under ¼ inch around the raw edges and press. Repeat for the other ear. Slip-stitch the ears to the head where indicated on the pattern.

8. For each antler, place two 7 × 9-inch felt pieces together. Using the marker, transfer the antler's

What You Need

- ½ yard of tan wool fabric for the body
- 8-inch square of tan evenweave fabric for the inner ears
- Two 2-inch squares of black felt for the hooves
- Four 9 × 12-inch pieces of brown felt for the antlers
- Matching sewing thread
- Polyester fiberfill
- Cardboard toilet tissue tube
- Hot glue gun and glue sticks
- Fine-point fabric marker
- Two 12-inch-long chenille stems
- 8-inch length of 1½-inch-wide red ribbon for the collar
- Nine ⅜-inch-diameter jingle bells for the collar
- One skein of yellow embroidery floss
- Soft-sculpture doll needle
- Two ½-inch-diameter four-hole blue buttons for the eyes
- ½-inch-diameter red shank button for the nose

solid and dashed lines to the felt. Sew on the sewing (dashed) line as indicated on the pattern, leaving the bottom edge open. Cut out the antlers on the cutting (solid) line, cutting away all markings. Insert one chenille stem into each antler for stiffness and shaping. Slip-stitch the antlers in place just behind the ears, having the side with the lowest antler at the back of the ear.

9. Wrap the red ribbon around the puppet's neck, turning under the raw ends and covering the overlapping fabric edges. Slip-stitch the ribbon ends together. Evenly space and sew the jingle bells to the center of the ribbon to create a collar.

10. Knot an 18-inch length of six-strand yellow floss and thread it through the doll needle. Insert the needle into the head at the eye dot, through the head, and out through the other eye dot. Run the needle up through a hole of one blue button and down through the opposite hole, then back through the head and out the first eye dot. Thread another button on the floss and pass the needle back through the head and the other button, crisscrossing the thread. Pass back through the head and the button, pulling the floss tightly to indent the eye area. Knot tightly.

11. Sew the red button nose in place where indicated on the pattern.

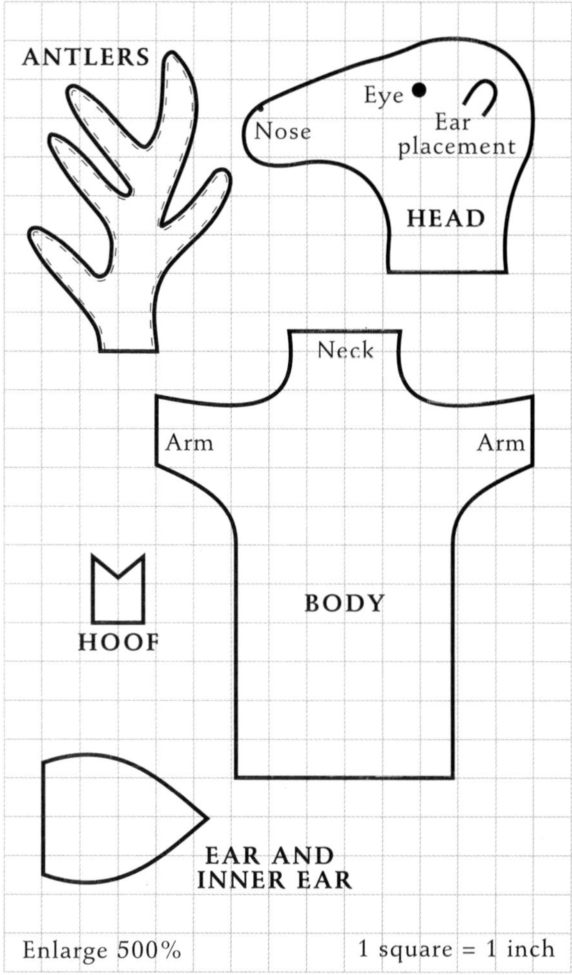

RUDOLPH THE REINDEER PUPPET PATTERNS

Money-Saving Tip

If your bazaar attracts families with younger children, remember that cost may be the deciding factor as to whether or not they make a craft purchase at your booth. Most families have limited resources but are usually willing to buy if the price is right and if the price reflects the quality. Keep this in mind as you tailor your crafts to your audience.

The Rudolph the Reindeer Puppet would look just as cute in felt as in wool, and will cost you much less in supplies. To save money on buttons, satin stitch the eyes and nose with brightly colored tapestry wool. Instead of nine jingle bells on the collar, use just five. You can cut corners and still create handsome crafts. By making smart substitutions, both you and your buyers will come out savers!

Warm Woolen Mittens

Every child loves to stay out in the snow and wintry cold to skate or sled. Keep their little hands warm while they play with a pair of warm, hand-knit mittens. These scalloped-edged and leather-palmed versions knit up fast and make great additions to a nostalgic winter bazaar.

Warm Woolen Mittens

WHAT YOU NEED

RED SCALLOPED-EDGED MITTENS

- One 3-ounce skein of red sportweight yarn, either wool or acrylic
- Set of double-pointed needles, size 5 or size to obtain gauge indicated
- 3 stitch markers
- Stitch holder
- Size F aluminum crochet hook
- 1 yard of 1/8-inch-wide white satin ribbon
- Tapestry needle

GREEN LEATHER-PALMED MITTENS

- One 3-ounce skein of green sportweight yarn, either wool or acrylic
- Set of double-pointed needles, size 5 or size to obtain gauge indicated
- 3 stitch markers
- Stitch holder
- Two 4 × 4½- (4½ × 5½-, 5 × 6½-) inch pieces of lightweight green leather
- Leather punch or awl
- Tapestry needle
- Heavy sewing thread to match leather

Red Scalloped-Edged Mittens

SIZE

Directions are for child's size small (3 × 5-inch finished palm size, excluding thumb). Changes for the featured size medium (3½ × 6-inch finished palm size, excluding thumb) and size large (4 × 7-inch finished palm size, excluding thumb) follow in parentheses.

WHAT YOU DO

1. Gauge: Knitting every round (rnd) for stockinette stitch (st st), 10 sts and 15 rnds = 2 inches.

2. Cast on 30 (36, 42) sts. Arrange 10 (12, 14) sts on each of 3 dpns; place a marker (pm) to indicate beginning of rnd; keeping sts untwisted, join. Work around in k 1, p 1 ribbing for 3½ inches. K 3 rnds.

3. For thumb gusset: K 5 sts; pm, (slip horizontal running thread between last st and next st onto left needle, k in back lp of this new st—M 1 made), k 2, M 1, pm; k 23 (29, 35) sts. Slipping markers for remainder of mitten, k 2 rnds on the 32 (38, 44) sts. Rnd 4: K 5 sts, sl marker, M 1, k to next marker, M 1, sl marker, k to end of rnd—34 (40, 46) sts. Rnds 5–6: Knit. Rep rnds 4–6 until there are 40 (48, 56) total sts or 10 (12, 14) sts between markers. K 5 sts, place next 10 (12, 14) sts onto a stitch holder for thumb; cast on 2 sts; k rem 25 (31, 37) sts. K around on 32 (38, 44) sts until mitten measures 3 (4, 5) inches from top of ribbing.

4. To decrease for top: K 4 sts, k 2 tog, pm, (k 4 sts, k 2 tog) for 4 (5, 6) times more, k 2—27 (32, 37) sts. Rnds 2–3: Knit. Rnd 4: K 3, k 2 tog, sl marker, (k 3, k 2 tog) for 4 (5, 6) times more, k 2—22 (26, 30) sts. Rnds 5–6: Knit. Rnd 7: (K 2, k 2 tog) for 5 (6, 7) times, k 2—17 (21, 25) sts. Rnds 8–9: Knit. Rnd 10: (K 1, k 2 tog) for 5 (7, 8) times, k 2 (0, 1)—12 (14, 17) sts. Rnds 11–12:

Knit. Rnd 13: (K 2 tog) around, ending k 0 (0, 1) st—6 (7, 9) sts rem. To finish, cut yarn, leaving a 6-inch tail. Thread tail into the tapestry needle and back through remaining sts; pull up to close top opening; secure in place.

5. For thumb: Return 10 (12, 14) sts to needles with 4 (5, 6) sts on each of 2 dpn and 2 sts on 3rd dpn; pick up and k 3 sts along mitten edge—13 (15, 17) sts. K 8 (10, 12) rnds. K 1, k 2 tog around—7 (8, 9) sts. K 1 rnd. K 1 (0, 1), k 2 tog around—4 (4, 5) sts. Finish as for top of mitten.

6. For scalloped edge: With the right side facing and using the crochet hook, join yarn in any st along ribbed edge (draw up a lp, ch 1). Work 23 (27, 31) sc evenly spaced around; at end, sl st in beginning sc. Ch 1, sc in same st, * 3 dc in next sc, sc in next sc; rep from * around, ending last rep sl st in beg sc. Fasten off. Weave in loose ends.

7. Repeat Steps 1 through 5 for the second mitten.

8. Cut the ribbon in half. Thread one length into the tapestry needle and weave it through the wrist stitches of a mitten, about 3/4 inch from the edge. Repeat for the remaining mitten.

Time-Saving Tip

Finding time to knit a pair of mittens may be impossible with your busy schedule. After many years of crafting for bazaars, I realized that huge blocks of time are hard to come by. So I hit upon an idea that may work for you.

Always keep an in-progress pair of mittens at your bedside. If it takes you about a half hour to really settle into bed, you could probably knit 10 to 20 rows, especially if it's an easy pattern to follow. This way, you'll have time to wind down and accomplish something in the process. You may even be able to finish a pair of mittens about every 10 days. Even if you skip a few nights, you'd be surprised at how much you complete. Keep this routine going for a year, and you'll have 30 pairs of mittens by the time the next bazaar rolls around!

Green Leather-Palmed Mittens

Size

Directions are for child's size small (3 × 5-inch finished palm size, excluding thumb). Changes for the featured size medium (3½ × 6-inch finished palm size, excluding thumb) and size large (4 × 7-inch finished palm size, excluding thumb) follow in parentheses.

What You Do

1. Repeat Steps 1 through 5 and Step 7 of the Red Scalloped-Edged Mittens.

2. Make a pattern for the leather palm by tracing a child's hand onto paper. Trim the pattern to be slightly smaller than the surface of the mitten. Cut a left and a right piece of leather by flopping the pattern for the different hands. Punch holes all around the edge of the leather pieces about 1/8 inch from the edge and at 1/8-inch intervals. Taking care not to sew the mitten closed, sew one piece of leather to the palm side of each mitten, using the tapestry needle and thread.

Holiday Tree Skirt and Trimmings

Simple materials are often all you need to create and sell memorable Christmas accessories. Crafted from dime-store felt or Styrofoam, the snowman and Santa ornaments are easy enough for the kids to make by the dozens. The Button-Bedecked Tree Skirt is simple to craft, too, and just the right size for a customer's tabletop tree.

Country Snowman Ornament

Size

6 inches tall

What You Do

1. Roll each of the balls against a hard, flat surface to flatten their rounded shapes in order to give the appearance of a "hand-packed" snowball; leave some lumpiness for a realistic look.

2. Glue the small ball to the medium one. Glue the medium ball to the large ball to create the snowman body.

3. From the felt, cut a 2½-inch-diameter circle for the hat brim, a 1-inch-diameter circle for the hat top, and a ¾ × 4-inch strip for the hat. Glue the short ends of the hat strip together to form a felt ring. Glue the small circle to one side of the ring, pushing it slightly inside the ring to give the look of a crumpled hat. Glue the other side of the ring to the center of the larger circle to form the hat brim. Glue the ribbon around the hat, trimming away any excess. Add the gold thread at the back of the hat for a hanger, then glue the hat in place atop the head.

4. Break the toothpick in half and paint one half orange. Let it dry, then insert the wide end of the painted toothpick in the head for the carrot nose.

5. Push the black seed beads into the snowman, using two for the eyes, five for the mouth, and six for the buttons.

6. Insert the twigs into the sides of the middle ball for the arms.

7. Fringe the ends of the gold fabric strip for about ½ inch, then tie the scarf around the snowman's neck.

WHAT YOU NEED

COUNTRY SNOWMAN ORNAMENT

- 1½-, 2-, and 3-inch-diameter Styrofoam balls for the body
- Low-temperature glue gun and glue sticks
- Scrap of brown felt for the hat
- 4-inch length of ¼-inch-wide red satin ribbon for the hat band
- 10-inch length of metallic gold thread for the hanger
- Toothpick for the "carrot" nose
- Orange acrylic paint
- Paintbrush
- 13 black seed beads for the "coal" eyes, mouth, and buttons
- Two 2-inch-long twigs for the arms
- 1 × 8-inch piece of gold evenweave fabric for the scarf

STAND-UP SANTA ORNAMENT

- 7-inch square of red felt for the body
- Scraps of green and pale pink felt for the mittens, holly, and face
- ⅜ × 10-inch strip of white felt for the trim
- Matching sewing thread
- Hot glue gun and glue sticks
- Red and black puff paint with fine-tip applicator for the holly berries and eyes
- Small piece of polyester fiberfill for the beard
- 8-inch length of ⅛-inch-diameter red cord for the hanger
- ¾-inch-diameter white pom-pom for the hat

Stand-Up Santa Ornament

SIZE

6 inches tall

WHAT YOU DO

1. Enlarge the **Stand-Up Santa Patterns** on page 48 as directed in "Enlarging Patterns" on page 238.

2. From the red, cut one body. From the green, cut two mittens and two holly leaves. From the pink, cut one face. From the white, cut one 3-inch length for thc hat trim and onc 7 inch length for the jacket trim.

3. Using a ¼-inch seam allowance, sew the sides of the body together to form a cone shape, then turn it to the right side.

4. Referring to the pattern for placement, glue the face and mittens in place. Glue the small strip around the cone at the top of the face for the hat trim. Glue the holly leaves in place at the top of the hat trim. Glue the large strip to the base of the cone.

5. Add three red puff paint holly berries and black puff paint eyes. Let dry thoroughly.

6. Glue the fiberfill below the face to form Santa's beard.

7. Fold the cord in half and sew the ends to the pom-pom to create a hanger, then glue the pom-pom to the top of Santa's hat.

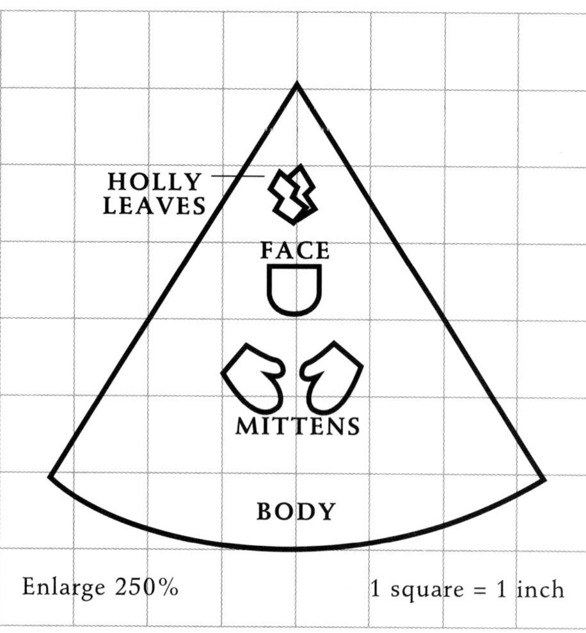

STAND-UP SANTA PATTERNS

Button-Bedecked Tree Skirt

SIZE

28 inches in diameter

WHAT YOU DO

1. To draft a 28-inch-diameter circle for the tree skirt, fold the paper square into quarters. Lay the quartered square on top of the cardboard or corkboard so you can stick the pushpin in securely. Tie one end of the string to the pencil. Stretching the string taut, tie a knot near the opposite end of the string so that the distance between the point of the upright pencil and the knot is exactly the radius measurement (14 inches). Insert the pushpin into the newly tied knot, then stick the pin in the corner of the folded paper square. Holding the pencil perpendicular to the pattern surface and keeping the string taut, swing the pencil around to draft the one quarter of the 28-inch circle. See the **Circle Diagram.** Repeat this step to draft a 4½-inch circle (the radius is 2¼ inches) for the tree skirt opening. Cut through all four layers of the paper on both drawn arcs. Unfold the paper. Cut along one fold line, then cut ¼ inch to each side of the fold line to create the tree skirt opening.

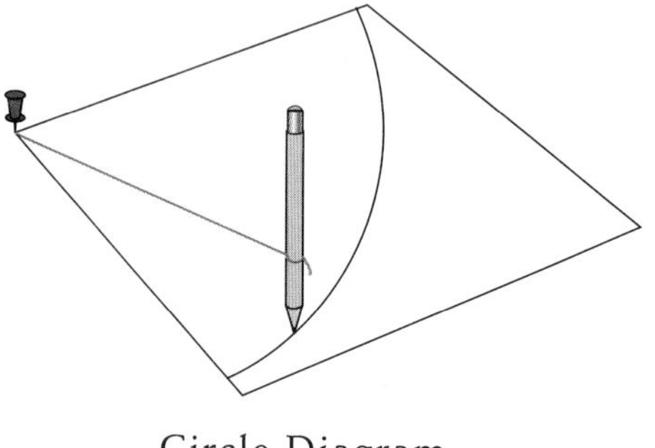

Circle Diagram

2. From the red, cut one tree skirt, using the drafted circle as a pattern.

3. Enlarge the **Christmas Tree Pattern** as directed in "Enlarging Patterns" on page 238. From the green, cut seven Christmas trees.

4. Using spray adhesive, lightly spray the wrong side of the trees and position them on the tree skirt, evenly spacing them around the tree skirt.

5. Using six strands of green floss and referring to "Stitch Details" on page 243, work blanket stitches around each tree; use a different shade of green floss for each tree. Using six strands of white floss, work blanket stitches around the tree skirt edges.

6. Using three strands of floss, randomly sew 12 to 15 buttons on each tree for the ornaments.

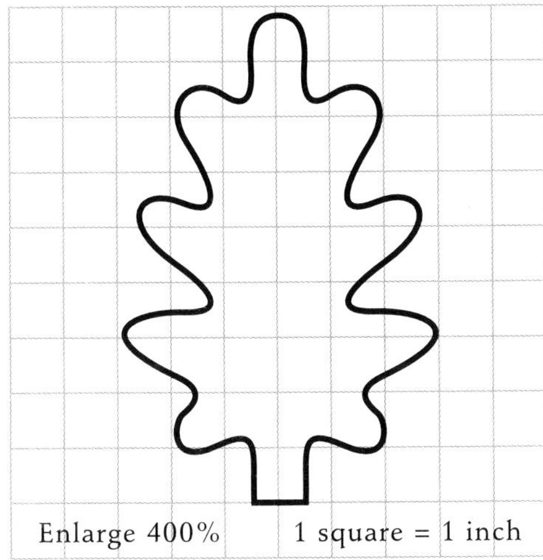

CHRISTMAS TREE PATTERN

WHAT YOU NEED

BUTTON-BEDECKED TREE SKIRT

- 29-inch square of paper
- Large piece of cardboard or corkboard
- Pushpin
- 34-inch length of string
- Sharp pencil
- 30-inch square of red felt for the tree skirt
- Seven 6 × 9-inch pieces of green felt for the trees
- Spray adhesive
- Seven skeins of embroidery floss in assorted shades of green
- Three skeins of white embroidery floss
- Sharp tapestry needle
- About 95 white and cream odd-lot buttons for the ornaments

MONEY-SAVING TIP

Buttons are often the most expensive component of a project. You may think the Button-Bedecked Tree Skirt is an unprofitable bazaar choice if you don't have access to a huge button jar or a great sale. Don't despair! Just substitute less-costly supplies for the buttons. Give the tree skirt a country look with cream pom-poms or sew on charms for an antique look. Skip the embellishments altogether and have a rustic look. Don't let a long materials list or a costly supply deter you from choosing one of the crafts in this book for your booth. Perhaps you have a bag of jingle bells from a close-out sale years ago; go ahead and sew them on! Just take a few minutes to poke around your craft closet and see what you can find!

Festive Fingertip Towels

Cross-stitch is always a popular item at bazaars—both for the contributors to stitch and the buyers to buy! These Jolly Santa, Jingle Bells, and Northern Pines motifs are easy to stitch onto purchased towels. They take just an evening or two and will bring a truly festive look to the buyer's holiday decorating. Sell them separately, or tie two or three together with a Christmassy ribbon to sell as a set at your booth.

SIZE

Northern Pines motif is 1 × 1⅜ inches
Jolly Santa motif is 1⅝ × 1⅞ inches
Jingle Bells motif is 1¾ × 2¼ inches

WHAT YOU NEED

- Cranberry, white, and evergreen velour 14-count fingertip towels*
- One skein of embroidery floss for each color in the **Color Keys**
- Size 22 or 24 tapestry needle

**See the "Buyer's Guide" on page 244 for ordering information.*

WHAT YOU DO

1. Find the center of the cross-stitch band on each towel and mark it with a pin. Find the centers of the **Northern Pines Chart,** the **Jolly Santa Chart,** and the **Jingle Bells Chart** on pages 52 and 53 by connecting the arrows.

2. Work the Northern Pines motif on the cranberry towel, the Jolly Santa motif on the white towel, and the Jingle Bells motif on the evergreen towel. Matching the centers of the charts and the cross-stitch bands on the towels, and using two strands of embroidery floss, begin cross-stitching at the center point, working outward until the entire design is complete.

3. Backstitch the fur trim on Santa with one strand of black. Referring to "Stitch Details" on page 243, work French knot eyes with one strand of black.

4. Wash and press the completed cross-stitch towels as directed in "Washing and Pressing" on page 241.

TIME-SAVING TIP

Do you lose momentum when you're stitching by having to stop and thread a new length of floss in your needle? You can save precious time by threading five needles for each color of floss you're using for your project. Avid needleworkers have used this time-saving tip for many years, and you'll find it's helpful for even small cross-stitch projects.

To keep your threaded needles tangle-free, make a small floss keeper. You'll need a 5-inch square of Styrofoam, a 5-inch square of graph paper, a pen, and tacky glue. Mark a grid on the graph paper, having the grid lines 1 inch apart. In each 1-inch grid block, write one of the floss color numbers you'll be using for the project. Glue the wrong side of the paper grid to the Styrofoam and let it dry thoroughly. Then, thread your needles and stick them into the appropriate block. This way, you'll only need to reach for a new needle instead of having to stop to thread one as you work. You'll save time and aggravation as well.

NORTHERN PINES COLOR KEY

	DMC	Anchor	J. & P. Coats	Color
•	906	256	6256	Med. Parrot Green

125

20

NORTHERN PINES CHART

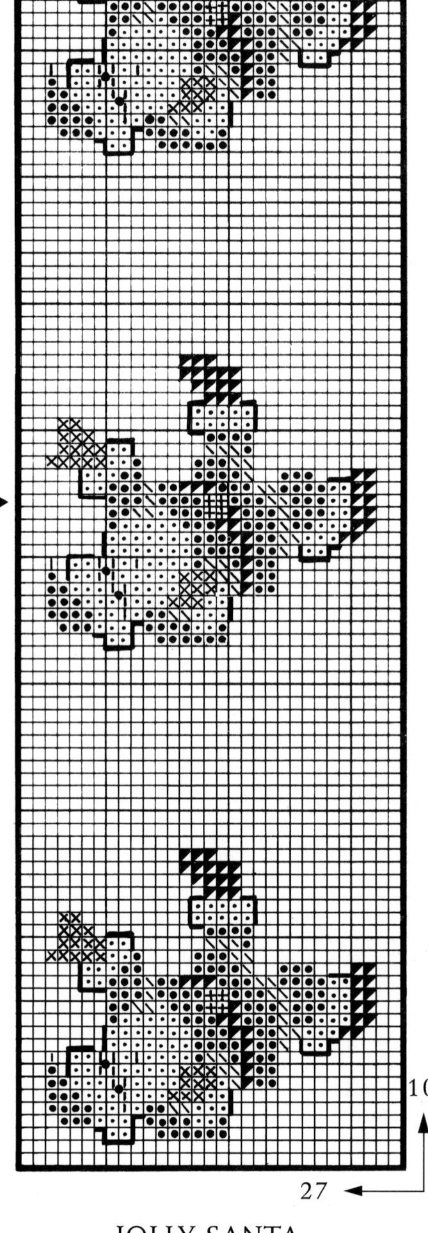

101

27

JOLLY SANTA CHART

JOLLY SANTA COLOR KEY

	DMC	Anchor	J. & P. Coats	Color
•	White	2	1001	White
	310	403	8403	Black
●	321	9046	3500	Christmas Red
◥	646	8581	8500	Dk. Beaver Gray
†	676	891	——	Lt. Old Gol
/	815	43	3000	Med. Garn
×	906	256	6256	Med. Parro Green
–	945	881	3335	Sportsman Flesh

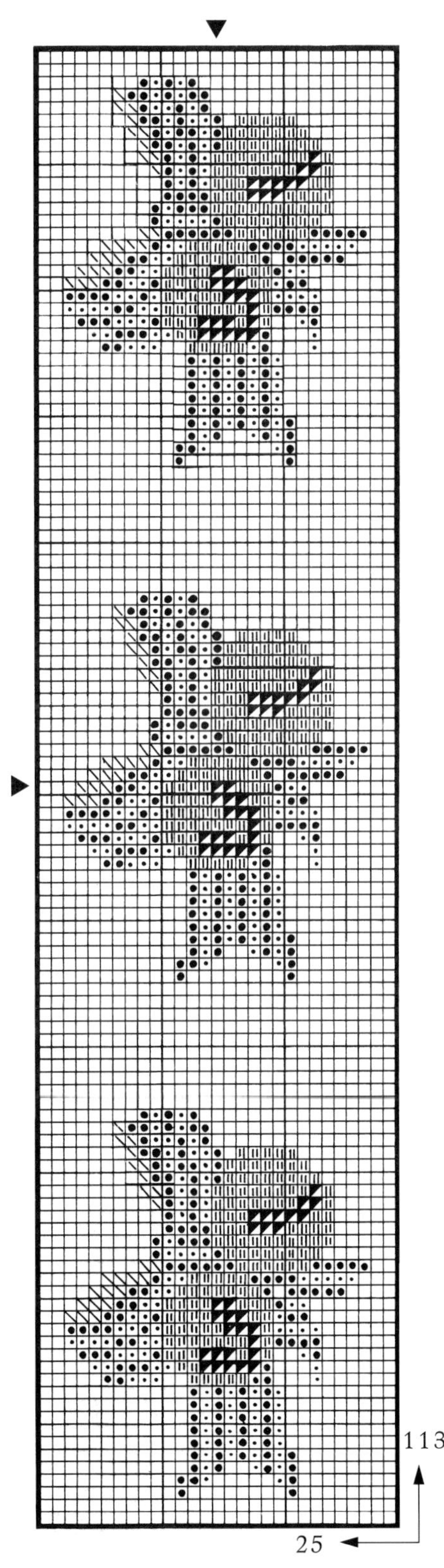

JINGLE BELLS CHART

JINGLE BELLS COLOR KEY

	DMC	Anchor	J. & P. Coats	Color
•	White	2	1001	White
●	321	9046	3500	Christmas Red
◥	420	374	5374	Med. Brown
=	676	891	——	Lt. Old Gold
/	815	43	3000	Med. Garnet

Gifts from Heaven and Earth

Celestial motifs and earth and sky colors inspire crafts that sparkle with imagination. These projects will provide you with a host of ideas for your holiday booth. This shining bazaar collection is sure to star in any seasonal display.

Heavenly Bodies

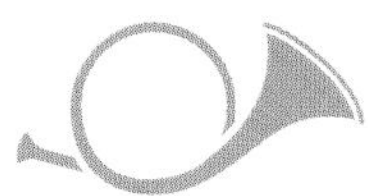

These celestially inspired ornaments are sure to cause a sparkle in the eyes of customers. The antique-finished Shooting Star Ball and the tin Crescent Moon Ornament can be made in a twinkling. Whip up a whole galaxy to display in your holiday crafts booth.

Shooting Star Ball

Size

About 5 inches high

What You Do

1. Remove the metal cap and hook from the Christmas ball.

2. Mix a solution of 1/4 cup of bleach and 1/4 cup of water and stir thoroughly.

3. To "antique" the gold ball, pour 1 teaspoon of the bleach-and-water solution into the ball, swish it around, then pour it out immediately. The bleach will react with the gold finish, dissolving it and leaving a smoky glass finish with gold-accented areas. The longer you leave the bleach solution in the ball, the more gold will be removed, so it is important to keep the bleach-and-water solution in the ball for just a few seconds. Set the ball aside to dry. Replace the cap and hook.

4. Cut the star garland into four pieces, each about 7 inches long. Holding the star garland lengths together as if they were one, fold them in the center. Apply a drop of hot glue to the folded area and insert it into the hole of the Christmas ball cap; see the **Star Garland Diagram.**

Star Garland Diagram

What You Need

Shooting Star Ball

- 2½-inch-diameter gold glass Christmas ball
- Bleach
- Water
- ¾ yard of metallic gold star garland
- Hot glue gun and glue sticks
- 3-inch piece of gold tinsel
- 8-inch length of ⅛-inch-wide metallic gold ribbon for the hanger

5. Wrap and glue the tinsel around the cap to hide it, tucking under the tinsel ends.

6. Loop the ribbon through the cap wire and tie the ends together to form a hanger.

Project Pointers

Glass Christmas balls provide a blank canvas for the bazaar crafter. If you like the swished-bleach look of the Shooting Star Ball, take it one step further by spray painting the inside of the ball. Choose one or two color spray paints that coordinate with the existing color ball. After antiquing the ball with the bleach and water, let the ball dry thoroughly. Insert the spray can nozzle a fraction of an inch into the ball's neck. Quickly press and release the nozzle to lightly dust the inside of the ball with paint. Lightly spray a second color if desired.

For a more contemporary effect, splatter the outside of a deep blue or red ball with silver or gold paint. Then accent with the shooting star topper for a dramatic look. For a kid-style decoration that even the little tykes can afford, buy garland with hearts, snowflakes, musical notes, or snowmen for the toppers. Bend the garland lengths into playful loops and glue them inside the ball cap. Kids will love them since they're sparkly and fun!

WHAT YOU NEED

CRESCENT MOON ORNAMENT

- 6 × 9-inch piece of lightweight craft tin*
- Tin snips or craft scissors
- 9 × 12-inch piece of corrugated cardboard
- Burnishing tool or stylus
- Yellow, blue, red, and green translucent glass paint†
- Awl
- 8-inch length of ⅛-inch-diameter silver cord for the hanger

* *Available at craft and hobby shops or school supply stores.*

† *See the "Buyer's Guide" on page 244 for ordering information.*

Crescent Moon Ornament

SIZE

8 inches high

WHAT YOU DO

1. Enlarge the **Crescent Moon Ornament Pattern** as directed in "Enlarging Patterns" on page 238.

2. Using a pencil, trace the pattern lightly onto the tin. Using the tin snips or craft scissors, cut out the ornament. Lay the ornament face down on the cardboard.

3. Working from the back of the ornament and using the burnishing tool or stylus, burnish or indent the cheek, lips, nose, and eyelids where indicated on the pattern. Take care not to push through the tin. Turn the ornament over. Working from the front, burnish or indent the eye in the same manner.

4. Using the translucent paints, paint the moon yellow, the eye blue, and the cheek and lips red; leave the paint somewhat blotchy to give the ornament a weathered appearance. Allow the paints to dry. Add green dots in a random pattern on the yellow portion of the ornament.

5. Punch a hole with the awl at the top of the crescent moon. Thread the silver cord through the hole and knot it for a hanger.

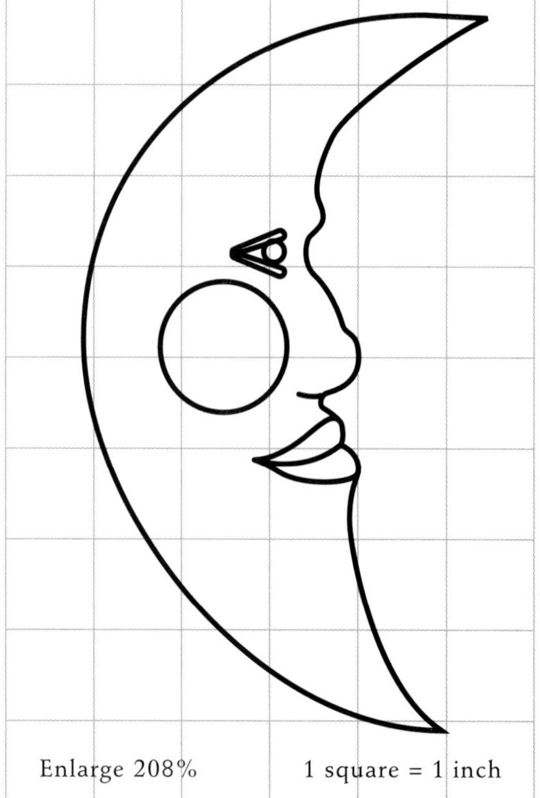

CRESCENT MOON ORNAMENT PATTERN

Beaded Stars

Quick and easy to craft, these jewel-studded stars will twinkle and shine when displayed in a mantel of greens or tied to the branches of a towering tree. A variety of inexpensive craft beads and beads from old costume jewelry catch the light and reflect the joy of the holiday season.

Beaded Stars

WHAT YOU NEED

- 24-gauge wire (35 inches for a 4-inch star, 45 inches for a 6-inch star, or 55 inches for an 8-inch star)
- Wire cutters
- Iridescent craft beads in assorted sizes and colors (100 for a 4-inch star, 150 for a 6-inch star, or 200 for an 8-inch star)
- Pearls by the yard or beaded holiday garland in a coordinating color (3 yards for a 6-inch star or 5 yards for an 8-inch star)
- Spray paint in a coordinating color (optional)
- 8-inch length of ¼-inch-wide braid for the hanger (optional)

SIZE

4 to 8 inches across

WHAT YOU DO

1. Use the point of the wire cutters to make a small bend at one end of the wire to prevent the beads from falling off while working. The size and number of points (five or six) in the star can be easily adjusted to fit your supplies and needs.

2. Alternating the size and color of beads in a random fashion, string the beads onto the wire. For a 4-inch star, string 24 inches of beads. For a 6-inch star, string 30 inches of beads. For an 8-inch star, string 40 inches of beads. After stringing the desired length, bend the working end of the wire to prevent the beads from falling off.

3. Make a bend in the wire to form one point of the star (4 inches from one end for the 4-inch star,

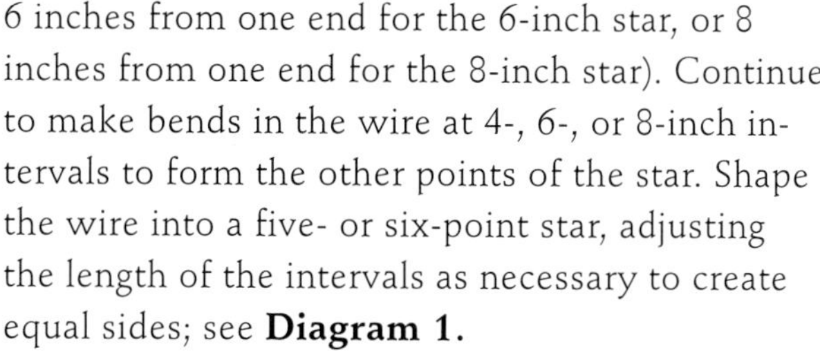

6 inches from one end for the 6-inch star, or 8 inches from one end for the 8-inch star). Continue to make bends in the wire at 4-, 6-, or 8-inch intervals to form the other points of the star. Shape the wire into a five- or six-point star, adjusting the length of the intervals as necessary to create equal sides; see **Diagram 1.**

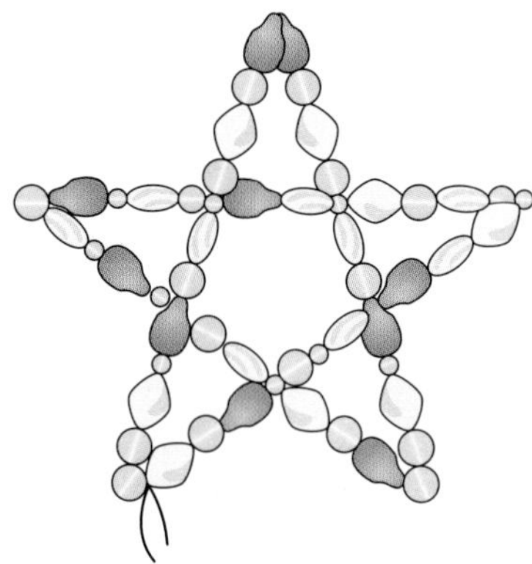

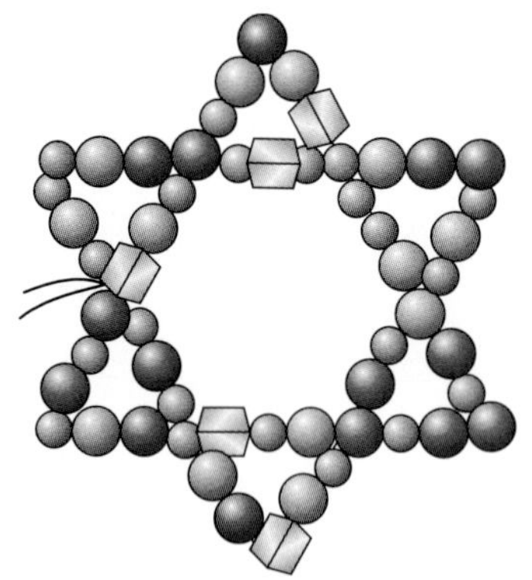

Diagram 1

4. Twist the wire ends together to secure the star shape. Trim away any remaining wire.

5. Cut several 1-inch lengths of wire and secure the star at all intersections to hold the shape.

6. Beginning at the top point of the 6- or 8-inch stars, wrap the pearls or the beaded garland around the strung beads; see **Diagram 2.** If desired, wrap the beaded garland around the star a second time. Trim away any excess pearls or garland. Secure the intersections with wire by wrapping it around both the beaded star shape and the beaded garland.

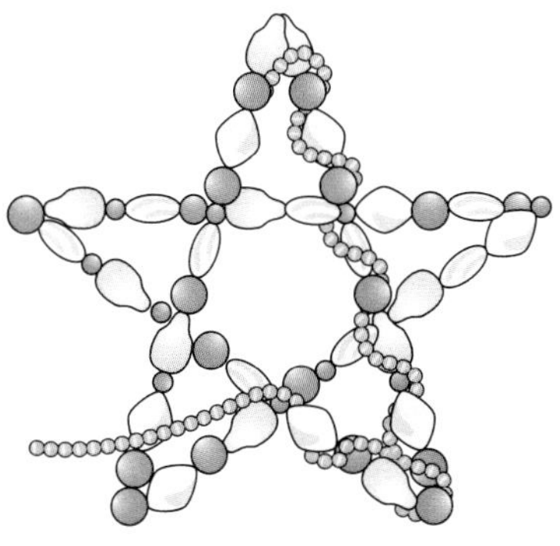

Diagram 2

7. Working in a well-ventilated area and using the spray paint, lightly "dust" the beaded star with paint to give it a spatter-painted effect.

8. Tie the braid hanger to the top point of the star, if desired, to use the star as an ornament.

TIME-SAVING TIP

These beaded stars are great bazaar gifts since the materials are inexpensive and they take only 20 to 30 minutes to make. You can shave a few minutes off your crafting time by making a star form instead of bending the star shape by hand.

You'll need a 10-inch square of scrap wood and five or six 2-inch-long nails. Using the ***Star Form Diagrams*** *as a guide, mark the location of the nails for the 4-, 6-, or 8-inch beaded star. Pound one nail into each marked spot.*

After you've strung the beads for each star, wrap the bead strand around the form, following a five- or six-point star pattern, as shown in the ***Shaping Diagrams.*** *Secure the bead strand ends and intersections with short lengths of wire.*

To remove the star from the form, pull out each nail. If you try to remove the star without first removing the nails, you may distort the shape.

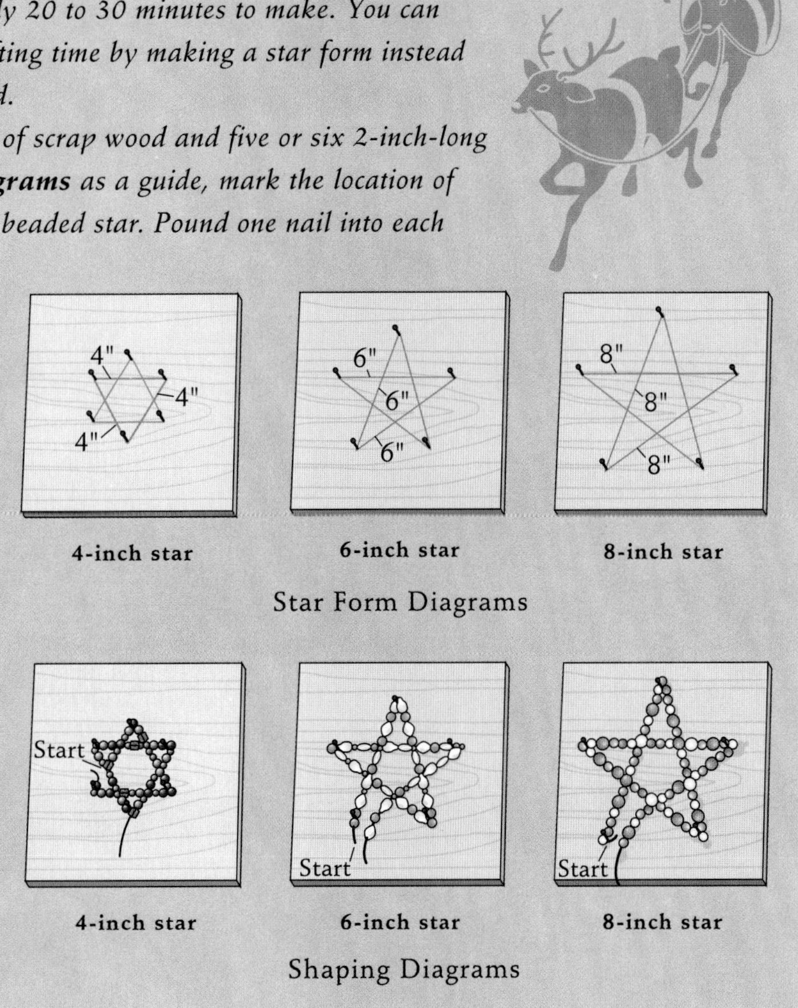

4-inch star | **6-inch star** | **8-inch star**

Star Form Diagrams

4-inch star | **6-inch star** | **8-inch star**

Shaping Diagrams

Golden Accents

Serve up the holidays with unquestionable style. The decorative Touch-of-Gold Bowl, Planet Earth Bowl, Beaded Bowl, and Bead-Wrapped Ball have plenty of pizzazz yet are easy to craft.

Touch-of-Gold Bowl

Size

8 inches in diameter

What You Do

1. Using the scrap wood and the paint, practice spraying a mist on the wood's surface in a well-ventilated area. Determine the pressure needed on the paint nozzle and the length of spray time necessary to obtain a light coating of paint. Do not cover the grain of the wood entirely with the paint.

2. Place the bowl on a clean, flat surface. Lightly spray a mist of paint onto the bowl, allowing the wood grain to show through the paint. Paint a second coat if necessary.

3. Using the paintbrush, seal the entire bowl with polyurethane, following the manufacturer's directions. Let it dry thoroughly.

Planet Earth Bowl

Size

8 inches in diameter

What You Do

Note: This bowl should be used for displaying nonedible items only. To clean, wipe it with a slightly damp cloth. Do not immerse it in water. It is important to let customers know how to use and care for the bowl by attaching a note and discussing its upkeep with them when it is purchased.

1. Squeeze the paint onto the saucer or palette. Using a brush, paint the interior of the bowl with the paint; do not paint the rim of the bowl. When the painting is complete, wash the saucer and brush with soap and water before the paint dries.

2. While the paint is still wet, lay the gold leaf onto the painted surface of the bowl to abstractly resemble the continents and oceans. Using a dry brush, press the leaf in place. Lift off unstuck, overlapping sections. Apply a small amount of paint to the top layer of leaf and reapply torn pieces of leaf to form a slightly layered look. Continue the process until a pleasing effect has been achieved. Let the bowl dry thoroughly.

3. Using the third paintbrush, seal the entire bowl with polyurethane, following the manufacturer's directions. Allow the bowl to dry thoroughly.

Beaded Bowl

SIZE

12½ inches in diameter

WHAT YOU DO

1. Lay the bowl upside down on a clean, flat surface.

2. Beginning at the edge of the flat bottom surface of the bowl, glue the silver garland around the edge of the bowl's bottom.

3. Continue to wrap and glue the silver garland around the curved outer surface of the bowl. Start the gold garland one or two rows below the rim of the bowl and continue onto the rim. Cut any excess garland.

WHAT YOU NEED

TOUCH-OF-GOLD BOWL

- Scrap wood
- Metallic gold spray paint
- 8-inch-diameter unfinished wooden bowl*
- Clear, waterproof polyurethane
- 1-inch-wide paintbrush

* *See the "Buyer's Guide" on page 244 for ordering information.*

PLANET EARTH BOWL

- Medium blue acrylic paint
- Saucer or palette
- 8-inch-diameter unfinished wooden bowl*
- Three 1-inch-wide paintbrushes
- 5 to 8 sheets of imitation gold leaf
- Clear, waterproof polyurethane

* *See the "Buyer's Guide" on page 244 for ordering information.*

BEADED BOWL

- 12-inch-diameter unfinished wooden bowl*
- 50-yard spool of silver bead garland
- Hot glue gun and glue sticks
- 4 to 6 yards of gold bead garland

* *See the "Buyer's Guide" on page 244 for ordering information.*

WHAT YOU NEED

BEAD-WRAPPED BALL

- 3½-inch-diameter Styrofoam ball
- 6-inch length of ⅛-inch-diameter gold or silver cord for the hanger
- Low-temperature glue gun and glue sticks
- 3½ yards of gold or silver bead garland

Bead-Wrapped Ball

SIZE

4 inches in diameter

WHAT YOU DO

1. Poke a small hole in the foam ball using the point of a pencil. Hot-glue the ends of the cord into the hole to form a loop for hanging.

2. Poke another small hole at the hanger and insert the end of the bead garland length into the hole; hot-glue it in place.

3. Wrap the garland length around the ball in a clockwise motion, hot-gluing it in place as you proceed. Continue covering the ball by applying small amounts of glue to the ball and laying the garland over the glue to secure; press the garland firmly into the hot glue.

4. Once the ball is completely covered, poke a small hole in the bottom of the ball for the garland end. Cut off the excess garland, then hot-glue the end in the hole.

PROJECT POINTERS

If the bazaar at which you sell your wares is a country bazaar, forget the glitz of silver and gold. Turn the Beaded Bowl and Bead-Wrapped Ball into charming home-style crafts. Use wooden bead garlands for a natural look or red or green bead garlands for a traditional slant. Browse your local craft or holiday store for ideas. You'll find pearlized garlands and round-and-square bead garlands that would make nice accents for these easy projects.

If you're a patient crafter and know that your customers are looking for works of art when buying handcrafts, you may want to offer decorated bowls of a high caliber. Strategically arrange lengths of gold garland to form shapes, such as circles, on the bowl's side. Then fill in the unadorned areas with rows of silver garlands cut to fit.

The wooden bowls used in these projects can often be picked up for a few dollars at garage sales, flea markets, or auctions. If you are fortunate enough to find older bowls, clean them thoroughly before painting and finishing them; it may also be necessary for you to sand them smooth before accenting them.

If you cannot find used bowls, unfinished bowls can be ordered from the Weston Bowl Mill; see the "Buyer's Guide" on page 244. Seconds are available at a very reasonable price and are perfect for painted country bowl projects.

Jeweled Candles

Turn run-of-the-mill candles into dazzling bejeweled gems to sell in your holiday craft booth. Add a few inexpensive jewels around the top, create a simple mosaic or polka-dot pattern, or go all out and encrust the entire candle surface for a diamond-studded Christmas decoration for all to enjoy.

Size

Jewels are ½ to 1 inch high

What You Do

1. Choose the pattern you wish to use. I glued oval jewels about 1½ inches apart along the top edge of the 6-inch-diameter candle. I alternated round jewels on the tall 3-inch-diameter candle and created a mosaic pattern on the shortest candle since it used quite a few jewels.

2. Glue the plastic jewels to the candle in your prearranged pattern, embedding them slightly where the hot glue has softened the candle.

What You Need

- 3-, 4-, and 6-inch-diameter candles, about 3 to 6 inches high
- Decorative oval, round, and square plastic beveled jewels
- Hot glue gun and glue sticks

Crocheted Choirboy

Any holiday tree will sing with a diminutive crocheted choirboy. And, of course, his heavenly look is perfect for a church bazaar. Stitch up a whole choir in a variety of colors for different tastes and color schemes.

Size

5 inches tall

What You Do

1. Gauge: Working in rnds of sc, 8 sts and 8 rnds = 1 inch.

2. Using the desired gown color, ch 45. Being careful to keep ch untwisted, join with sl st in beginning ch to form a ring.

3. Rnd 1: Ch 1, sc in each ch around; join with sl st to first sc—45 sc. Rnds 2 and 3: Ch 1, sc in each sc around; join. Rnd 4: Ch 1, * sc in 13 sc, (draw up a lp in each of next 2 sc, yo and draw through all 3 lps on hook—sc 2 tog made); repeat from * twice more—42 sc; join. Rnds 5–7: Ch 1, sc in each sc around; join. Rnd 8: Ch 1, (sc in 12 sc, sc dec) 3 times—39 sc; join.

4. Working dec rnds as est, rep rnds 5–8 until 12 sc remain. To complete: Cut thread, leaving a 5-inch tail. Thread tail into tapestry needle and back through sts. Pull up to close opening; secure.

5. For the head: Rnd 1: With light peach, ch 2, work 8 sc in 2nd ch from hook; join with sl st to first sc. Rnd 2: Ch 1, work 2 sc in each sc around—16 sc; join. Rnds 3–7: Ch 1, sc in each sc around; join. At end of Rnd 7, stuff head snugly with cotton balls. Rnd 8: Ch 1, sc 2 tog around—8 sts; join. Rnd 9: Ch 1, sc in each sc around; join. Complete as for gown.

6. For the lace robe: Beg at neck edge with white, ch 20; join with sl st to form ring. Rnd 1: Ch 1, work 32 sc in ring; join. Rnd 2: Ch 4 (counts as dc, ch 1), dc in same st, * skip 1 sc in next sc (dc, ch 1, dc—V-st made); rep from * around—16 V-sts; join. Rnd 3: Sl st in next ch-1 sp, ch 3 for first dc, in same ch-1 sp (dc, ch 2, and 2 dc), in next 3 ch-1 sps (2 dc, ch 2, and 2 dc) for sleeve; for robe front, (V-st in next ch-1 sp) 4 times; for 2nd sleeve, in next 4 ch-1 sps (2 dc, ch 2, and 2 dc); for robe back (V-st in next ch-1 sp) 4 times; join with sl st in top of beg ch-3. Rnd 4: Skip 4 ch-2 sps of sleeve, sl st in ch-1 sp of next V-st, ch 4 (counts as dc, ch 1), dc in same ch-1 sp, (V-st in ch-1 sp of next V-st) 3 times, skip 4 ch-2 sps of next sleeve, (V-st in ch-1 sp of next V-st) 4 times; join in 3rd ch of beg ch-4. Rnd 5: Sl st to next ch-1 sp, ch 3 for first dc, in same ch-1 sp (dc, ch 1, 2 dc), (2 dc, ch 1, 2 dc) in ch-1 sp of each V-st around; join. Rnd 6: Sl st to next ch-1 sp, ch 3 (counts as dc), in same sp (dc, ch 1, 2 dc), * ch 1, in next ch-1 sp (2 dc, ch 1, 2 dc); rep from * around; join. Rnd 7: Sl st to next ch-1 sp, ch 3 for first dc, in same sp (dc, ch 1, 2 dc), * ch 2, skip ch-1 between groups, in next ch-1 sp (2 dc, ch 1, 2 dc); rep from * around; join. Rnd 8: Sl st to next ch-1 sp, ch 3 for first dc, in same sp (dc, ch 2, and 2 dc), * ch 2, sc in ch-2 sp between groups, ch 2, in next ch-1 sp (2 dc, ch 2, 2 dc); rep from * around; join. Fasten off and cut the thread.

7. Cover the cardboard with waxed paper for a base, then form sheets of waxed paper into small cone shapes for a choirboy form. Using the paintbrush, paint starch on the gown and lace robe, then place them onto the cone shapes. Stretch the gown and robe into the desired position and pin the lower edges to the cardboard.

WHAT YOU NEED

- J. & P. Coats South Maid Cotton Knit and Crochet Thread, Art. D. 54: one ball each of white #1 and light peach #424 for the lace robe and face, and one ball of purple #458, true blue #482, or wood violet #495 for the gown
- Size 6 (1.8 mm) steel crochet hook or size to achieve gauge
- Tapestry needle
- Cotton balls for stuffing
- 4-inch square of cardboard
- Waxed paper
- Paintbrush
- Liquid starch for stiffening
- Rustproof straight pins

8. For the hanger, cut a 4-inch length of light peach and thread it into the tapestry needle. Form a loop at the top of the head, securing it with a few short stitches.

PROJECT POINTERS

You could sell the choirboys in sets of three so customers could add them to their manger scene. You can also make the choirboys larger or smaller by changing the crochet hook size. And wouldn't the choirboys make nice door prizes on the day of the bazaar? To attract more buyers, give away one as a door prize every 15 minutes. Or have a whole tree of crocheted choirboys at the bazaar entrance to set a spirited mood.

Circles and Stars

This trio of craft projects takes advantage of vintage and inexpensive items and is easy enough for the youngest booth participants to make. The Button Vase and Button Garland make use of mismatched white and cream buttons while the shiny Stand-Up Star is cut from metallic gold posterboard.

Button Vase

SIZE

8 inches high

WHAT YOU DO

1. Mark a line around the carton 8 inches from the bottom of the carton and cut off the top.

2. Working in a well-ventilated area, spray paint the inside and outside of the carton with several light coats.

3. Glue the buttons to each side of the carton, covering the entire surface of the vase, arranging the buttons in informal rows.

4. Using the polyurethane and working in a well-ventilated area, spray the inside and outside of the vase to add durability.

5. To display at your booth, cut a block of floral foam to fit the inside base, then insert dried flowers into the foam; if you prefer fresh flowers, you may insert a water-filled glass jar in the vase.

WHAT YOU NEED

BUTTON VASE

- Empty, clean ½-gallon paper milk container or similar-size cardboard box
- Off-white spray paint
- About 200 assorted-size white and cream buttons
- Hot glue gun and glue sticks
- Spray polyurethane
- 4-inch square of floral foam (optional)
- Dried flowers (optional)
- Glass jar (optional)
- Fresh flowers (optional)

BUTTON GARLAND

- ⅛-inch-wide cream satin ribbon in length desired
- Blunt-point tapestry needle
- Antique bone or odd-lot white or cream buttons, about 12 per yard

Button Garland

SIZE

Length as desired

WHAT YOU DO

1. Thread one end of the ribbon into the eye of the tapestry needle.

2. Referring to the **Button Threading Diagram,** thread the needle and ribbon through both holes of a button, sliding the button down the ribbon to about 6 inches from the other end of the ribbon. For buttons that have four holes, thread the ribbon through two of the holes.

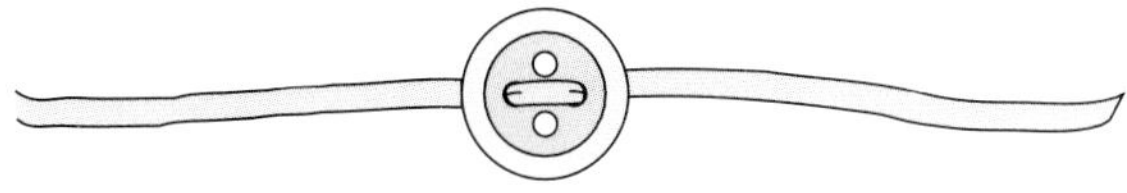

Button Threading Diagram

3. Continue to thread buttons onto the ribbon, spacing them in a random pattern. You can try placing them anywhere from 3 to 8 inches apart until the ribbon is complete.

4. For your booth, wrap the garland on cardboard tubes and sell it by the foot or by the yard.

WHAT YOU NEED

STAND-UP STAR

- Template plastic for the pattern
- Two 6-inch squares of double-sided metallic gold posterboard for the star
- Craft knife with extra blades

Stand-Up Star

SIZE

6 inches high

WHAT YOU DO

1. Enlarge the **Stand-Up Star Pattern** as directed in "Enlarging Patterns" on page 238.

2. From the template plastic, cut one star. The template plastic is more durable than paper and will withstand repeated use.

3. From the posterboard, cut two stars, using the craft knife for a clean cut and changing blades as necessary.

4. Using the craft knife and the pattern as a guide, cut on the dotted line for one star and the dashed line for the remaining star to create the interlocking slits. Slide one star's interlocking slit into the other and adjust the stars at right angles to stand.

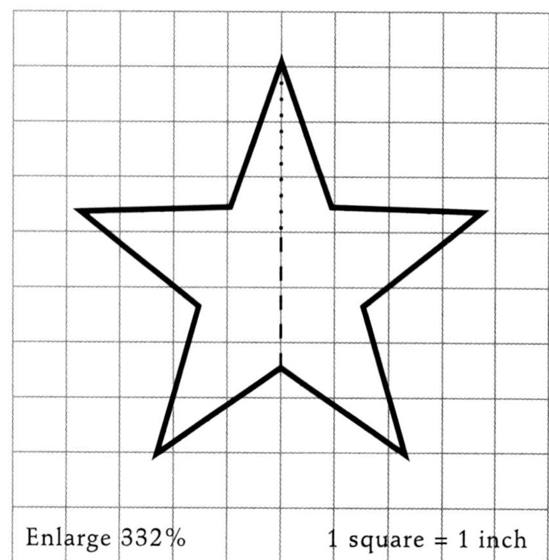

STAND-UP STAR PATTERN

PROJECT POINTERS

If you haven't tried to marbleize paper, this stand-up star would make a good starter project. You'll need watercolor paper, a large aluminum pan, 1 gallon of liquid starch, 1½-inch-wide newspaper strips, acrylic paints, plastic cups, an eyedropper, toothpicks, and a small squeegee. Pour about 1½ inches of starch into the pan. Skim the surface with newspapers and skim between each marbleization. Place about 2 tablespoons of paint into a cup and thin slightly with water. Fill the eyedropper with paint, then float drops onto the surface of the starch. If the paint spreads, it's too thin. If it sinks, it's too thick. If your first attempt isn't correct, just skim it off and try again.

Float new colors on top of the first color, then carefully swirl a toothpick on the surface to create patterns; do not disturb the starch. Hold the sheet of paper with your fingertips and lower it onto the surface of the liquid. Hold the paper still for 5 seconds, then lift and place it, painted side up, on a flat surface. Let the marbleized paper set for 15 minutes, then squeegee off the excess paint. Dry thoroughly. Repeat for the other side of the paper.

Blue Velvet Stocking

This richly textured stocking will add a touch of class to any holiday bazaar booth. Plush velvet and multicolored stripe fabrics are trimmed and tasseled with gold for a truly opulent look.

Size

18 inches long

What You Do

Note: All seam allowances are ½ inch.

1. Enlarge the **Stocking Pattern** on page 73 as directed in "Enlarging Patterns" on page 238.

2. From the velvet, cut one stocking and one stocking reverse so the stripes of the stocking run vertically. From the stripe, cut one 9 × 17-inch strip for the cuff and one 3 × 6-inch strip for the hanger both with the stripes running vertically.

3. With the right sides together, sew the stockings together, leaving the top edge open. Grade

WHAT YOU NEED

- ⅝ yard striped blue velvet fabric for the stocking
- ⅜ yard multicolored stripe fabric for the cuff and hanger
- Matching sewing thread
- ½ yard of ⅜-inch-diameter gold upholstery cord
- 3½-inch-long gold tassel

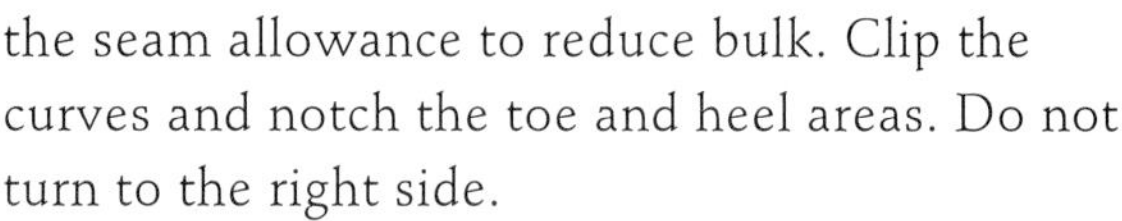

the seam allowance to reduce bulk. Clip the curves and notch the toe and heel areas. Do not turn to the right side.

4. With right sides together, sew the short ends of the cuff together to form a loop; see **Diagram 1.** Press the seams open. With wrong sides together, fold the loop in half lengthwise.

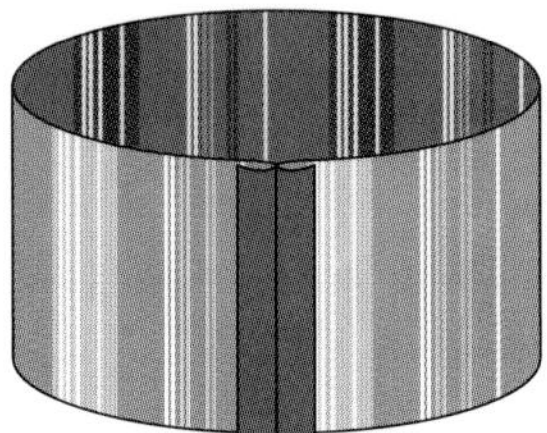

Diagram 1

5. Slip the cuff over the stocking, having the raw edges aligned and the seam of the cuff at the back seam of the stocking. Sew around the top edge of the stocking, as shown in **Diagram 2.** Trim the seam allowance.

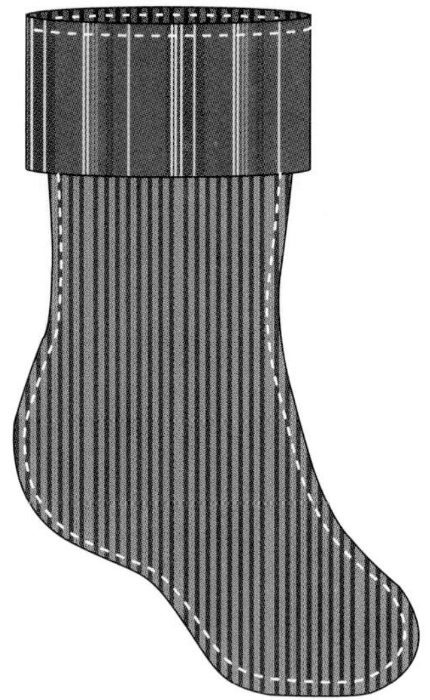

Diagram 2

6. Turn the stocking to the right side. Fold the cuff to the outside and press.

7. With right sides together, fold the strip for the hanger in half lengthwise. Sew along the long raw edge. Turn it to the right side and press. Fold the hanger in half crosswise and slip-stitch it to the inside of the stocking at the back seam.

8. Slip-stitch the gold cord to the lower edge of the cuff. Hand tack the tassel to the cord about 2 inches from the back seam; see **Diagram 3.**

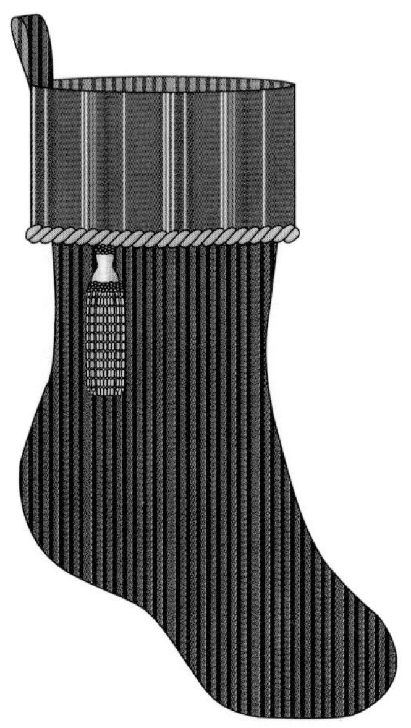

Diagram 3

Money-Saving Tip

Since this stocking uses just two coordinating fabrics, it's a sure moneymaker if you have a stockpile of scrap fabric. Make the stocking out of a pretty calico and add a solid color broadcloth cuff. Or cut the stocking from a solid color wool and the cuff from faux sheepskin. Do you have scraps of dress fabrics as well? If so, go for the romantic look and use floral polyesters for the stocking and lace yardage for the cuff. Appeal to sophisticated buyers with winter white linen for the stocking and slinky gold lamé for the cuff. You could also purchase a royal blue satin for the body of the stocking and accent it with a printed paisley fabric. Just dig deep into your fabric baskets and create a whole collection of holiday stockings for every customer's taste.

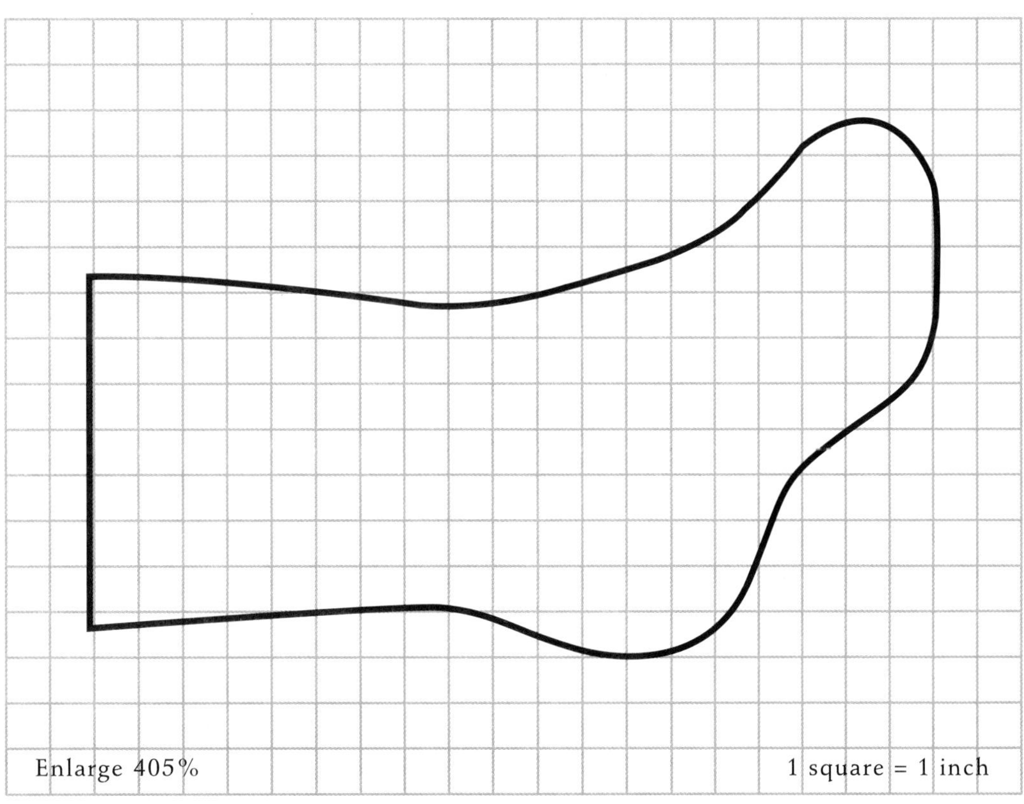

STOCKING PATTERN

Celestial Pillows and Sachets

The Golden Weave Pillow, Blue Velvet Celestial Sachets, and colorful Bargello Pincushion are easy to make, yet special enough to display throughout the holidays or give as gifts.

Golden Weave Pillow

SIZE
$11\frac{1}{2} \times 14\frac{1}{2}$ inches

WHAT YOU DO

Note: All seam allowances are $\frac{1}{4}$ inch.

1. From the ribbon, cut twenty-three 12-inch lengths and fifteen 15-inch lengths. Set aside the remaining ribbon; you may need to cut additional lengths to cover the pillow base.

2. Lay the pillow base on a flat surface.

3. Lay the twenty-three 12-inch ribbon lengths side by side vertically on top of the pillow base to form the warp; do not overlap the edges. See the **Warp Diagram.** If necessary, cut additional ribbon lengths to cover the pillow base. Baste across the ends to secure them in place.

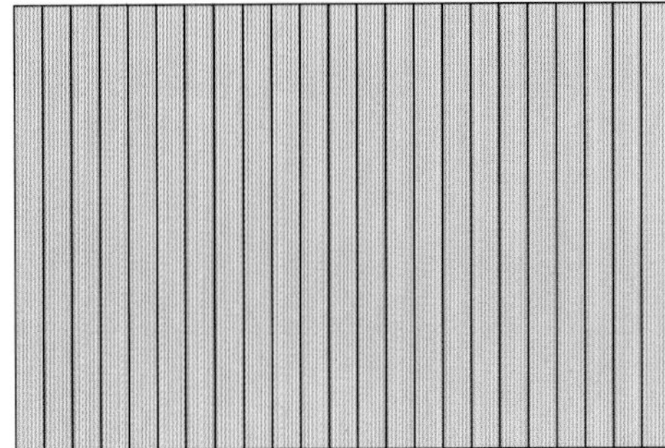

Warp Diagram

4. To make the pillow front, start at the lower left corner and weave one 15-inch ribbon length over and under the warp lengths to form the weft, as shown in the **Weft Diagram.** Continue weaving ribbon lengths over and under until the pillow front is complete. If necessary, cut additional ribbon lengths to cover the pillow front. Baste across the ends to secure them in place.

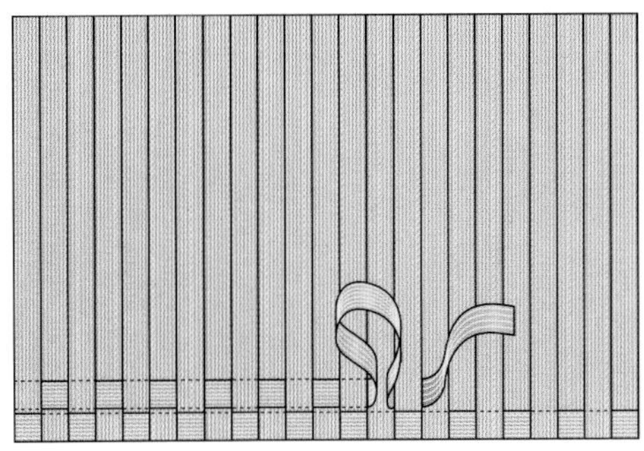

Weft Diagram

5. With right sides together, sew the pillow front and back together, leaving a 5-inch opening along one side for turning.

6. Turn the pillow right side out and press lightly. Stuff the pillow with the fiberfill, then slip-stitch the opening closed.

7. Tape the ends of the upholstery cord to prevent raveling. Knot one end of the cord, hiding the taped end. Beginning at the center bottom of the pillow, slip-stitch the cord around the pillow, covering the seam edge; knot the cord at each corner and at the center top of the pillow as you proceed, referring to the **Upholstery Cord Diagram.** As you approach the center bottom again, tape the cord to prevent raveling, then clip away the excess. Hide the taped end behind the first knot and slip-stitch it in place.

What You Need

Golden Weave Pillow

- 15 yards of ⅝-inch-wide metallic gold grosgrain ribbon
- 12 × 15-inch piece of gold cotton fabric for the pillow base
- Matching sewing thread
- 12 × 15-inch piece of midnight blue satin fabric for the backing
- Polyester fiberfill
- 2 yards of ½-inch-diameter metallic gold upholstery cord
- Cellophane tape

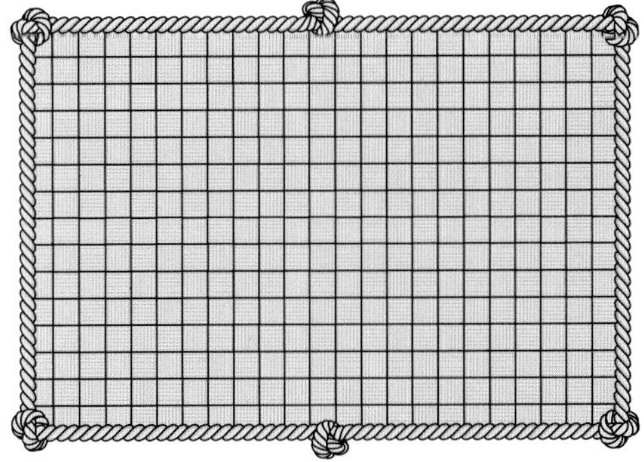

Upholstery Cord Diagram

WHAT YOU NEED

BLUE VELVET CELESTIAL SACHETS

- Two 6-inch squares of blue velvet for each sachet
- Matching sewing thread
- Lavender, cloves, pine, or other scented herbs or potpourri for each sachet
- ¾-inch gold star button for each sachet
- 2-inch-long gold moon button for the star-and-moon sachet
- ⅔ yard of ½-inch-diameter metallic gold upholstery cord for the corded sachet
- Cellophane tape

Blue Velvet Celestial Sachets

SIZE

5½ and 6 inches square

WHAT YOU DO

1. For each sachet, place the right sides of the velvet together and sew around 3½ sides, using a ¼-inch seam allowance; leave an opening for turning along the bottom edge on the star-and-moon sachet and along the top edge for the corded sachet. Clip the corners to reduce bulk.

2. Turn each sachet to the right side and fill with herbs or potpourri. For the star-and-moon sachet, slip-stitch the opening closed. For the corded sachet, slip-stitch part of the opening closed, leaving the center top open.

3. For the star-and-moon sachet, sew the buttons to the front of the sachet, as shown in the photograph on page 74.

4. For the corded sachet, tape the ends of the upholstery cord to prevent raveling. Insert the taped end of the cord into the opening. Slip-stitch the cord around the sachet, covering the seam edge. As you approach the center top again, tape the cord to prevent raveling, then clip away the excess. Insert the end into the opening, then slip-stitch the opening closed. Sew the star button to the center top of the sachet, as shown in the photograph on page 74.

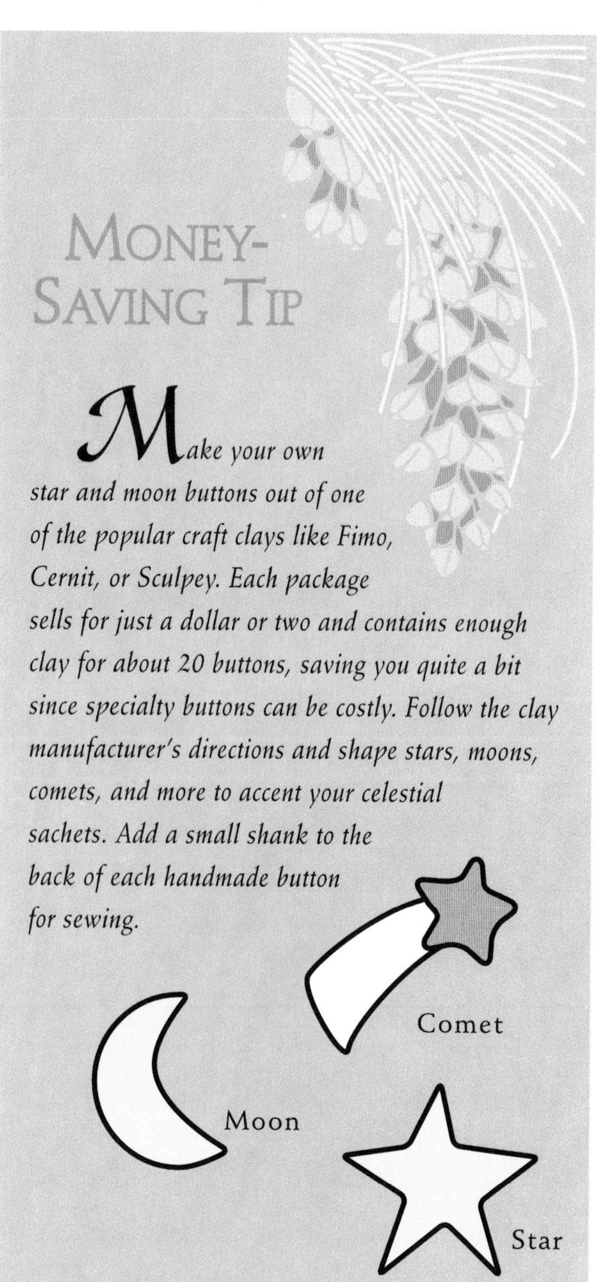

Bargello Pincushion

Size

5 inches square

What You Do

1. Using the indelible marker, mark a 5½-inch square in the center of the needlepoint canvas to form the stitching parameters.

2. Following the **Bargello Pincushion Chart** and using all three plies of the leaf green tapestry wool, work the first row of the bargello pattern across the canvas. Following the established pattern, fill in the triangular spaces above the first row with light blue. Continue the bargello pattern below the first row in the following color order: turquoise, teal, light blue, navy, light avocado, dark flesh, pale green, spring green, olive, gold, midnight blue, and dark flesh. Trim the bargello to 5½ inches square.

3. With right sides together, sew the bargello to the backing, using a ¼-inch seam allowance; leave an opening for turning. Grade the seam allowance to reduce bulk.

4. Turn the pincushion to the right side. Stuff with pellets, then slip-stitch the opening closed.

What You Need

Bargello Pincushion

- 7-inch square of 10-mesh needlepoint canvas
- Indelible marker
- One skein of 3-ply tapestry wool for each color in the **Color Key**
- Size 20 tapestry needle
- 5½-inch square of turquoise velvet fabric for the backing
- Matching sewing thread
- Plastic pellets for stuffing

Color Key

DMC Floralia

7037	Olive	7485	Gold
7166	Dk. Flesh	7580	Lt. Avocado
7301	Lt. Blue	7597	Turquoise
7317	Midnight Blue	7607	Teal
7341	Spring Green	7615	Navy
7344	Leaf Green	7755	Pale Green

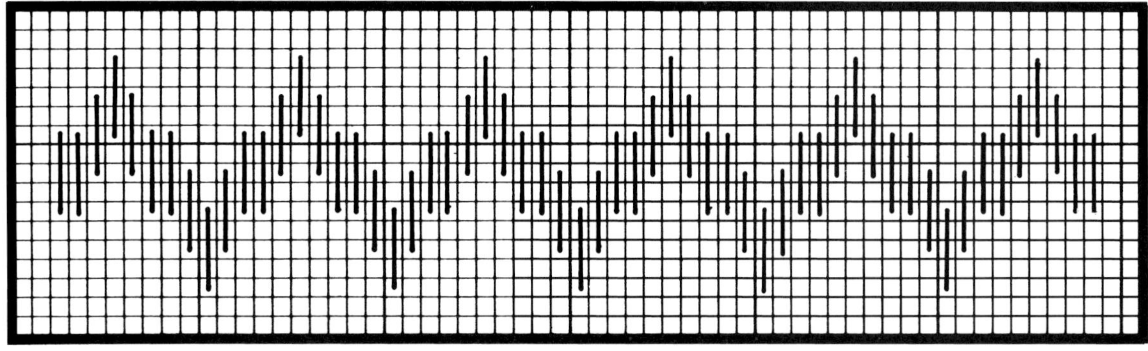

BARGELLO PINCUSHION CHART

Angels on High

For many folks, angels symbolize the true meaning of the Christmas holiday season. Here, the stylized Gabriel Angel Ornament and the Angel in a Gilded Frame showcasing a holiday greeting card call out to those who favor this time-honored religious icon.

Gabriel Angel Ornament

SIZE

10¼ inches tall

WHAT YOU DO

1. Enlarge the **Gabriel Angel Ornament Pattern** as directed in "Enlarging Patterns" on page 238.

2. In a well-ventilated area, spray the wrong side of the decorative papers with the adhesive. Adhere one to each side of the posterboard.

3. Lay the angel pattern on the covered posterboard and trace around it. Using the craft knife, cut out the angel just inside the traced line, cutting away any markings. Also cut out the area between the chin and arm. Change blades as necessary.

4. Using an awl, poke a hole at the top of the ornament. Thread the cord through the hole and knot it for the hanger.

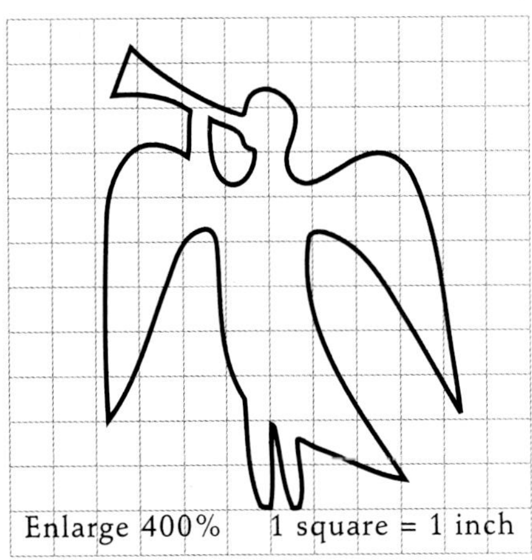

GABRIEL ANGEL ORNAMENT PATTERN

WHAT YOU NEED

GABRIEL ANGEL ORNAMENT

- Two 11-inch square sheets of decorative oriental paper or small-print gift wrap
- Spray adhesive
- 11-inch square of coordinating color posterboard
- Craft knife with extra blades
- Awl
- 8-inch-length of ⅛-inch-diameter gold cord for the hanger

ANGEL IN A GILDED FRAME

- 8 × 10-inch wooden frame with glass, backing, and stand
- Quick-drying gold sizing*
- Two ½-inch-wide paintbrushes
- 5 sheets of imitation gold leaf
- 4 × 6-inch holiday card with angel motif
- 8 × 10-inch coordinating color mat board
- Spray adhesive

** See the "Buyer's Guide" on page 244 for ordering information.*

Angel in a Gilded Frame

SIZE

8 × 10 inches

WHAT YOU DO

1. Remove the backing and glass from the frame. Thoroughly clean the frame and allow it to dry.

2. Using the paintbrush, brush the gold sizing onto the frame and let it dry for at least three hours. When it is completely dry, lay the gold leaf on the top and sides of the frame, pressing the leaf lightly with a clean, dry brush. Tear away any excess leaf, then reposition it on another section. Smooth all edges of the leaf. Continue until the frame is covered or until a pleasing effect is achieved.

3. Using the spray adhesive, adhere the wrong side of the card to the right side of the mat board.

4. Reassemble the frame.

Muslin Country Angel

A touch of country charm christens this doll-like muslin angel. Her hand-sculpted face, clove eyes, and yellow yarn hair give her plenty of homespun personality. Your customers will surely want to make her a part of their holiday celebration.

Size

18 inches tall

What You Do

Note: All seam allowances are $\frac{1}{4}$ inch unless otherwise indicated.

1. Enlarge the **Muslin Country Angel Patterns** on page 85 as directed in "Enlarging Patterns" on page 238.

2. From the unbleached muslin, cut two bodies, two heads, two legs, and two arms. From the linen, cut one bodice, one skirt, and two bloomers. From the evenweave, cut two 11-inch squares for the wings. From the scrap of felt, cut one heart.

3. With the right sides together, fold each leg in half where indicated by the thin line on the pattern. Using the cream thread, sew along one short (foot edge) and one long edge to form the leg, leaving one short edge (body edge) open for turning. Turn each leg to the right side and stuff lightly with fiberfill. Using brown thread, sew across the lower portion of each leg where indicated by the dotted line to define the ankle. Define the toe in the same manner. Set the legs aside.

4. With the right sides together, fold each arm in half where indicated on the pattern. Using the cream thread, sew along one short (hand edge) and one long edge to form the arm, leaving one short edge (body edge) open for turning. Turn each arm to the right side and stuff lightly. Using brown thread, sew across the lower portion of each arm where indicated by the dotted line to define the wrist.

5. With the right sides facing, pin the arms to the body where indicated by the dots on the pattern; see **Diagram 1.** Baste in place.

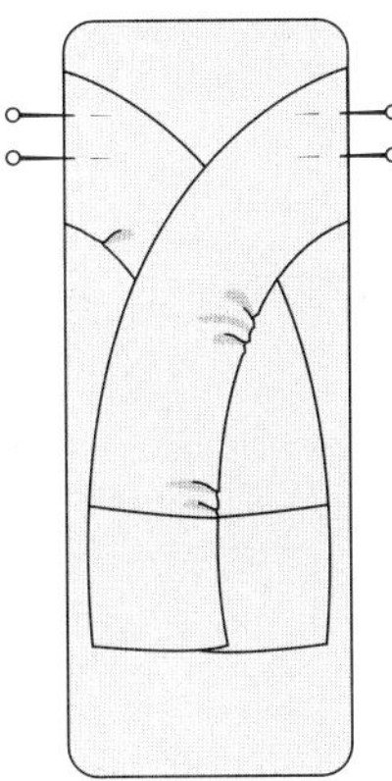

Diagram 1

6. With the right sides together and having the arms tucked inside, sew the bodies together, leaving the bottom edge open for turning. Turn to the right side. Turn under 1/4 inch along the bottom edge and press.

7. With the leg seams facing inward, insert the top of the legs 1/4 inch inside the lower edge of the body where indicated by the dots on the pattern. Referring to **Diagram 2** on page 82, pin the legs to the body, then slip-stitch them in place. Lightly stuff the body, then slip-stitch the opening closed.

What You Need

- 1/4 yard of unbleached muslin for the body
- 1/4 yard of white linen fabric for the dress and bloomers
- 3/8 yard of tan evenweave fabric for the wings
- Small scrap of red felt for the heart
- Cream, brown, and tan sewing thread
- Polyester fiberfill
- Hot pink and yellow tapestry wool for the mouth and hair
- Sharp-point tapestry needle
- 2 whole cloves for the eyes
- Fabric glue
- Powder blusher for the cheeks
- 8-inch length of 1/4-inch-wide elastic for the bloomers
- 3/4 yard of 1/2-inch-wide tatted or scalloped-edged cotton lace for the trim
- 8-inch length of 1/4-inch-wide white satin ribbon for the shoulder straps
- 3/8 yard of fusible web
- 12-inch length of metallic gold star garland for the halo
- 5-inch-long gold plastic trumpet or desired musical instrument*

* *Available at craft or party supply stores.*

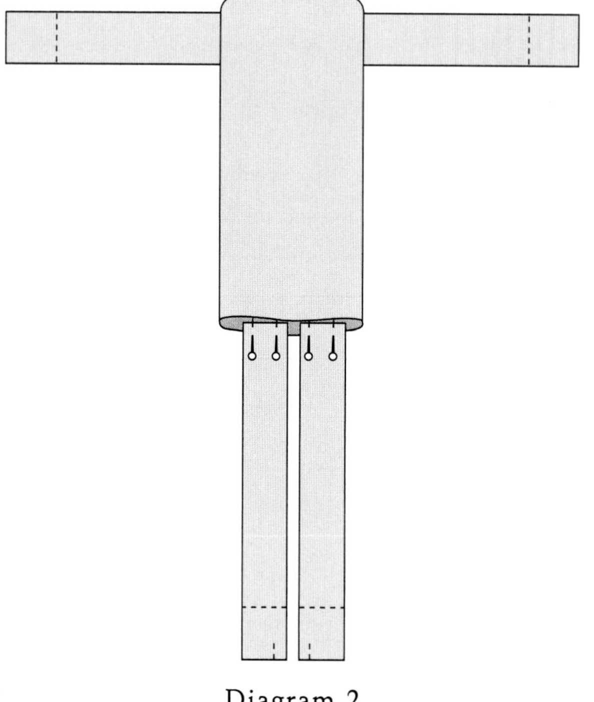

Diagram 2

8. With the right sides facing, sew the heads together, leaving an opening for turning. Clip the curves. Turn the head to the right side and press lightly; do not press the head flat. Stuff the head lightly, then slip-stitch the opening closed.

9. Referring to the pattern, create the nose by pinching the face front fabric in the center and satin stitching across the bottom of the nose using tan thread; see "Stitch Details" on page 243. Use small running stitches along both sides of the pinched fabric to define the nose. For the mouth, make a series of ¼-inch-long satin stitches with the pink tapestry wool about ¼ inch below the nose. Using a tapestry needle, poke holes in the face for eyes. Add a drop of glue to the stem of each clove and insert one into each eye hole. Blush the outer cheek area with the powder blusher.

10. For the hair, cut twenty-five 3-inch lengths of yellow tapestry wool. Thread one length through the tapestry needle, then insert the needle in and out through the top seam of the head, leaving a 1¼-inch tail. Insert the needle back in the original "in" hole, then bring it back out through the original "out" hole; see **Diagram 3.**

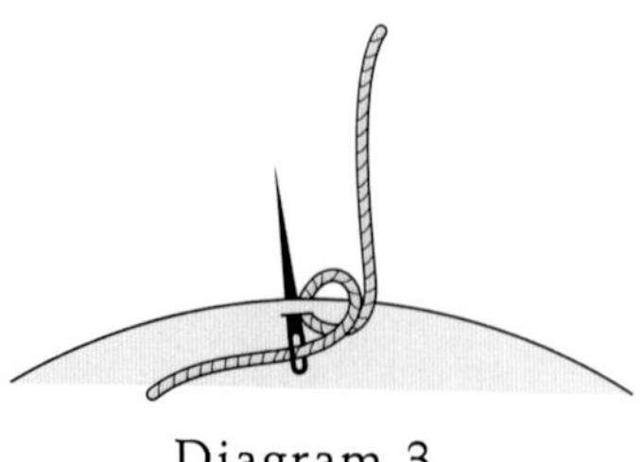

Diagram 3

11. Continue to add yarn strands until the top half of the head is covered with hair, as shown in **Diagram 4.** Separate the plies of the yarn, if desired, to give the hair more fullness.

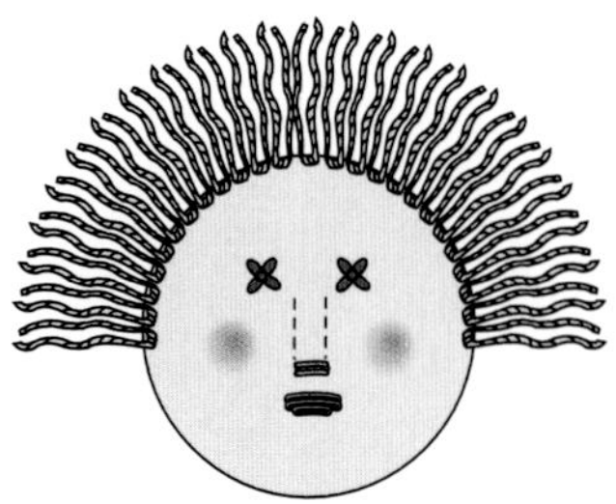

Diagram 4

12. Referring to **Diagram 5** and using the dashed line on the body pattern as a guide, slip-stitch the head to the body. Set the angel aside.

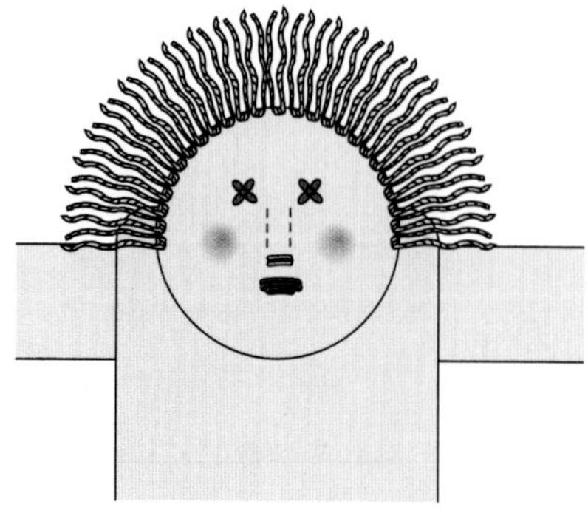

Diagram 5

13. With the right sides together, sew the bloomers together along the side seams and inseam. Clip the inseam curve. Turn under ½ inch along the waist edge and press. Topstitch around the waist edge ⅜ inch from the folded edge to form the elastic casing, leaving about 1 inch open to insert the elastic. Referring to **Diagram 6,**

insert the elastic, sew the ends together, then finish sewing the casing seam.

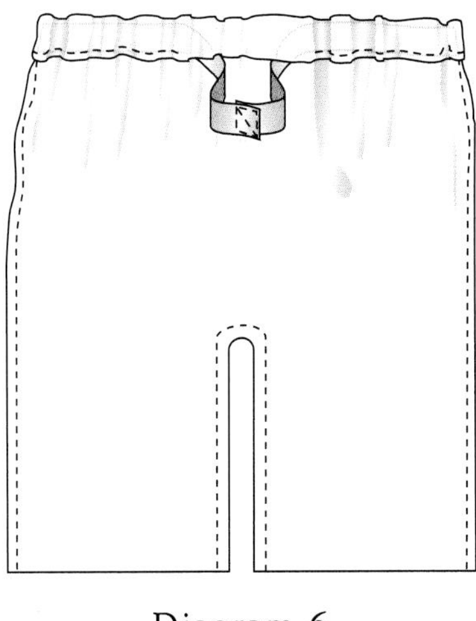

Diagram 6

14. From the lace trim, cut two 4-inch lengths. Turn the bloomers to the right side. Turn under ¼ inch along each leg opening and press. Referring to **Diagram 7,** topstitch one length to each leg opening. Place the bloomers on the angel.

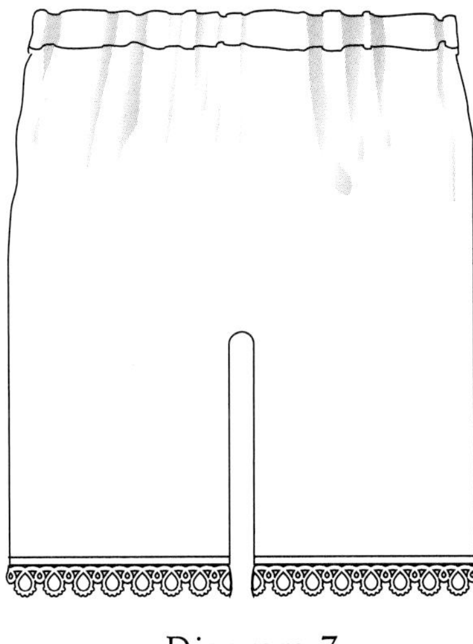

Diagram 7

15. From the remaining lace trim, cut one 7-inch length and one 10-inch length. Turn ¼ inch to the wrong side along one long edge of the bodice and the skirt. Press. Topstitch the 7-inch length of trim to the turned-under edge of the bodice for the neck trim and the 10-inch length to the turned-under edge of the skirt for the hem trim.

16. Run a gathering thread along the untrimmed long edge of the skirt. Pull up the gathers to fit the untrimmed long edge of the bodice. Pin the bodice to the skirt to form the dress, as shown in **Diagram 8,** then sew the seam.

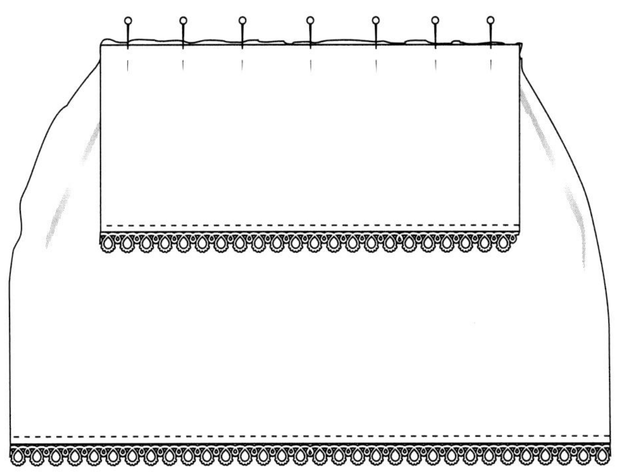

Diagram 8

17. With the right sides together, fold the dress in half and sew the back seam. Turn the dress to the right side and place it on the angel.

18. Cut the ribbon in half for the shoulder straps. Referring to **Diagram 9,** place one strap over each shoulder, then slip-stitch each strap end to the dress.

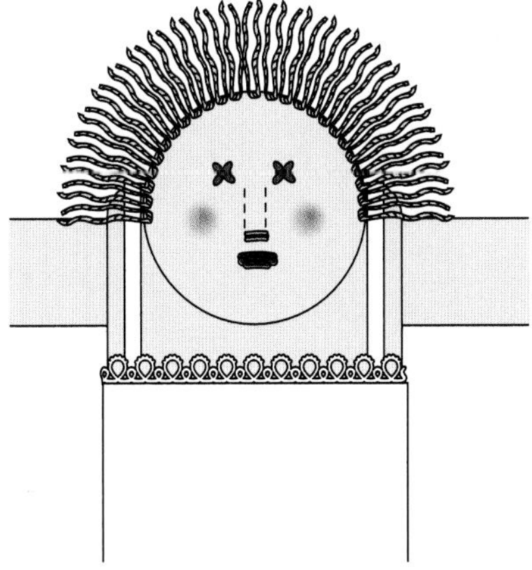

Diagram 9

19. Slip-stitch or glue the red felt heart to the left side of the bodice where indicated on the bodice pattern.

20. Following the manufacturer's directions, fuse the fusible web to the wrong side of one 11-inch square of evenweave for the wings. Remove the paper backing and then fuse the web side of the first square to the wrong side of the remaining square. From the fused evenweave square, cut out one set of wings. Slip-stitch the wings to the back of the angel, tacking the wings through the angel's dress.

21. For the halo, curl the garland into a 2-inch-diameter circle and tack it to the back of the head. Slip the trumpet onto the angel's right arm, then slip-stitch the hands together at the top edge.

TIME-SAVING TIP

As you craft in quantity, you'll find many ways to cut the time you spend on each project. For example, many bazaar crafters use a rotary cutter to cut out layers of pattern pieces at the same time. Other crafters substitute glue for hand stitching whenever possible, especially if it doesn't affect the overall look or quality of the craft.

When I began crafting the Muslin Country Angel in quantity, I discovered another way to save time. I often use lace-trimmed linen napkins or handkerchiefs for the angel's outfit, so I can eliminate the steps of turning under the raw edges and topstitching the tatted lace onto the linen. I position the patterns on the napkin so the tatted-lace edges form the decorative trims on the bodice, skirt, and bloomers. I've included a pattern layout below for you to use as an example.

I also save a step by using a heavyweight canvas for the wings instead of fusing two lighter-weight pieces of fabric together. To vary the look of my angels, I often dip the canvas in liquid starch and shape the heart-shape piece into wings for added interest. You can even skip the elastic in the waistband of the bloomers and tie a ribbon sash around the top instead to keep the bloomers in place.

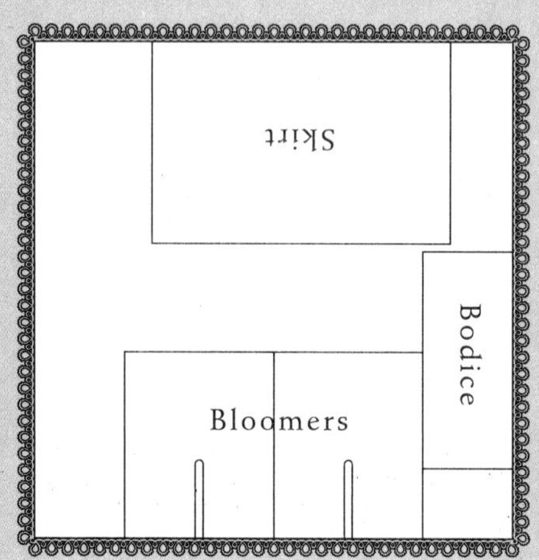

Try different assembly-line methods to find one that's right for you. As you craft each individual project, you'll discover shortcuts that you may be able to adapt for other craft bazaar projects as well.

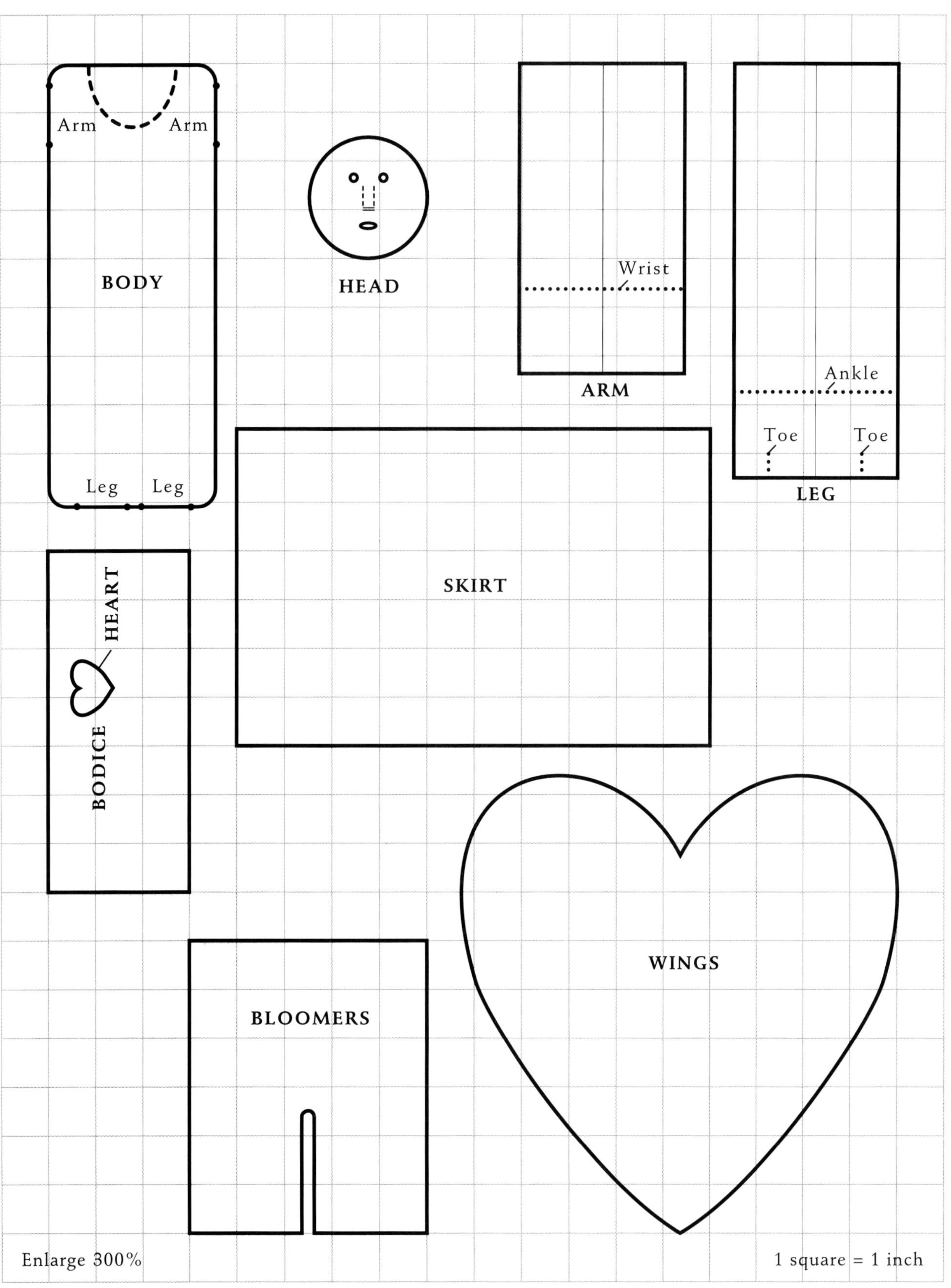

MUSLIN COUNTRY ANGEL PATTERNS

Hand-Printed Wrapping Paper

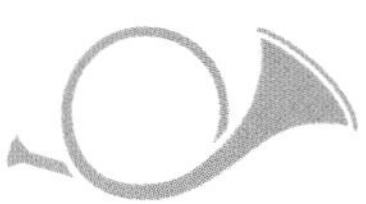

A little paint and the simplest of tools can transform sheets of ordinary colored paper into one-of-a-kind gift wraps. Get the whole family in on the act and let them express their creativity with checks, stars, circles, rubbed-in clouds, and grids. Sell the wraps individually or packaged as a set at your benefit.

SIZE
20 × 28-inch sheets

WHAT YOU NEED

- 20 × 28-inch sheets of medium-weight paper in a variety of colors, such as gray, turquoise, royal blue, and sage green
- Metallic gold and white acrylic paint
- Dry sponge, jar lid, paper towel or cloth rag, and scrap of 4-count quickpoint canvas for printing
- Saucer or palette
- Metallic gold and white spray paint

WHAT YOU DO

1. Lay the paper to be printed or painted on a clean, flat surface.

2. For the checkerboard paper, use the gray paper and metallic gold acrylic paint. From the sponge, cut a 1-inch square. Squeeze about 3 tablespoons of paint onto a saucer or palette. Dab the sponge into the paint, then press it to the paper, beginning in one corner. Continue along the edge to create a row, leaving 1 inch between prints. Continue over the entire paper surface, alternating the prints for a checkerboard effect. When you are finished, wash the saucer with soap and water before the paint dries.

3. For the star paper, use the turquoise paper and the white acrylic paint. From the sponge, cut one **Full-Size Star Pattern.** Squeeze about 3 tablespoons of paint onto a saucer or palette. Dab the sponge into the paint, then press it to the paper. Continue printing stars randomly over the surface of the paper. When you are finished, wash the saucer with soap and water before the paint dries.

FULL-SIZE STAR PATTERN

4. For the circles paper, use the royal blue paper and metallic gold acrylic paint. Squeeze about 3 tablespoons of paint onto a saucer or palette. Dab the rim of the jar lid into the paint and press it to the paper. Continue printing circles in a random manner over the surface of the paper. When you are finished, wash the saucer with soap and water before the paint dries.

5. For the cloud paper, use the royal blue or turquoise paper and the white acrylic paint. Squeeze about 3 tablespoons of paint onto a saucer or palette. Very lightly dab a paper towel or cloth rag into the paint. Lightly rub the paint onto the surface of the paper, creating cloudlike formations. Continue until the entire surface is covered. When you are finished, wash the saucer with soap and water before the paint dries.

6. For the grid paper, use the sage green paper and metallic gold and white spray paints. Working in a well-ventilated area, lay the quickpoint canvas on top of the paper, then spray with the gold paint. Do not move the canvas. Lightly spray the same area with the white paint. Reposition the canvas scrap and repeat until the entire surface is covered.

Star-Studded Tabletop Accessories

These stellar napkins and place mat will ensure that holiday customers leave the booth starry-eyed. The Star Border Napkin, Bead-Edged Napkin, Sparkly Stars Napkin, and Stars All Around Place Mat start with purchased materials and are accented for holiday flair. For an additional touch of glitz, the Golden Twig Wreath is gilded for use as a napkin ring or ornament.

Star Border Napkin

SIZE

Motif is 1 inch high

WHAT YOU DO

1. Trace the **Full-Size Star Pattern** onto the Mylar. To cut the star, place the Mylar on the glass and tape it with the masking tape to secure. Holding the craft knife like a pencil, carefully cut out the star on the tracing line. Cut toward you, turning the glass as you cut. If your knife should slip, mend both sides of the cut with masking tape. Change blades as necessary.

2. Referring to the **Star Border Placement Diagram,** position the stencil in one corner of the napkin about 1½ inches from each edge, having the star slightly off-point. Tape the stencil in place with artist's tape.

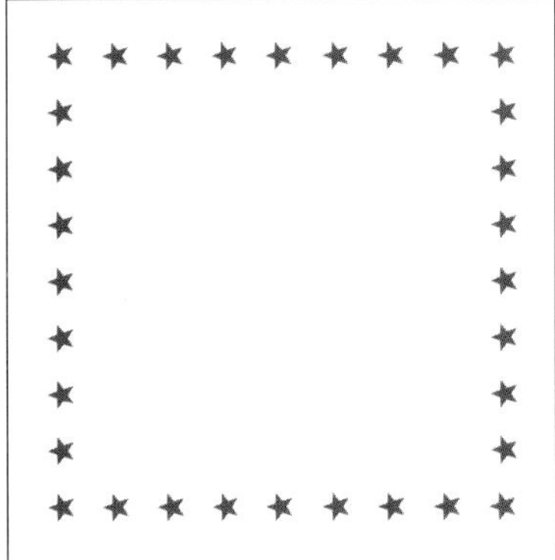

Star Border Placement Diagram

3. Place 2 tablespoons of paint on the saucer or palette. Dip the tip of the stencil brush into the paint, then dab it on the paper towels until the brush is almost dry. Holding the brush perpendicular to the surface, brush over the cutout areas with a circular motion, working over the stencil edges. Always allow the paint to dry on one star before moving on to avoid smearing the paint.

4. After you've finished stenciling the entire napkin, wash the brush and saucer with soap and water before the paint dries.

WHAT YOU NEED

STAR BORDER NAPKIN

- Stencil Mylar
- 4-inch square of glass with masked or filed edges
- Masking tape
- Craft knife with extra blades
- 20-inch square white napkin
- White artist's tape
- Royal blue fabric paint
- Saucer or palette
- 1-inch-diameter stencil brush
- Paper towels

BEAD-EDGED NAPKIN

- 18-inch square royal blue napkin
- 2⅛ yards of gold bead garland
- Gold sewing thread

FULL-SIZE STAR PATTERN

Bead-Edged Napkin

SIZE

18 inches square

WHAT YOU DO

1. Beginning in one corner of the napkin, whipstitch the garland to the edge of the napkin by stitching between every bead; see the **Whipstitch Diagram** on page 90.

WHAT YOU NEED

SPARKLY STARS NAPKIN

- Stencil Mylar
- 4-inch square of glass with masked or filed edges
- Masking tape
- Craft knife with extra blades
- 18-inch square white napkin
- White artist's tape
- Metallic gold fabric paint
- Saucer or palette
- 1-inch-diameter stencil brush
- Paper towels

GOLDEN TWIG WREATH

- 6-inch-diameter twig wreath
- Quick-drying gold sizing*
- Two ½-inch-wide paintbrushes
- 3 sheets of imitation gold leaf
- 8-inch length of ⅛-inch-wide metallic gold ribbon for the hanger (optional)

* *See the "Buyer's Guide" on page 244 for ordering information.*

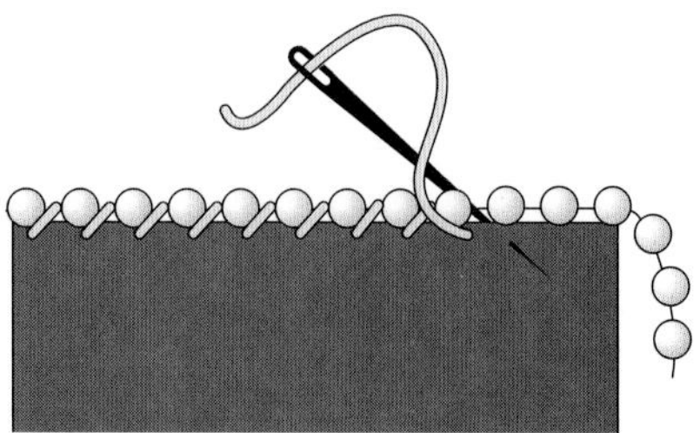

Whipstitch Diagram

2. Continue stitching evenly around the napkin, being careful to keep the napkin and garland at the same tautness to prevent puckering.

Sparkly Stars Napkin

SIZE

Motif is 1 inch high

WHAT YOU DO

1. Repeat Step 1 of the Star Border Napkin on page 89.

2. Referring to the **Sparkly Stars Placement Diagram,** position the stencil on one corner of the napkin, then tape it in place with artist's tape.

Sparkly Stars Placement Diagram

3. Repeat Step 3 of the Star Border Napkin.

4. Stencil the remaining stars, as shown in the diagram, or repeat the stars in a random pattern across the entire napkin.

5. Repeat Step 4 of the Star Border Napkin.

Golden Twig Wreath

SIZE

6 inches in diameter

WHAT YOU DO

1. Using a paintbrush, brush the gold sizing onto the wreath, coating as many of the twigs as possible. Let the wreath dry for one to three hours.

2. When the wreath is completely dry, lay the gold leaf on top of the wreath and, with a clean, dry paintbrush, press the leaf to the coated twigs. Tear away any unused gold leaf, then reposition it on another section of the wreath. Continue until the entire wreath is covered or until a pleasing effect is achieved. Brush away any crumbs of gold leaf. Firmly press the gold leaf edges to the twigs.

3. Tie the ribbon hanger to the top of the wreath, if desired, to use the wreath as an ornament.

Stars All Around Place Mat

Size

Motif is 1 inch high

What You Need

Stars All Around Place Mat

- Stencil Mylar
- 4-inch square of glass with masked or filed edges
- Masking tape
- Craft knife with extra blades
- 12 × 17-inch royal blue place mat with diagonal corners
- White artist's tape
- White fabric paint with gold glitter
- Saucer or palette
- 1-inch-diameter stencil brush
- Paper towels

What You Do

1. Repeat Step 1 of the Star Border Napkin on page 89.

2. Referring to the **Stars All Around Placement Diagram,** position the stencil on one side of the place mat about 1 inch from the edge. Tape the stencil in place with artist's tape.

Stars All Around Placement Diagram

3. Repeat Step 3 of the Star Border Napkin.

4. Continue stenciling around the border of the place mat, spacing the stars about 1½ inches apart.

5. Repeat Step 4 of the Star Border Napkin.

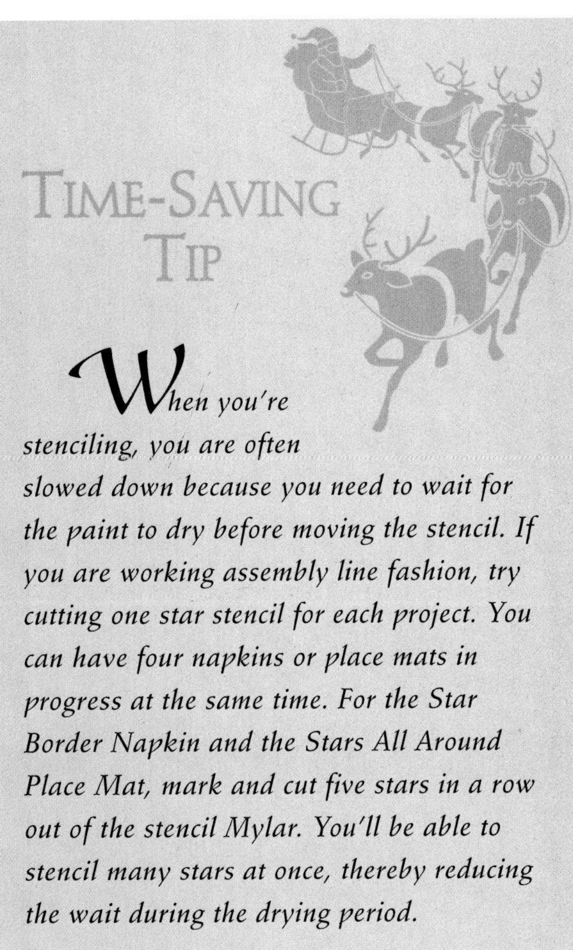

Time-Saving Tip

When you're stenciling, you are often slowed down because you need to wait for the paint to dry before moving the stencil. If you are working assembly line fashion, try cutting one star stencil for each project. You can have four napkins or place mats in progress at the same time. For the Star Border Napkin and the Stars All Around Place Mat, mark and cut five stars in a row out of the stencil Mylar. You'll be able to stencil many stars at once, thereby reducing the wait during the drying period.

Dainty Tree Treasures

Tiny Golden Acorns and Cross-Stitch Noel Ribbons are perfect holiday party favors that can later adorn the tiniest tree branches. For your booth, gild the wooden acorns by the dozen and stitch the banner on gold mesh ribbon.

Golden Acorn

SIZE

About 2 inches high

WHAT YOU DO

1. Working in a well-ventilated area and using the metallic gold paint, spray the acorn. Let it dry thoroughly.

2. Fold the gold cord in half and insert it in the bead. Knot one end and allow the bead to rest on the knot, adding a dab of glue to secure it in place. Glue the knot of the bead to the top of the acorn cap.

3. Using the silver paint, decorate the acorn cap with random dots. Hang the acorn to dry.

WHAT YOU NEED

GOLDEN ACORN

- Wooden acorn*
- Metallic gold spray paint
- 8-inch length of 1/16-inch-diameter gold cord for the hanger
- 13 mm metallic gold bead for the acorn top
- Hot glue gun and glue sticks
- Metallic silver puff paint with fine-tip applicator

** See the "Buyer's Guide" on page 244 for ordering information.*

CROSS-STITCH NOEL RIBBON

- 10-inch length of 2-inch-wide metallic gold wire mesh ribbon
- 2 × 5-inch piece of 14-count waste canvas
- One skein of embroidery floss for the color in the **Color Key**
- Size 22 or 24 tapestry needle
- Plant mister
- Tweezers

Cross-Stitch Noel Ribbon

SIZE

Motif is 1 × 2¼ inches

WHAT YOU DO

1. Find the center of the ribbon and mark it with a pin. Find the center of the **Cross-Stitch Noel Ribbon Chart** by connecting the arrows.

2. Baste the waste canvas to the center of the ribbon. Matching the centers of the chart and the ribbon, and using three strands of floss, work the design over the ribbon mesh, using the waste canvas holes as a stitch guide.

3. Trim the waste canvas close to the cross-stitch. Dampen the canvas with the plant mister, then let it stand a few minutes to soften the canvas sizing. Using tweezers, carefully draw out the canvas threads one at a time.

4. Clip the ribbon ends in a "V" shape. Crimp the wire edges of the ribbon into the desired shape for use on a table as a party favor or nestled in the branches as a tree ornament.

COLOR KEY

	DMC	Anchor	J. & P. Coats	Color
•	826	161	7180	Med. Blue

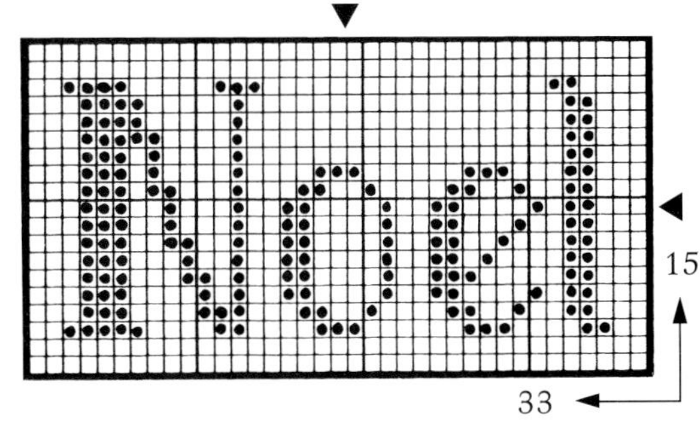

CROSS-STITCH NOEL RIBBON CHART

Southwestern Star Tree Topper

Touches of turquoise, silver, and cactus-colored fabrics give this treetop ornament a subtle taste of the old Southwest. Belled and beribboned and laden with vintage charm, its heirloom quality is sure to attract sophisticated buyers to your holiday crafts booth.

SIZE

19 inches across

WHAT YOU NEED

- One 12-inch square each of five coordinating turquoise and green fabrics for the star points
- Matching sewing thread
- Polyester fiberfill
- 7-inch-diameter antique white doily with crocheted edging
- Matching buttonhole twist thread
- Thirty $\frac{3}{8}$-inch-diameter silver jingle bells
- 5 yards of $\frac{1}{2}$-inch-wide turquoise satin ribbon for the bows
- 3-inch-diameter costume jewelry brooch for the center accent
- 8-inch length of 24-gauge wire for the hanger

WHAT YOU DO

Note: All seam allowances are $\frac{1}{4}$ inch.

1. Enlarge the **Star Points Pattern** on page 96 as directed in "Enlarging Patterns" on page 238.

2. From each fabric, cut two star points for the star front and back.

3. On a flat surface, position the points into a star front and back, arranging the different fabrics until you have pleasing combinations.

4. Select two adjacent star points from the star front arrangement. With the right sides together, sew the two star points together along one short side; see **Diagram 1.**

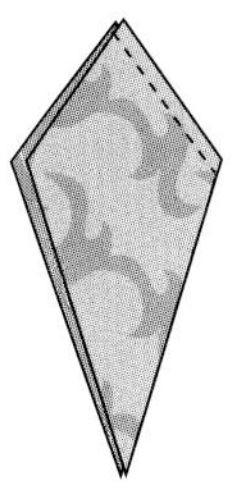

Diagram 1

5. With right sides together, sew a third star point to the second along one short side. Continue in this manner until the five star points have been sewn into a star shape, as shown in **Diagram 2.**

Diagram 2

6. Repeat Steps 4 and 5 for the star back.

7. With the right sides together, sew the star front and back together, leaving an opening along one long edge for turning.

8. Clip the points and corners, then turn the star to the right side; press.

9. Begin stuffing the star by pushing small amounts of fiberfill into the tip of each star point. Continue stuffing each point, stuffing firmly so it does not sag, then fill in the star center. Slip-stitch the opening closed.

10. Starch and press the doily, then slip-stitch it to the center of the star front.

11. Using buttonhole twist, sew five bells to each star point, as shown in **Diagram 3** on page 96. Repeat for the other four points.

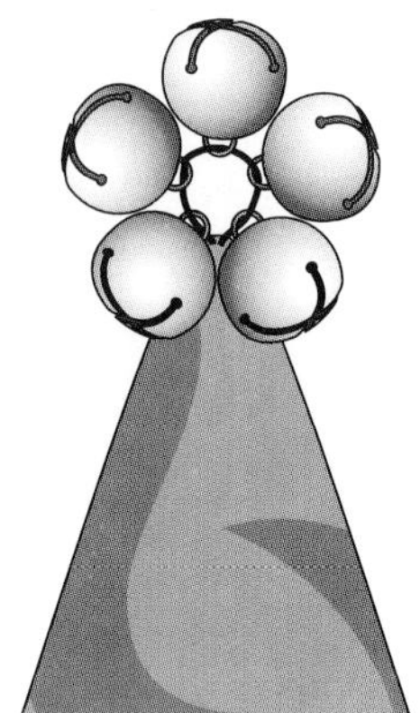

Diagram 3

12. Cut the ribbon into five 1-yard lengths. "Figure eight" each length into a two-loop bow, then secure the center with a 10-inch length of buttonhole twist; see **Diagram 4.** Using the buttonhole twist ends, sew the bows to the star point intersections. Sew one bell to the center of each bow. Clip any excess buttonhole twist.

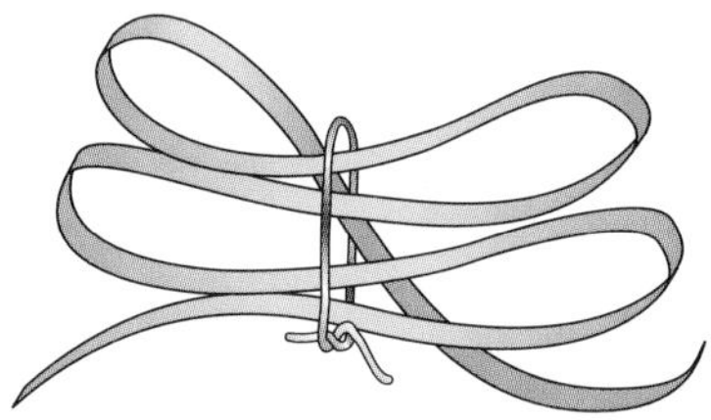

Diagram 4

13. Sew or pin the brooch to the center of the star.

14. Loop the center of the wire to form the branch holder, then bend each end back over itself, as shown in **Diagram 5.**

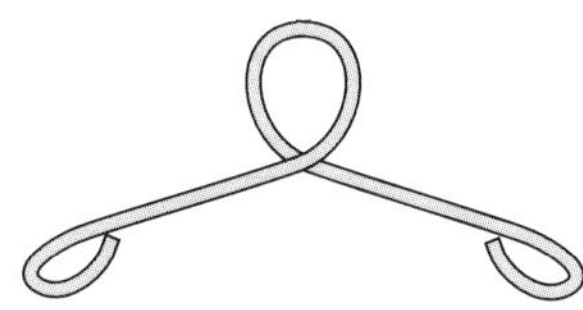

Diagram 5

15. Using the buttonhole twist, hand tack each end of the wire to the back of the topper; see **Diagram 6.**

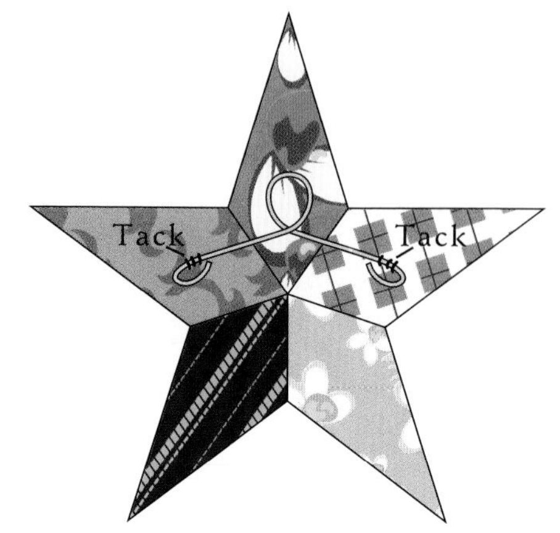

Diagram 6

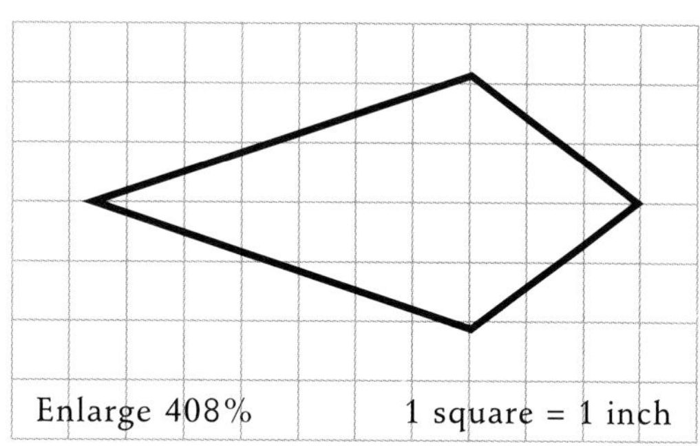

STAR POINTS PATTERN

PROJECT POINTERS

The shoppers in your area may appreciate traditional colors for their holiday decorations. Skip the turquoise and green fabrics and opt instead for scraps of red and green to complete your star tree toppers.

Gold or silver lamé would make an elegant statement in any customer's home; winter white velvet would be ideal for the bazaar buyer with a contemporary decor.

You may want to have two or three samples in your booth and take orders. This way, you won't waste the time making tree toppers in colors that may not sell.

Serving Up Elegance Set

Holiday parties will take on a special light with the addition of this striking Verdigris Serving Tray and the Golden Swirl Towel—both use easy techniques with high visual impact.

Verdigris Serving Tray

Size

$13\frac{1}{2}$ inches in diameter

What You Do

Note: This tray should be used for display purposes or transport of serving pieces. Food should not be placed directly on it. To clean, wipe it with a slightly damp cloth. Do not immerse it in water. It is important to let customers know how to use and care for the tray by attaching a note and by discussing its upkeep with them when they make their purchase.

1. Sand the tray smooth, then wipe it with the tack cloth.

2. Working in a well-ventilated area and using the gold paint, spray all sides of the tray; allow it to dry. Repeat if necessary to cover.

WHAT YOU NEED

VERDIGRIS SERVING TRAY

- 13½-inch-diameter unfinished wooden tray*
- Fine-grit sandpaper
- Tack cloth
- Metallic gold spray paint
- Patina Blue Liquid Finishing Solution*
- Two 1-inch-wide paintbrushes
- Clear, waterproof polyurethane

** See the "Buyer's Guide" on page 244 for ordering information.*

GOLDEN SWIRL TOWEL

- Cream 11-count prefinished kitchen towel with evenweave border
- One skein of wound metallic filament for the color in the **Color Key**
- Size 22 or 24 tapestry needle

3. Using a paintbrush, brush the finishing solution on the center of the tray. Place the tray on a level surface where it can sit undisturbed. Allow it to dry for 18 hours, checking periodically for progress. The solution is watery and needs to evaporate to create the weathered, crusted texture.

4. Once the solution has evaporated, determine whether the result is pleasing. If it is not, reapply the solution as desired to create stronger texture and color; let it dry thoroughly. Repeat as necessary until the desired effect is achieved.

5. Lightly brush off any loose flakes and crustation. Using the second brush, apply the polyurethane, following the manufacturer's directions. Let it dry thoroughly.

PROJECT POINTERS

Change the look of the towel from sophisticated to Victorian to country with a simple color change! For a romantic look, use rose-colored floss (DMC 335, Anchor 38, or J. & P. Coats 3283) or slate blue (DMC 3760, Anchor 169, or J. & P. Coats 7161). For a traditional Christmas feel, use jolly red floss (DMC 321, Anchor 9046, or J. & P. Coats 3500) or tree green (DMC 699, Anchor 923, or J. & P. Coats 6228).

Add a bit of drama by using three shades of floss. The first and fifth swirls should be the lightest shade, the second and fourth swirls should be the medium shade, and the middle swirl should be the darkest shade. I've chosen four color combinations that would be perfect for a holiday towel. For a soft look, a family of mauves would look perfect. Use DMC 3689, 3688, and 3687; Anchor 49, 66, and 68; or J. & P. Coats 3086, 3087, and 3088. The country blue look is also popular. Choose DMC 3325, 3755, and 334; Anchor 129, 140, and 977; or J. & P. Coats 7977, 7976, and 7975. The red range could be DMC 902, 498, and 321; Anchor 897, 1005, and 9046; or J. & P. Coats 3083, 3000, and 3500. The holiday green shading uses DMC 909, 910, and 911; Anchor 923, 229, and 205; or J. & P. Coats 6228, 6031, and 6205.

If you have other color schemes you'd like to offer to your customers, just pick three shades of any floss color family and stitch the swirls in color order, randomly, or in repeating groups.

Golden Swirl Towel

SIZE

Motif is 1 × 13⅛ inches

WHAT YOU DO

1. Find the center of the evenweave border and mark it with a pin. Find the center of the **Golden Swirl Towel Chart** by connecting the arrows.

2. Matching the centers of the evenweave border and the chart, cross-stitch the design using three strands of filament.

3. Wash and press the completed towel as directed in "Washing and Pressing" on page 241.

COLOR KEY

	J. & P. Coats	Color
●	5363	Old Gold

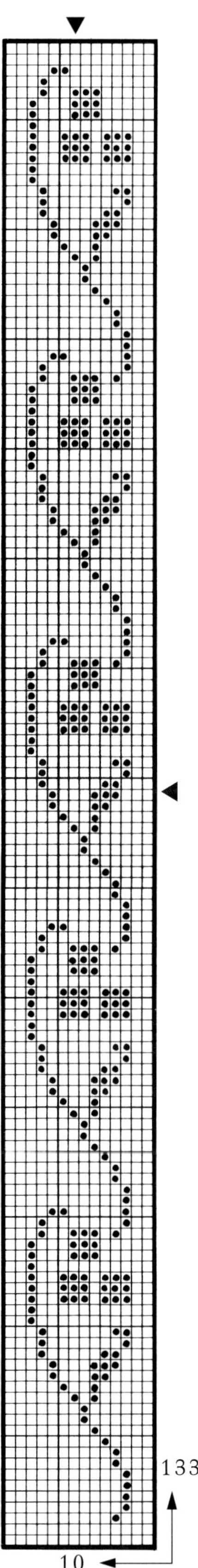

GOLDEN SWIRL TOWEL CHART

Victorian Elegance

Step into a world of elegance and romance with these satin, brocade, and beaded gifts and ornaments to make and sell. You'll find a selection of Victorian-inspired crafts that will charm and delight your holiday customers.

"Junk" Jewelry Kissing Ball

Dripping with "pearls" and other gems gleaned from antique stores, flea markets, and a once-forgotten jewelry box, this holiday bauble is a great way to show off sparkling "jewels" that are no longer in vogue. It can be hung in a doorway as a mistletoe substitute or on a sturdy branch for all to admire.

Size

About 5 inches in diameter

What You Do

1. Poke a small, deep hole in the foam ball using the point of a pencil. Fold the cord in half and glue the ends of the cord into the hole to form a loop for hanging.

2. Using the ball-head straight pins, attach the beaded appliqués to the ball to cover most of the ball's surface.

3. Using the pins or the glue gun, attach the larger pieces of jewelry to the ball, covering any bare areas of Styrofoam first.

4. Attach the smaller pieces in the same manner, covering any bare patches first. Allow the jewelry chains, pendants, and dangle earrings to hang free from the ball for added interest.

5. Tie the ribbon in a bow, then pin it to the ball near the hanging cord. Bend and twist the wire edges of the ribbon to create a three-dimensional effect. Cut the ribbon ends in a "V" shape.

What You Need

- 4-inch-diameter Styrofoam ball for the base
- 8-inch length of ⅛-inch-diameter silver cord for the hanger
- Low-temperature glue gun and glue sticks
- About 50 colored ball-head straight pins for attaching the jewelry
- 3 to 5 beaded appliqués to cover the base
- 30 to 50 pieces of costume jewelry, such as bracelets, pendants, pins, earrings, barrettes, and brooches, to cover the ball
- 1 yard of 1½-inch-wide pink wire-edged ribbon for the bow

Time-Saving Tip

The larger the jewelry piece you use for the "Junk" Jewelry Kissing Ball, the less space you have to cover and the less time you spend on crafting each one. Use link bracelets, beaded chokers, watch faces, and pretty barrettes to cover large sections of the ball, then fill in with chunky clip-on earrings and odd-size brooches. The remaining small areas can be covered with petite charms, slinky chains, and post earrings. Of course, your supply of junk jewelry should contain pieces of all sizes to complete the project. You could also theme your kissing ball by using only gold or silver jewelry pieces or make it a collector's ball by using jewelry from just one era, such as Art Deco, the War Years, or the 1960s. Either way, be on the lookout for oversize (and even gaudy!) jewels since they'll make the most interesting and glitzy kissing ball when combined.

Ribbon Barrettes

What little girl, or mom for that matter, could resist these fanciful ribbon barrettes, hair combs, and headband for special holiday occasions? The Rosette Hair Comb, Blue Ribbon Hair Comb, Cord-Wrapped Barrette, Gathered Ribbon Barrette, Ribbon Candy Barrette, and the Gold-Spangled Headband transform snippets of colorful ribbon and ordinary combs and clips into a fashionable bonanza of holiday bazaar bargains.

Rosette Hair Comb

Size

Rosette is 1½ inches wide

What You Do

1. For each rosette, refer to the **Rosette Diagram** and coil one end of the ribbon around itself to create the flower center. Form the outer petals by twisting the ribbon one-half turn every inch; bring each twisted section to the base of the rosette and slip-stitch it in place. Hand tack through the entire base to secure each rosette.

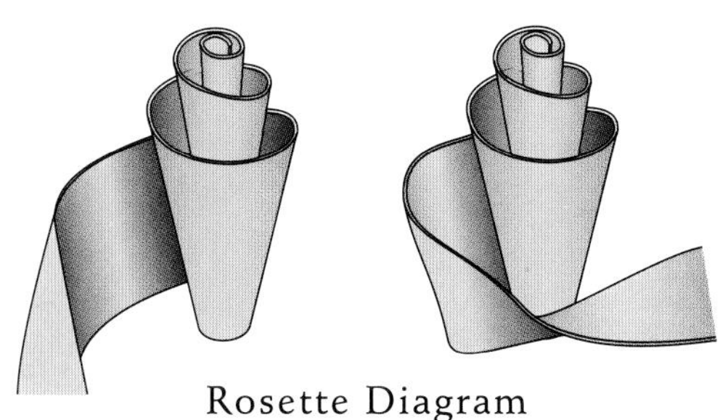

Rosette Diagram

2. Glue the ribbon rosettes to the top of the comb.

Blue Ribbon Hair Comb

Size

Ribbon loops are 1 inch high

What You Do

1. Beginning at one end of the comb and leaving a 3-inch tail, pull the ribbon up through the first tooth of the comb, nestling the ribbon as tightly as possible at the top of the tooth. Wrap the ribbon around the top of the comb creating a 1-inch loop, then pull the ribbon up through the third tooth.

2. Continue creating 1-inch loops across the comb, skipping every other tooth of the comb.

3. After threading the ribbon through the last tooth, cut the ribbon, leaving a 3-inch tail. Cut the ends of the ribbon in a "V" shape.

What You Need

Rosette Hair Comb

- Three 12-inch lengths of 1½-inch-wide French wire ribbon in variegated shades of purple and pink
- Matching sewing thread
- 3½-inch clear plastic hair comb
- Hot glue gun and glue sticks

Blue Ribbon Hair Comb

- 3½-inch clear plastic hair comb
- 1 yard of 1½-inch-wide light blue French wire ribbon with a gold edge

Cord-Wrapped Barrette

- ⅜ yard of ¼-inch-diameter pink upholstery cord
- Cellophane tape
- 4-inch-long metal barrette
- Hot glue gun and glue sticks

Cord-Wrapped Barrette

Size

4 inches long

What You Do

1. Secure each end of the upholstery cord with tape to prevent raveling. Glue one end of the cord to the underside of the barrette, taking care not to block the barrette closure.

2. Wrap the cord tightly around the entire length of the barrette top.

3. Cut any excess cord and glue the end to the underside of the barrette.

WHAT YOU NEED

GATHERED RIBBON BARRETTE

- ½ yard of 1-inch-wide magenta French wire ribbon with a gold edge
- Metallic gold thread
- 4-inch-long metal barrette

RIBBON CANDY BARRETTE

- Pink acrylic paint
- Saucer or palette
- 1-inch-wide sponge paintbrush
- 1 × 4-inch piece of heavy artist's paper
- Hot glue gun and glue sticks
- 4-inch-long metal barrette
- ⅞ yard of 1½-inch-wide variegated pink French wire ribbon

Gathered Ribbon Barrette

SIZE

7 inches long

WHAT YOU DO

1. Cut the ribbon in half, then place one length on top of the other. To form the barrette sleeve, use the gold thread to sew running stitches about 1/16 inch away from each long edge of the ribbon, starting and stopping 1½ inches from each ribbon end; see the **Ribbon Diagram.**

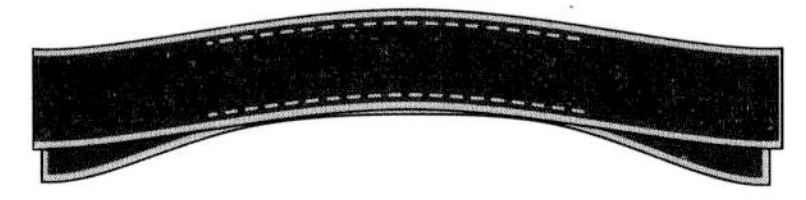

Ribbon Diagram

2. Clip all four ribbon ends in a "V" shape.

3. Slide the sleeve onto the barrette, gathering and bunching it to create a pleasing arrangement and to close the barrette.

Ribbon Candy Barrette

SIZE

About 7 inches long

WHAT YOU DO

1. Squeeze the paint onto the saucer or palette, then using the sponge brush, paint both sides of the paper and allow it dry. After painting the paper, wash the saucer and brush with soap and water before the paint dries.

2. Glue the paper strip to the top of the barrette.

3. Referring to the **Looping Diagram** and leaving about 4 inches of ribbon free, glue one end of the ribbon to the first 2 inches of paper. Fold the ribbon to create a 3-inch-high loop, then a 2-inch-high loop, gluing the lower fold of the loop to the paper. Make a 1-inch-high loop, a 2-inch-high loop, then a 3-inch-high loop in the same manner.

Looping Diagram

4. Glue the ribbon end to the paper, leaving a 4-inch tail.

5. Crinkle the loops by manipulating the ribbon's wire edge.

6. Cut the ribbon ends in a "V" shape.

Gold-Spangled Headband

SIZE

Headband accent is 4½ inches long

WHAT YOU NEED

GOLD-SPANGLED HEADBAND

- 2½ yards of ½-inch-wide metallic gold ribbon
- ½-inch-wide headband
- Hot glue gun and glue sticks
- 1 yard of ⅝-inch-wide metallic gold flat braid
- 8-inch length of 24-gauge wire
- ⅝ yard of ¼-inch-wide metallic gold flat braid
- ⅝ yard of 9 mm gold bead garland
- Three ¾-inch-diameter gold glass Christmas balls

WHAT YOU DO

1. Glue one end of the ribbon to the inside of the headband at one lower edge. Wrap the ribbon around the headband, overlapping the edges. Trim the excess ribbon and glue the end in place.

2. Make a three-loop bow with the wide gold braid and wire it to the headband about 5 inches from one end; do not cut the wire ends. See the **Three-Loop Bow Diagram.**

Three-Loop Bow Diagram

3. Cut the narrow gold braid in half and the bead garland into three equal lengths. Pinch the braid and bead garland lengths in the center and attach them to the headband over the bow, twisting the wire ends tightly to secure the bow grouping in place. Cut the ribbon ends diagonally.

4. Glue the Christmas balls to the center of the bow grouping.

PROJECT POINTERS

Displaying barrettes and hair combs can be somewhat tricky. If customers can't tell what an item is, they won't buy it. A pretty basket of hair combs might look great on the table, but from 5 feet out, it would resemble the cutting floor of a ribbon factory.

Be innovative when displaying hair wares. Make a brightly colored velvet bolster to display headbands. The bolster's round shape allows the headbands to remain upright in your booth. Display barrettes on a wide velvet ribbon with a decorative double bow at the top. Just clip the barrettes onto the ribbon length to create an eye-catching booth accent. Spatter paint a piece of Styrofoam in a color to match your hair combs. Then stick the teeth of the combs into the base for a snappy presentation.

Opulent Grape Cluster

This beribboned grape ornament has an elegance all its own—so befitting of the long-ago Victorian era. For marking the celebrations of today, the ornament can be clustered in a wreath or hung from a tree branch.

SIZE
About 5 inches long

WHAT YOU DO

1. Clean the balls with the lint-free cloth to remove dust.

2. Pour the paint into the plastic container, stirring thoroughly. Holding each ball firmly by the hanger, dip the entire ball into the paint. Hold each ball over the container to let the excess paint run off, then hang the ball to drip dry over the newspaper.

3. String four Christmas balls onto the center area of the silver wire, then twist the wire to create the grape cluster end; see **Diagram 1.**

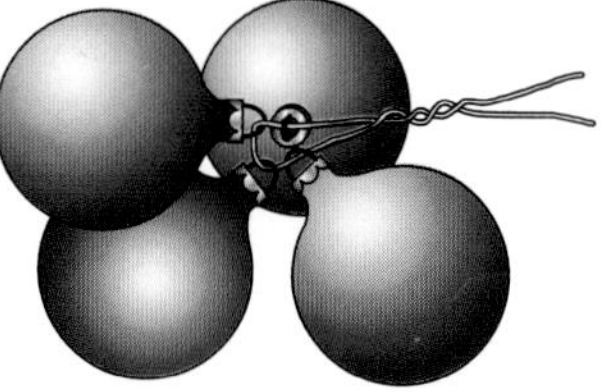

Diagram 1

4. Continue to form the cluster by adding three balls at a time to each wire, then twist the wire ends together to secure this grape layer in place. Curve the cluster as you continue to add balls to create a realistic-looking cluster; see **Diagram 2.** After adding the remaining balls, twist the wire ends, but do not trim them.

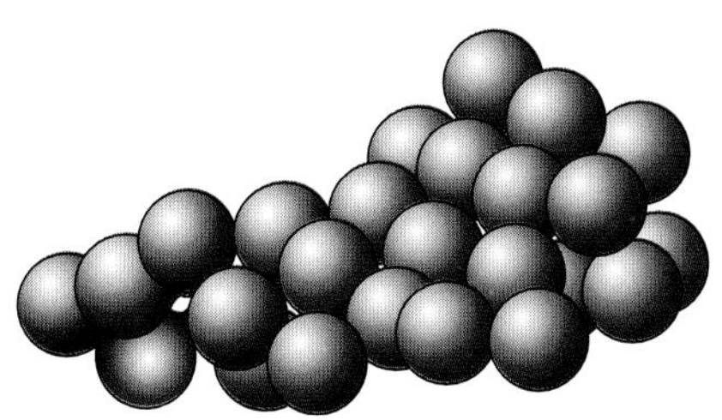

Diagram 2

5. Enlarge the **Grape Leaf Pattern** as directed in "Enlarging Patterns" on page 238.

6. From the craft paper, cut two grape leaves. Punch a hole in the stem area of each leaf. Fold each leaf accordion-style to create the veins, referring to the thin lines on the pattern.

7. Holding both wire ends together as if they were one, thread the leaves onto the wire ends leaving ½ inch of wire free between the grape cluster ornament and the leaves in order to attach the hanger. Twist the wire ends to secure, then clip any excess wire. Separate the leaves to give the cluster more dimension.

8. Wrap the fuchsia ribbon around the wire between the cluster and the leaves, then tie a bow. Clip the ribbon ends in a "V" shape.

9. Wrap the cream ribbon around the wire near the leaves and tie a knot for the hanger.

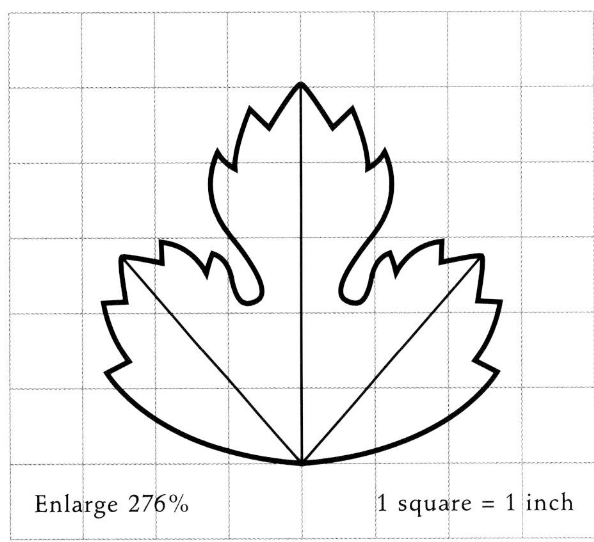

GRAPE LEAF PATTERN

WHAT YOU NEED

- About thirty ¾-inch-diameter silver glass Christmas balls
- Lint-free tack cloth
- Violet translucent glass paint*
- Plastic container at least 2 inches wide and 2 inches high
- Newspaper
- ½ yard of 24-gauge silver wire
- 9 × 12-inch sheet of violet craft paper for the leaves
- Paper punch
- ⅝ yard of 1½-inch-wide fuchsia French wire ribbon for the bow
- ½ yard of ⅛-inch-wide cream satin ribbon for the hanger

* *See the "Buyer's Guide" on page 244 for ordering information.*

PROJECT POINTERS

Displaying the grape ornaments can be challenging. Having them flat on a table will be boring and dangling them from an artificial tree branch won't do them justice. So get creative with your displays.

Cover a large piece of cardboard with silver lamé fabric, then accent the edges with pretty purple ribbon. Pin the grape ornaments to the display with ball-head pins.

Or spray paint sturdy wire mesh with silver paint, then weave miniature tinsel around the border; hang the ornaments by tying them on the mesh.

Christmas Birds and Babies

Stitch a whole flock of birds using the Brocade Bird Patterns or a nursery of newborns like the Sweet Dreams Doily Baby. Each makes use of rich fabric and doily scraps.

Brocade Bird

Size

$4\frac{1}{2}$ inches tall

What You Do

1. Enlarge the **Brocade Bird Patterns** as directed in "Enlarging Patterns" on page 238.

2. From the fabric, cut two bodies, two tails, and one gusset, taking advantage of the patterns in the fabric to create a feathered look.

3. Place the right sides of the bodies together. Using a $\frac{1}{4}$-inch seam allowance and referring to the **Sewing Diagram,** sew the bodies together, sewing from the large dot under the beak, around the top of the head, and down the back to the tail area. Also sew from the small dot at the derrière up to the tail area of the bird. Leave the straight edge of the tail open.

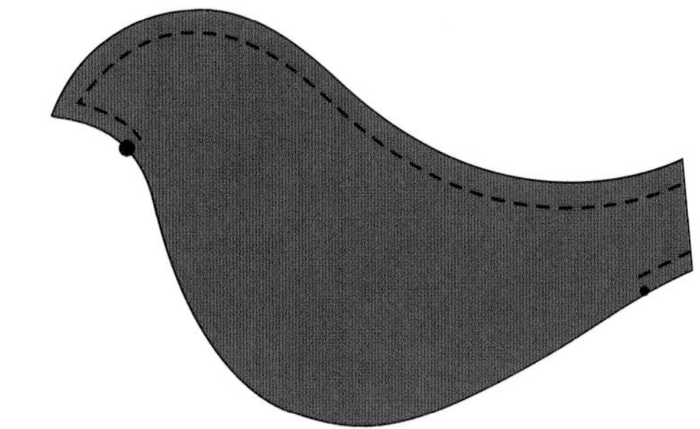

Sewing Diagram

4. Sew the gusset to one side of the body, matching the large and small dots and easing in any fullness. Leave the other side open for stuffing.

5. Turn the bird to the right side and stuff with fiberfill. Slip-stitch the gusset closed.

6. With right sides together and using a ¼-inch seam allowance, sew the tail pieces together, leaving an opening at the bottom. Turn the tail to the right side, but do not stuff it.

7. Slip the tail over the tail opening of the body, overlapping the edges by ½ inch; slip-stitch the tail in place.

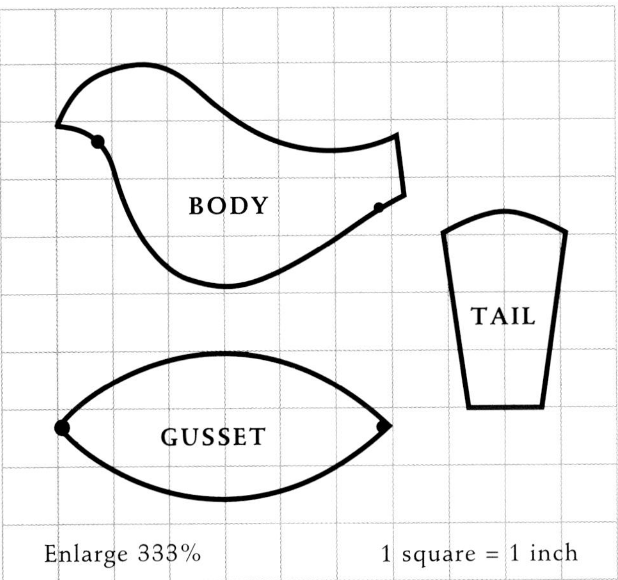

BROCADE BIRD PATTERNS

WHAT YOU NEED

BROCADE BIRD

- 9 × 12-inch piece of dark red brocade or upholstery fabric for the bird
- Matching sewing thread
- Polyester fiberfill

SWEET DREAMS DOILY BABY

- 10-inch-diameter crocheted-edged doily for the outfit
- Matching sewing thread
- 25 mm wooden bead for the head
- Black puff paint with fine-tip applicator for the eyes
- Rust or yellow embroidery floss for the hair
- Hot glue gun and glue sticks
- 8-inch length of 1/16-inch-diameter gold cord for the hanger
- Two 10 mm wooden beads for the hands
- ⅜ yard of ⅛-inch-wide cream satin ribbon for the bow

Sweet Dreams Doily Baby

SIZE

6½ inches tall

WHAT YOU DO

1. Press the doily and cut it in half. Set one half aside for now.

2. With the right sides together, fold one doily half in half again and sew along the raw edges to form the gown, using a ¼-inch seam allowance; see the **Gown Diagram.** Turn the gown to the right side and press so the seam is at the center back.

Gown Diagram

3. Hold the large bead so the holes form the baby's "ears." Using the paint, make two dots for eyes. Cut four 1-inch lengths of floss and glue them in place at the top of the head for hair, as shown in **Baby's Face Diagram.**

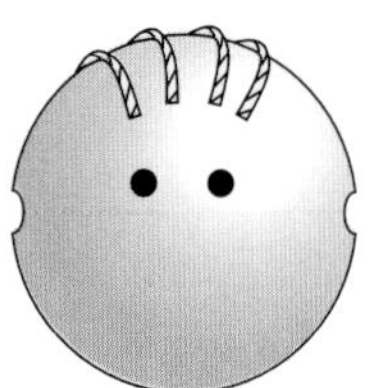

Baby's Face Diagram

4. Enlarge the **Bonnet Pattern** as directed in "Enlarging Patterns" on page 238.

5. From the reserved doily half, cut one bonnet; be sure to use the crocheted edging of the doily as the bonnet border. Lay the bonnet over the baby's head, pleating the excess fabric behind the head. Glue the bonnet in place so it covers the bead holes.

6. Fold the gold cord in half and glue it to the front side of the gown top for a hanger.

7. Glue the baby's head to the front side of the gown top, covering the ends of the hanger cord.

8. Glue one small bead, with the hole facing outward, at each side of the head for the hands.

9. Wrap the ribbon around the baby's neck and tie it in a bow.

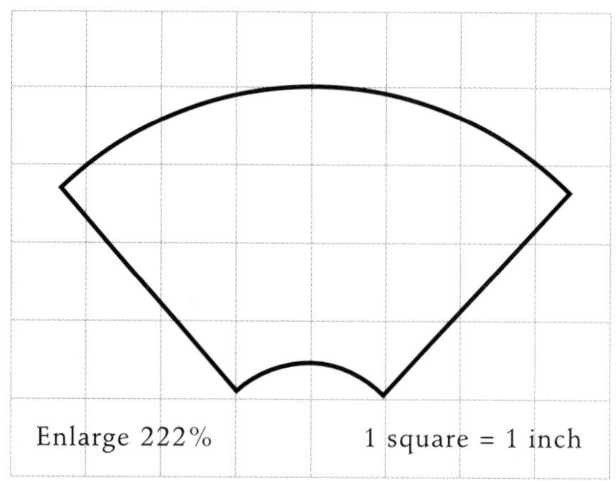

BONNET PATTERN

Money-Saving Tip

You may be able to find inexpensive doilies with crocheted edgings at discount or import stores for the doily baby's gown and bonnet. But an even thriftier idea would be to use paper doilies. They usually come eight to a package for just a dollar or two. You might even be able to find pastel doilies to add a little more color to the doily baby.

To craft with a circular paper doily, just cut the doily in half. Fold one half in half again with the cut edges at the center back. Make the bonnet in the same manner as for the fabric doily, pleating the excess paper behind the baby's head; you may want to cut away some of the paper layers for a nicer finish. To add decorative elements to your paper doily baby, blush the cheeks with pink paint, add a thin black marker eyebrow above each eye, then glue tiny bows or buttons to the gown front. And you have another bazaar best-seller that won't break your crafting supplies budget!

You can also craft Sweet Dreams Doily Babies with printed holiday doilies. These doilies are usually accented with holly leaves or poinsettia and would add an appropriate touch to a Christmastime bazaar.

Heartfelt Gifts

Christmas is a time for sharing and expressing thanks to loved ones and friends. Fill your booth with pretty Fabric-Covered Tins loaded with home-baked goods and loving Heart-in-Hand Ornaments for bazaar shoppers to buy and give as gifts of appreciation.

Fabric-Covered Tin

Size

7 inches in diameter

What You Do

1. From the fabric, cut a strip 1½ inches wider than the height of the tin and long enough to go around it (about 4½ × 22 inches for a 7-inch-diameter tin). Also cut a circle 1 inch larger than the lid size (about 8 inches for a 7-inch-diameter tin).

2. Press under ¼ inch along one long edge and one short edge of the strip. Using pinking shears, cut along the opposite long edge to create a decorative edge.

3. Position the strip on the tin with the long pressed edge at the bottom lip. Using the hot glue, glue it in place, leaving the short edges free. Glue the unpressed short edge to the tin, then glue the pressed edge over it to finish the "seam."

4. Hot-glue the 1 inch of fabric that extends above the tin to the inside of the tin, finger pressing the extension for a neat, finished look; be careful not to fray the pinked edge as you smooth the fabric.

WHAT YOU NEED

FABRIC-COVERED TIN

- 7-inch-diameter tin with a loose-fitting lid
- 1/4 yard of floral chintz fabric to cover the tin
- Pinking shears
- Hot glue gun and glue sticks
- Spray adhesive
- 3/4 yard of 3/8-inch-wide coordinating grosgrain ribbon for the lid

HEART-IN-HAND ORNAMENT

- 9 × 12-inch piece of fusible web
- 9 × 12-inch piece of light gray felt for the hand
- 5 × 9-inch piece of cardboard
- 4 × 7-inch piece of rust calico fabric for the heart
- Antique tatted- or lace-edged white handkerchief or napkin for the cuff
- 8-inch length of 1/8-inch-wide cream satin ribbon for the hanger
- Hot glue gun and glue sticks
- 3/8-inch-diameter white covered button for the cuff accent
- Matching sewing thread
- Polyester fiberfill
- 3/8-inch-diameter gold shank button

5. Using the spray adhesive, spray the wrong side of the circle, then center the circle on top of the lid, pressing it in place. Smooth any wrinkles by rubbing the fabric.

6. Clip about 1/8 inch into the selvage around the lid circle of fabric. Using the spray adhesive, glue it in place down the side of the lid to the lip, smoothing any wrinkles by rubbing the fabric. Clip away any excess fabric.

7. Glue the ribbon to the edge of the lid lip to cover the fabric edge.

PROJECT POINTERS

If you like to bake, fill your Fabric-Covered Tins with delicious brownie bars or bite-size gourmet cookies and sell them packaged to go. Line the tin with a wax-coated tissue paper or colored cellophane paper, leaving the top edges peeking over the top of the tin.

Cut your homemade goodies into small pieces so they fit nicely into the decorated container. Accent the "holes" with wrapped peppermint candies to give the presentation a more festive look. Fold the excess tissue paper over the top of the baked goods, then close the lid. Tie a large ribbon around the tin, then attach a tag to identify the tin's contents.

If you can buy your supplies in bulk or at a discount wholesaler's, baking for bazaars can be quite profitable. Since the covered tins are inexpensive to craft and are a great way to use scraps of fabric and ribbon, combine the two moneymaking projects for your next Christmas bazaar to the delight of hungry shoppers.

Heart-in-Hand Ornament

Size

8½ inches long

What You Do

1. Enlarge the **Heart-in-Hand Patterns** as directed in "Enlarging Patterns" on page 238.

2. Following the manufacturer's directions, fuse the fusible web to the felt.

3. From the cardboard, cut one hand. From the felt, cut one hand and one hand reverse. From the calico, cut two hearts. From the handkerchief, cut a 3 × 6-inch strip for the cuff, being sure to include a lace-edged corner, as shown in **Diagram 1.**

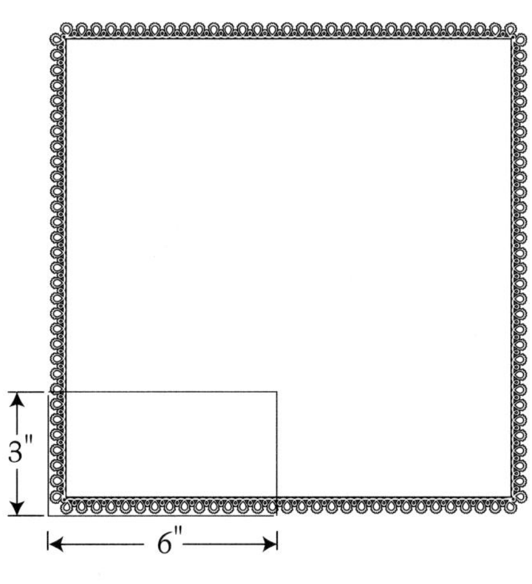

Diagram 1

4. Remove the paper backing from the felt hands and fuse one hand to the front and the back of the cardboard hand, following the manufacturer's directions.

5. Glue one end of the ribbon to the center front wrist and the other end to the center back wrist to create a hanger.

6. For the cuff, press under ½ inch on the two cut edges. With the lace at the pinkie finger and the lower edge and the long pressed edge about ¼ inch above the top of the hand, glue the cuff to the front of the hand; see **Diagram 2.** Wrap the cuff to the back of the hand and glue it in place. Sew or glue the white covered button to the cuff for accent.

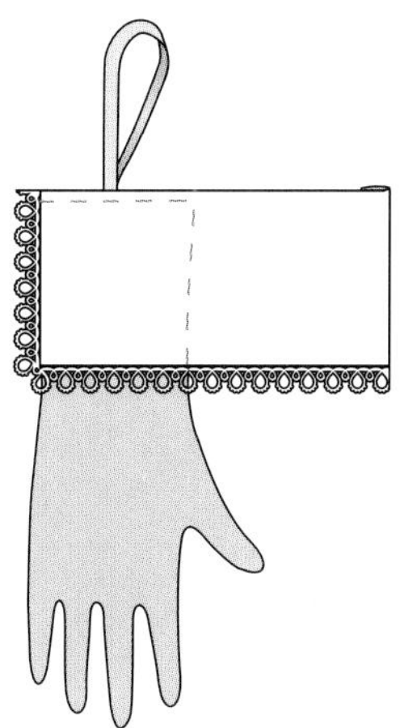

Diagram 2

7. With the right sides together and using a ¼-inch seam allowance, sew the hearts together, leaving an opening for turning. Clip the curves, turn it to the right side, and stuff lightly. Slipstitch the opening closed.

8. Sew the gold button to the center of the heart, pulling tightly to tuft the heart. Glue the heart to the palm area of the hand.

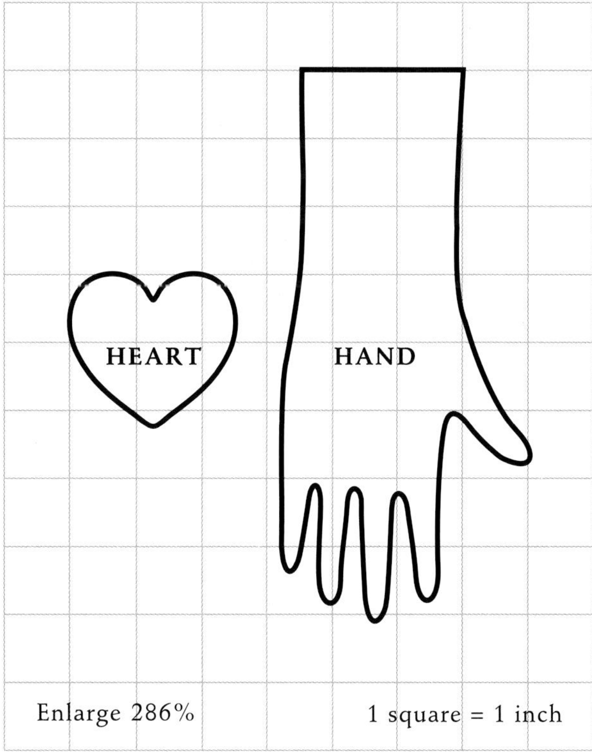

HEART-IN-HAND PATTERNS

Regal Boxes

These elegant boxes, covered in brocades and floral chintzes, make great storage containers or gift boxes. Their regal looks disguise their humble beginnings—ordinary oatmeal and detergent boxes.

Size

Rectangular box is 5½ × 6½ × 3 inches
Small container is 7½ inches high
Tall container is 9½ inches high

What You Do

Note: These directions give basic information on how to cover a box or container; adapt the steps for your individual project.

1. For round containers, cut one piece of fleece to fit around the side of the container and one piece to fit the lid. For rectangular boxes with a hinged lid, cut the fleece in two pieces—one for the sides and front and one for the back and lid. Hot-glue the fleece piece(s) to the containers or boxes.

2. Cut the fabric to fit around the side of the round container, adding 1 inch to all edges. For a hinged-lid box, cut the fabric in two pieces in the same manner as the fleece, adding 1 inch to all of the edges.

3. Fold under ¼ inch on each edge of each fabric piece and press. Referring to **Diagram 1,** wrap and glue the fabric to the containers, boxes, and lids, folding the excess fabric to the bottom and inside and overlapping the fabric ends at one corner; cut notches in a "V" shape for the lid.

Diagram 1

4. Cut a strip of heavy craft paper long enough to fit around the perimeter or sides of the lid of each box and wide enough to fit the height of the box lid. Cut a piece of fabric to cover the strip, adding ½ inch to all edges. Press under ½ inch on all edges and insert the paper strip; glue the folded-over edges in place. Glue the strip around the perimeter or sides of the box lid, as shown in **Diagram 2,** slightly overlapping the strip ends on the container lids.

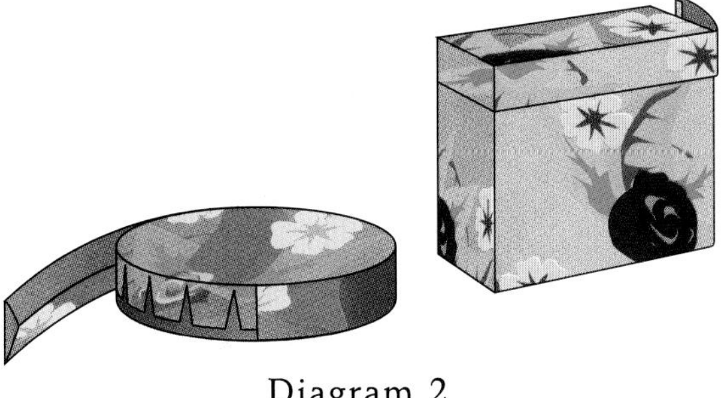

Diagram 2

5. If desired, glue a button to the lid. Hang a tassel from the button.

What You Need

- Empty oatmeal container or hinged concentrated detergent box
- ½ yard of thin fleece for each box
- Hot glue gun and glue sticks
- ½ yard of floral or brocade fabric for each box
- Heavy craft paper for each container rim
- Decorative ¾-inch-diameter button for a lid accent (optional)
- 4-inch-long tassel for an accent (optional)

Project Pointers

Kids love to have containers and keepers for all their little treasures. Gear some of your upholstered boxes to these young customers by choosing fun holiday prints or candy cane–stripe fabric.

Accent with huge plastic buttons or miniature ornaments. If you enjoy machine appliqué, fuse Christmas shapes like reindeer, trees, and snowflakes to the fabric, zigzag around the shapes, then hot-glue the decorated fabric to the boxes. For a special bazaar treat, sell the upholstered boxes filled to the brim with peppermint sticks or red and green lollipops.

Holiday Lights

These festive Jingle Bell and Beaded Candle shades are easy to craft and will add a touch of whimsy and intrigue to a shopper's holiday celebration.

Jingle Bell Candle Shade

Size

5 inches in diameter

What You Do

1. For the candle shade, use the drill to drill 32 evenly spaced holes around the lower rim of the shade. For the lamp shade, use the paper punch to punch 32 evenly spaced holes around the lower rim of the shade.

2. For the candle shade or the lamp shade, glue one end of the ribbon to the inside rim of the shade near one hole, then thread the ribbon through the hole. Thread a jingle bell onto the ribbon, leaving about 1 inch of ribbon hanging free to form a loop for the bell. Thread the ribbon back through the shade at the next hole, as shown in the **Jingle Bell Candle Shade Diagram.** Thread the ribbon out through the next hole, add a bell, and thread back through the shade at the next hole. Continue around the entire shade. Cut any excess ribbon and glue the end to the inside of the shade.

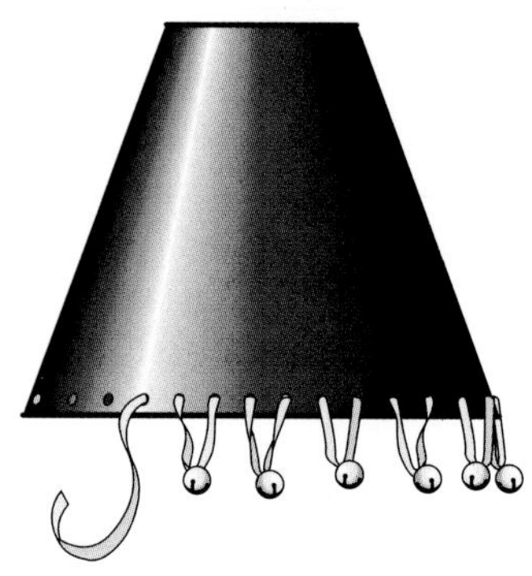

Jingle Bell Candle Shade Diagram

Beaded Candle Shade

SIZE
5 inches in diameter

WHAT YOU DO

1. For the candle shade, use the drill to drill 32 evenly spaced holes around the lower rim of the shade. For the lamp shade, use the paper punch to punch 32 evenly spaced holes around the lower rim of the shade.

2. For each length of fringe, cut a 10-inch length of black thread and thread the beading needle. Knot one end of the thread around a black seed bead. Thread the beads onto each fringe length in the following order: 1 pear-shape bead, 3 faceted round beads, 1 tube bead, 1 faceted rondelle bead, 1 faceted round bead, 1 faceted rondelle bead, 1 faceted round bead, 1 faceted rondelle bead, 1 faceted round bead, and 30 seed beads.

3. Referring to the **Beaded Candle Shade Diagram,** thread the end of the beaded thread through a hole in the shade and knot it securely. Cut any excess thread.

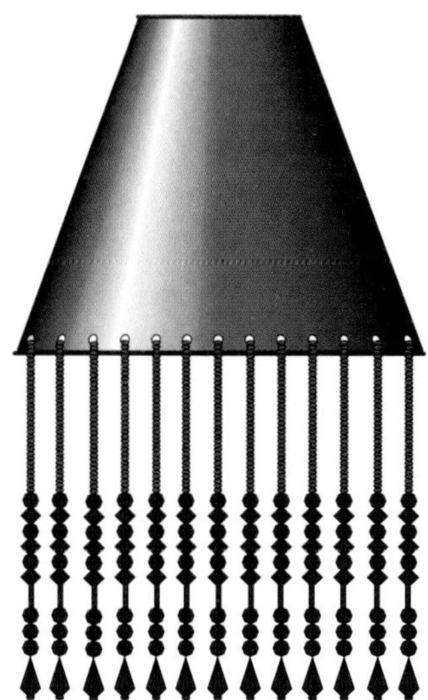

Beaded Candle Shade Diagram

4. Repeat Steps 2 and 3 for each hole to create a fringe around the shade.

WHAT YOU NEED

JINGLE BELL CANDLE SHADE

- Black metal candle shade or black paper lamp shade, 4 inches high and 5 inches in diameter
- Drill and 1/16-inch drill bit for the candle shade or paper punch for the lamp shade
- 2 yards of 1/8-inch-wide cream satin ribbon
- Epoxy glue
- Sixteen 3/8-inch-diameter silver jingle bells

BEADED CANDLE SHADE

- Black metal candle shade or black paper lamp shade, 4 inches high and 5 inches in diameter
- Drill and 1/16-inch drill bit for the candle shade or paper punch for the lamp shade
- Black sewing thread
- Beading needle
- About 1,000 black seed beads
- Thirty-two 12 × 8 mm black pear-shape beads
- One hundred ninety-two 4 mm black faceted round beads
- Thirty-two 12 mm black tube beads
- Ninety-six 6 mm black faceted rondelle beads

Fabric Accents

Crisp raw linen and vintage satins and silks make up these handsome home decorator items. The Standing Double Frame shows off a shopper's prized photographs while the Crazy-Quilt Heart Pillow will add comfort and elegance to any living room. Each will be welcome additions to a home accessories booth at your favorite holiday benefit.

Standing Double Frame

SIZE

6 × 8½-inch frames with 2 × 3-inch openings

WHAT YOU NEED

STANDING DOUBLE FRAME

- Six 6 × 8½-inch pieces of mat board for the frame fronts, backs, and stands
- Craft knife with extra blades
- ½ yard of tan linen fabric for the frame covering
- Two 6 × 8½-inch pieces of thin fleece for the frame padding
- Hot glue gun and glue sticks
- Dressmaker's shears
- Matching sewing thread
- Two 1-inch-diameter tan decorative buttons for the accents

WHAT YOU DO

1. Mark the photograph opening on two pieces of mat board, as shown in **Diagram 1.** Using a ruler to ensure a straight cut, cut out the openings with the craft knife, changing blades as necessary.

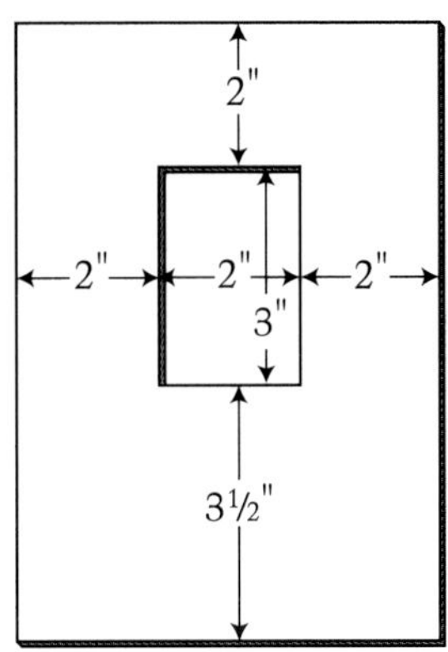

Diagram 1

2. From the fabric, cut six 7 × 9½-inch pieces for the frame fronts, frame bases, and frame backs. Also cut two 1½ × 8-inch strips for the hinges. Press the fabric well.

3. Glue one piece of fleece to each mat board with the photograph opening, then cut out the photograph openings.

4. Lay one piece of 7 × 9½-inch fabric, right side down, on a flat, clean surface. Place one fleece mat board, fleece side down, in the center of the fabric.

5. Fold the top edge of the fabric to the back of the mat board, then glue it in place. Fold and glue the opposite edge in the same manner, keeping the tension even. Repeat for the other two sides of the frame, trimming the corners as needed for a smooth fit.

6. Lay the covered mat right side down. Using the dressmaker's shears, make a small slit in the center of the fabric that covers the opening, then make mitered cuts to each corner of the opening, as shown in **Diagram 2.** For best results, the cuts must be precise and go directly into the center of each corner.

Diagram 2

7. Stretch the fabric flaps of the opening to the back of the frame and glue them in place. You may find it necessary to add a drop of glue at each corner. If you desire, press the clipped fabric corners with a warm iron. This forms one frame front.

8. Repeat Steps 4 through 7 for the second frame front. Set the frame fronts aside.

9. For the frame bases and frame backs, cover the four remaining pieces of mat board in the same manner as the frame fronts, repeating Steps 4 and 5.

10. To assemble the frame, glue the wrong side of each frame front to the right side of each frame base, leaving the bottom edge open so that photographs may be inserted in the frame; do not allow the glue to spread into the window. Press under heavy books to seal, allowing the glue to dry thoroughly before proceeding.

11. To create the hinges, fold each strip in half lengthwise with right sides together and press. Fold in the long raw edges and press again. Topstitch ⅛ inch from the long edges and fold into a hinge, as shown in **Diagram 3.**

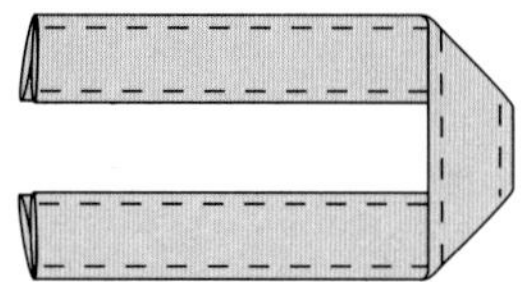

Diagram 3

12. Glue one hinge to the wrong side of each frame base, placing one hinge ¾ inch from the top edge of one frame and the other hinge ¾ inch from the bottom edge of the other frame; see **Diagram 4.**

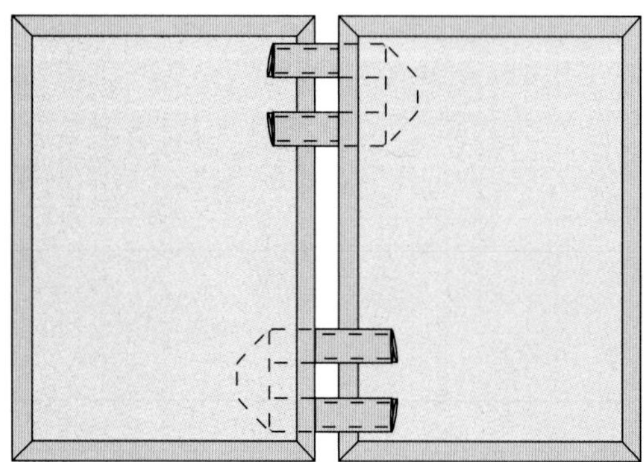

Diagram 4

13. Glue the wrong side of each frame base to the wrong side of each frame back, then press under heavy books to seal.

14. Lay the frames side by side. Lay the hinge from each frame over the other frame, then mark the position of each button. Referring to **Diagram 5,** sew the buttons in place through the top layer of fabric, then button the frames together using the hinges as buttonholes.

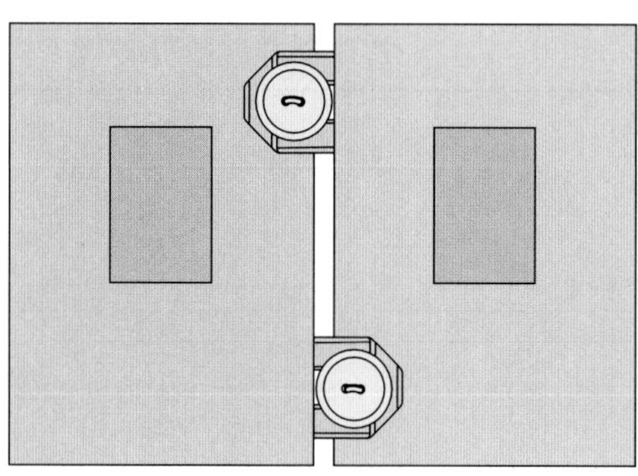

Diagram 5

PROJECT POINTERS

Go for the holly, jolly look at your booth and make the Standing Double Frame one of your big sales pushers! Purchase a bright holiday print for the frame front and back, then cover the frame base with a colorful pindot. Hot-glue piping around the perimeter of the frame and make the hinges out of grosgrain ribbon. Forget the sophisticated round buttons—choose 1¼-inch-long candy cane or Ol' Saint Nick buttons instead to fasten the hinges. Or buy bright red fabric and crisp white lace to craft festive frames. A red and white polka-dot button would add a touch of whimsy. Shoppers love Christmas-oriented decorations and gifts, and it's up to you to supply the yuletide cheer at a holiday bazaar with a table full of spirited crafts.

Crazy-Quilt Heart Pillow

SIZE

9 inches high

WHAT YOU DO

1. Enlarge the **Crazy-Quilt Heart Pillow Pattern** as directed in "Enlarging Patterns" on page 238.

2. From both the crazy quilt and the velvet, cut one heart.

3. With the right sides together and using a 1/4-inch seam allowance, sew the hearts together, leaving an opening for turning. Grade the seam allowance and clip the curves. Turn the pillow to the right side and stuff. Slip-stitch the opening closed.

4. Tape the ends of the upholstery cord to prevent raveling. Beginning at the top center of the heart, slip-stitch the upholstery cord around the pillow, covering the seam edge; end the cord by curling it into a knot and hiding the taped end. Hand tack the knot in place. Trim any excess cord.

WHAT YOU NEED

CRAZY-QUILT HEART PILLOW

- 12-inch square of a well-worn crazy quilt with Victorian embroidery for the pillow top*
- 12-inch square of blue velvet fabric for the pillow back
- Matching sewing thread
- Polyester fiberfill
- 1 1/8 yards of 1/2-inch-diameter metallic gold upholstery cord
- Cellophane tape

* *In order to preserve the historical value of antique quilts, be sure to use only tattered or torn examples or quilts in such disrepair that they are impossible to salvage otherwise.*

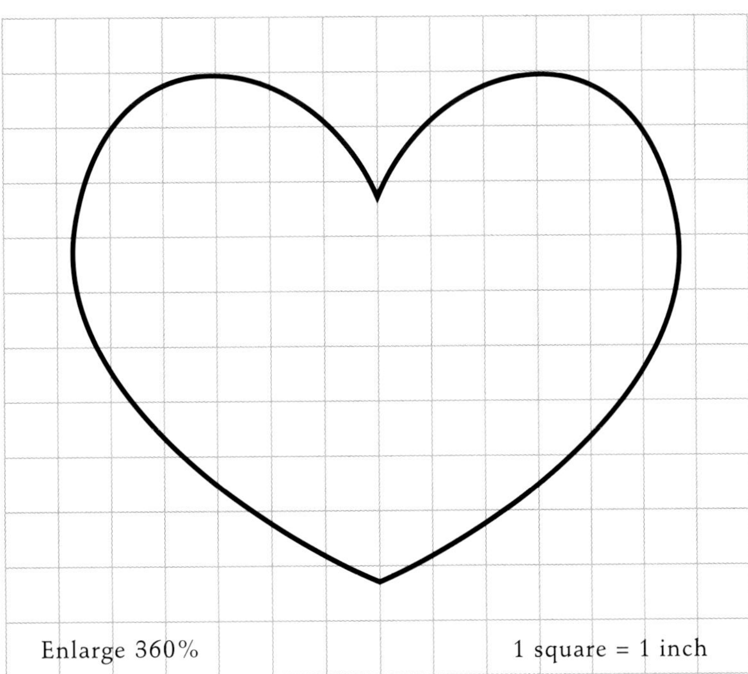

CRAZY-QUILT HEART PILLOW PATTERN

Belt-Buckle Brooches

Here's a simple way to accent rhinestone, pearl, gold, plastic, or Bakelite buckles. Just thread a length of pretty ribbon through the buckle, add a pin back, and you'll instantly have a brooch to dress up a blazer.

SIZE

4½ to 8½ inches long

WHAT YOU DO

1. Thread an appropriate-size ribbon through the slots of the belt buckle, then even out the ribbon ends by folding them down from the buckle. Clip the ends of the ribbon into diagonal slants or into a "V" point, as shown in the **Ribbon Diagram.**

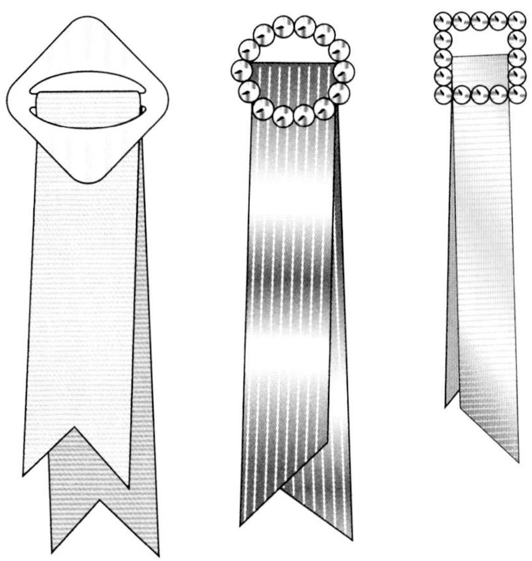

Ribbon Diagram

WHAT YOU NEED

- Old or unusual belt buckles, ¾ to 2 inches wide*
- 9- to 16-inch lengths of coordinating color satin or metallic grosgrain ribbon in widths to fit the buckles
- Hot glue gun and glue sticks
- Metal pin backs slightly smaller than buckle width

* *Available at flea markets, antique shops, and fabric or notions stores.*

2. Add a very small dot of hot glue near the fold of the ribbon to keep it from slipping out of the buckle.

3. Glue a pin back to the back of the ribbon behind the buckle.

4. Vary the ribbon lengths you offer on your brooches.

PROJECT POINTERS

Don't fret if you can't find antique belt buckles! Your local fabric or notions store has a great selection of buckles—in fact, two of the five buckles I used came right out of a fabric store's button case! You'll find brightly colored plastic buckles, pearl-look varieties, shiny black ones, as well as stitched leather beauties.

Choose ribbon that coordinates with the "theme" of your buckles. For instance, a kiddie ribbon with baby ducks would look great with a yellow plastic buckle if you want to target the younger market. Or add a length of suede ribbon to a leather buckle to give a sophisticated look for the adult buyer. Teens would love a metallic or Day-Glo ribbon on a funky buckle. These brooches are very inexpensive to make, but appeal to just about anyone. Display them on a large solid-color pillow for best sales results at your bazaar booth.

Sweetly Scented Drawer Sachets

Craft a variety of elegant sachets from brocade, linen, or floral scraps. Fill them with herbs, so the aromas will attract as much attention as their simple, stylish looks.

Size

5 to 8 inches high

What You Do

1. From each fabric, cut two same-size pieces. The sachets shown were cut 5 × 8 inches (olive), 4 × 6 inches (tan), 5½ × 7½ inches (sage green), 4½ × 7 inches (floral), and 4½ × 6 inches (pine green).

2. With right sides together and using a ¼-inch seam allowance, sew each sachet together around all four sides, leaving a 2-inch opening for turning and filling. Trim the seam allowances. Turn each sachet to the right side and press.

3. Fill each sachet with potpourri, then slip-stitch the opening closed.

4. Decorate the sachets as follows for each model shown or as you desire; see the **Embellishment Diagrams.** For the olive sachet, hand tack a tassel to each lower corner. For the tan sachet, hand tack a tassel to the center top. For the sage green sachet, poke a hole in the sachet center. Tape the cord ends to prevent raveling, then hot-glue one end of the cord into the hole. Wrap the cord around the glued end in a spiral, and slip-stitch the cord to the sachet until the spiral measures about 1½ inches across. Curve the cord toward the upper left corner, slip-stitching it in place. Use a seam ripper to make a small hole in the upper seam; insert the cord end. Slip-stitch the opening closed. For the floral sachet, hand tack a tassel to the center bottom. For the pine green sachet, tuft the center of the sachet with a button.

Embellishment Diagrams

WHAT YOU NEED

- Scraps of decorator fabrics, such as brocades, linens, or florals, for the sachets
- Matching sewing thread
- Lavender, clove, pine, or other scented potpourri or herbs
- Decorative tassels in desired color and size, a decorative button, and/or ½-yard length of ¼-inch-diameter upholstery cord for the accents
- Cellophane tape
- Hot glue gun and glue sticks

PROJECT POINTERS

Try selling premade gift baskets full of crafts at your booth. Make up three or four different ones for the first holiday bazaar of the year, then gauge the response. If they sell well, make additional baskets for the next bazaar. If sales could be better, substitute items in the basket to see if a different combination sells more successfully.

These easy sachets make excellent crafts for a romantic-style basket since they're quick and very inexpensive to make. Buy woven baskets, paint them, and add pretty ribbons. Fill the baskets with excelsior or Spanish moss, then nestle in a teapot ornament, a sparkling jeweled candle, a rosette hair comb, a sweetly scented drawer sachet, and a few trial-size lotions and shampoos with pretty labels.

You can also decorate bars of scented soap for the basket. Using pinking shears, cut an 8-inch square of pretty calico or striped fabric for each soap. Lay the fabric on a flat surface with the wrong side up. Place the soap in the center of the fabric, then wrap the fabric around the soap, pleating and folding the edges as necessary. Secure with a drop of hot glue. Accent the wrapped soaps with ribbons, sprigs of dried flowers, laces, buttons, and charms. The soaps will look beautiful when tucked in among the other romantic crafts. And you'll enjoy solid sales since people love the idea of ready-to-give gifts.

Vintage Silverware Tree Trims

Preserve an odd piece of silverware by transforming it into a fanciful ornament for the tree. Pick up old pieces of flatware, then add a ribbon and bells for a romantic ornament that will catch the eye of discriminating buyers.

Silver Spoon Ornament

Size

3½ inches long

What You Do

1. Bend the handle of the spoon backward in a graceful curve to create a hook to hang on a tree branch; see the **Handle Diagram.**

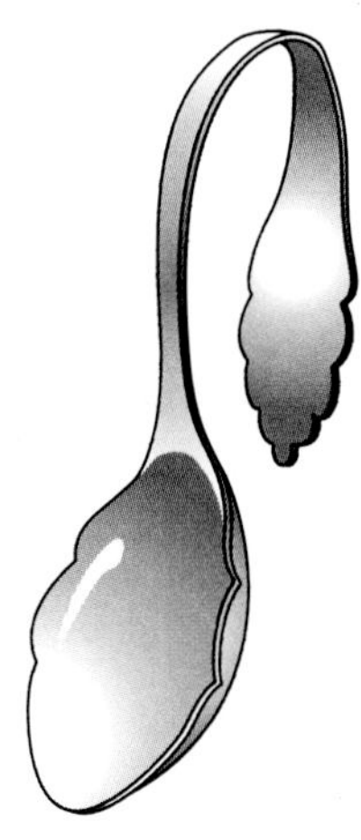

Handle Diagram

2. Thread the bells onto the wire and wrap it around the stem of the spoon just above the bowl. Twist the wire ends together, then trim the excess.

3. With the ribbon, tie a bow around the spoon's stem, covering the wire; cut the ends diagonally.

Dangling Fork Ornament

Size

7½ inches long

What You Do

1. Thread the bells onto the wire and wrap it around the stem of the fork about 1 inch above the pronged section. Twist the wire ends together, then trim the excess.

2. Cut the length of pink ribbon in half. Holding the two ribbon lengths as if they were one, tie a bow around the handle of the fork, covering the wire. Cut the ribbon ends in a "V" shape.

3. Tie the cream ribbon in a knot just below the wired bells, then pull the ribbon ends toward the back of the fork for the hanger. Holding both ribbon ends as if they were one, tie an overhand knot at the ribbon ends to form a hanging loop.

What You Need

Silver Spoon Ornament

- Silverware spoon with a decorative embossed pattern
- Four ½-inch-diameter silver jingle bells
- 3-inch length of 24-gauge silver wire for attaching the bells
- ½ yard of ⅝-inch-wide turquoise satin ribbon for the bow

Dangling Fork Ornament

- Three ¾-inch-diameter silver jingle bells
- 3-inch length of 24-gauge silver wire for attaching the bells
- Silverware fork with a decorative embossed pattern
- 1 yard of 1-inch-wide pink satin ribbon for the bow
- ½ yard of ⅛-inch-wide cream satin ribbon for the hanger

Money-Saving Tip

True antique flatware and ornate sterling silver pieces can be priced quite high. For just a few pennies, you can easily age inexpensive stainless flatware. Purchase everyday flatware forks and spoons, being sure to choose embossed styles with lots of detail. Starter sets for baby would also make cute ornaments. Apply a rough-surface acrylic base coat or sealer to each piece of flatware to prepare the surface for antiquing. Wipe on antiquing waterbase acrylic washes (available in craft stores), letting the antiquing settle in the nooks for highlights. Wipe off the excess, then allow the piece to dry. Seal the antiquing with an acrylic sealer.

Teatime Ornaments

These whimsical cutouts will add a spot of charm to a customer's dining room or kitchen Christmas tree. They're easy to make from scraps of fabric or wallpaper and are sure to whistle their way right out of your booth.

Size

5½ inches high

What You Need

- ³⁄₈ yard of floral or blue-and-white fabric or wallpaper
- Spray-Mount Artist's Adhesive*
- 12-inch square of white posterboard for one teapot and teacup
- Craft knife
- ½ yard of ⅛-inch-wide cream satin ribbon for the hangers
- Hot glue gun and glue sticks

** See the "Buyer's Guide" on page 244 for ordering information.*

What You Do

Note: When selecting fabrics, look for fabric that mimics the patterns and designs found in your favorite fine china and porcelain. Take care when purchasing fabrics so that the fabric patterns don't overwhelm the size of the teacups and teapots.

1. Enlarge the **Teatime Ornaments Patterns** as directed in "Enlarging Patterns" on page 238.

2. From the fabric, cut two 12-inch squares.

3. In a well-ventilated area, spray the wrong side of the fabric with the adhesive. Adhere one piece of fabric to each side of the posterboard.

4. Lay the teapot, teacup, saucer, and inner cup patterns on the covered posterboard, using the patterns in the fabric to best advantage. Trace around each pattern. Using the craft knife, cut out each piece just inside the traced line, cutting away any markings. Also cut out the areas in the teacup and teapot handles.

5. Cut the ribbon in half. Fold each length in half and hot-glue the ends to the back side of the teapot or teacup for the hanger.

6. Referring to the **Teacup Assembly Diagram** and using the hot glue, first glue the inner cup to the teacup and then the assembled teacup to the saucer.

Teacup Assembly Diagram

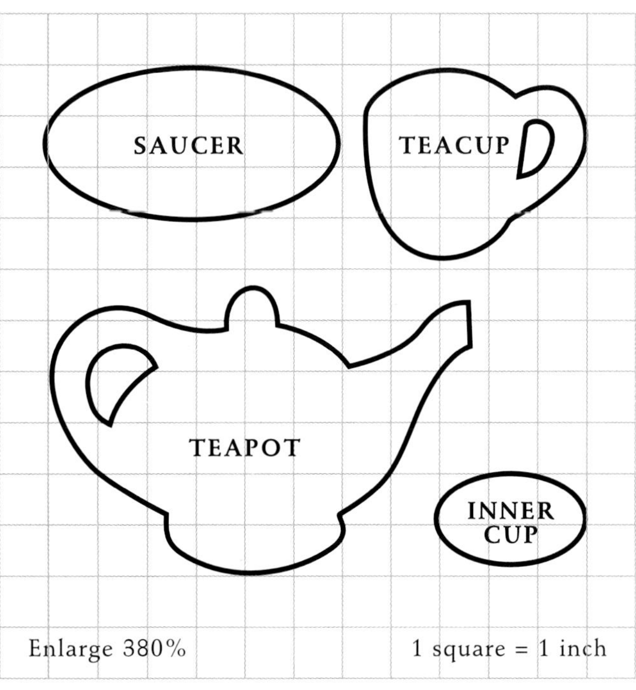

TEATIME ORNAMENTS PATTERNS

Necktie Fan Pillow

This striking pillow is crafted from father's cast-off neckties and makes a handsome addition to a customer's living room, den, or parlor. Choose ties of a similar width, but vary the patterns for a true Victorian crazy-quilt effect. A tassel and large decorative button complete the effect.

Size

About 14 inches high

What You Do

1. Enlarge the **Necktie Fan Pillow Pattern** as directed in "Enlarging Patterns" on page 238.

2. From the linen, cut one fan for the tie base. From the velvet, cut one fan for the pillow backing. Including the widest portion and the point of each necktie, cut a 12-inch length.

3. Using the pillow backing as a size reference, arrange the ties in a fan shape, paying attention to color and patch coordination; the tenth and eleventh ties should be at least 1 inch from the edges of the fan point when the fan shape is completed. Remove the center tie from the arrangement and place it in the center of the linen tie base fabric; see **Diagram 1.** Slip-stitch it in place.

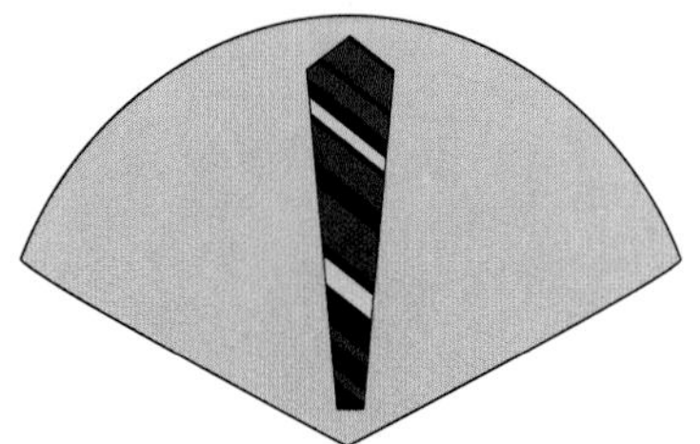

Diagram 1

4. Remove the second tie from the arrangement and place it on the left side of the first tie, overlapping the lower portion of the tie to accentuate the fan shape; see **Diagram 2.** Slip-stitch the tie in place.

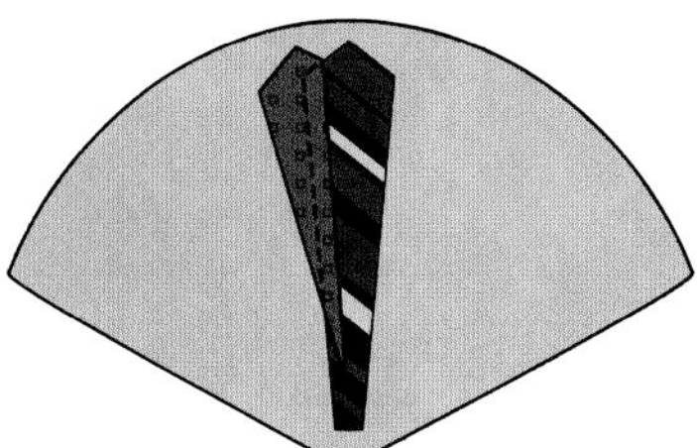

Diagram 2

5. Referring to **Diagram 3,** remove the third tie and place it on the right side of the first tie, overlapping the cut end. Slip-stitch the tie in place. Varying the width of each tie, continue placing and slip-stitching ties on either side of the first three ties to complete the pillow front.

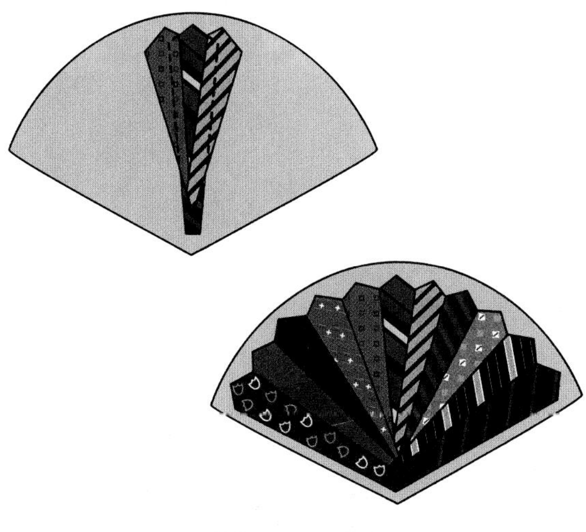

Diagram 3

6. With the right sides together, sew the pillow front to the pillow backing, using a ½-inch seam allowance; leave an opening for turning near the point of the fan. Clip the curves and grade the seam allowance if necessary. Turn the pillow to the right side and press.

7. Stuff the pillow firmly, but do not slip-stitch the opening closed.

What You Need

- ½ yard of tan linen fabric for the tie base
- ½ yard navy velvet fabric for the pillow backing
- 11 vintage neckties
- Matching sewing thread
- Polyester fiberfill
- 1⅝ yards of ⅜-inch-diameter metallic gold upholstery cord
- Cellophane tape
- 2-inch-diameter button
- 6-inch-long gold tassel

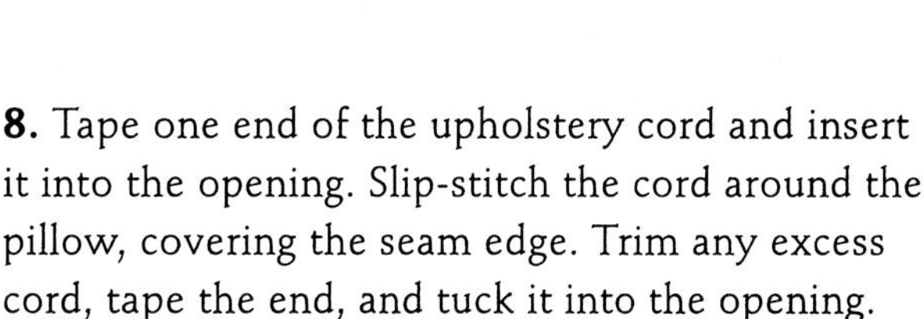

8. Tape one end of the upholstery cord and insert it into the opening. Slip-stitch the cord around the pillow, covering the seam edge. Trim any excess cord, tape the end, and tuck it into the opening. Slip-stitch the opening closed.

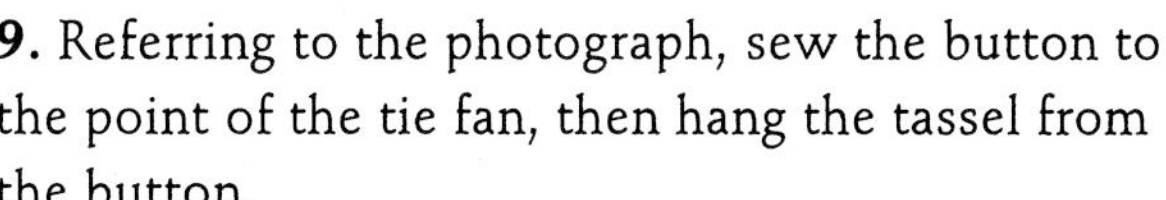

9. Referring to the photograph, sew the button to the point of the tie fan, then hang the tassel from the button.

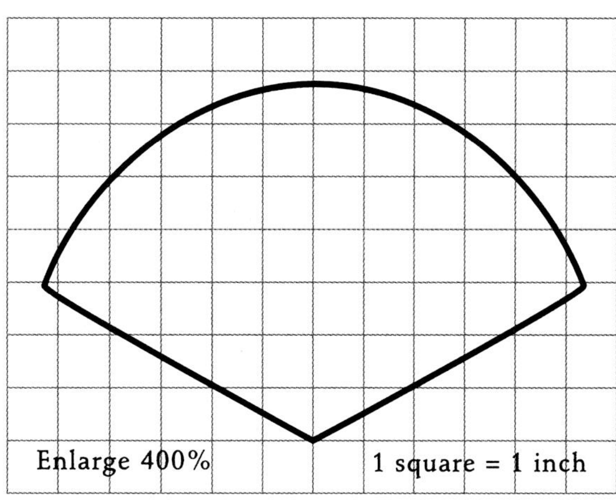

NECKTIE FAN PILLOW PATTERN

Romantic Rosebud Trims

The Rosebud Nosegay and the Rosebud Wreath are accented with miniature dried roses that are gathered together to delight the eye and the senses.

Rosebud Nosegay

Size

4 inches long

What You Do

1. Clip the rose stems to 3 inches in length, cutting the stems at an angle with the pruning shears.

2. Gather the roses together in a bouquet and wrap a 10-inch length of wire around the stems.

3. Cut a 1/4-inch-diameter hole in the center of the doily, then insert the rose stems in the hole to create a handle. Gather the bottom of the doily tightly around the stems. Working at the cut edge of the doily, securely wrap a 5-inch length of wire around the doily and stem tops to hold the doily gathers in place; see the **Doily Diagram.** Arrange the doily by folding the front area of the nosegay over to create a lip.

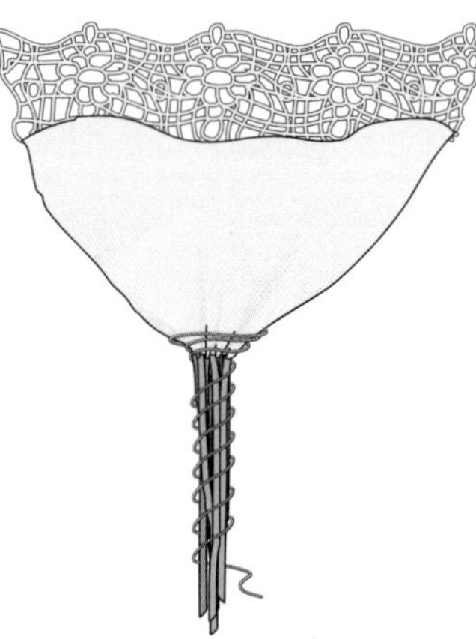

Doily Diagram

4. Glue one end of the wide satin ribbon over the wire at the base of the rose blossoms. Tightly wrap the ribbon around the wired stems to cover the handle; see the **Handle Diagram.** Cut any excess ribbon, turn under the raw end, then glue it to the back side of the handle.

Handle Diagram

5. Tie the fuchsia ribbon in a bow. Insert a 3-inch length of wire in the bottom of the bow, then insert the wire into the left side of the nosegay between the roses and the doily, placing the wire ends into the handle. Glue the wire in place if necessary.

6. Cut the narrow ribbon in half. Holding the two lengths as if they were one, tie the ribbon around the stem of the nosegay at the base of the doily to create the streamers.

Rosebud Wreath

Size

4 inches in diameter

What You Do

1. Glue one Christmas ball to the wreath, inserting the hanger end into the woven twigs of the wreath.

2. Glue two rosebuds below the ball with one pointing inward and one pointing outward. Nestle the two remaining gold balls below the rosebuds. Finish the wreath by gluing the four remaining rosebuds below the balls on the wreath; see the **Accent Diagram.**

What You Need

Rosebud Nosegay

- 18 dried pink miniature roses with stems
- Pruning shears
- ½ yard of floral wire
- 6-inch-diameter crocheted-edged white doily for the bouquet base
- ⅜ yard of 1-inch-wide cream satin ribbon for the handle
- Hot glue gun and glue sticks
- ⅜ yard of 1-inch-wide fuchsia French wire ribbon for the bow
- 1 yard of ⅛-inch-wide cream satin ribbon for the streamers

Rosebud Wreath

- Three ¾-inch-diameter gold glass Christmas balls
- 4-inch-diameter twig wreath
- Hot glue gun and glue sticks
- 6 dried red rosebuds
- 8-inch length of ⅛-inch-diameter gold cord for the hanger (optional)

Accent Diagram

3. Add a gold cord hanger, if desired, at the top of the wreath by wrapping the cord around the wreath and tying the ends together in a knot.

Painted Glass Balls

Turn ordinary dime-store glass Christmas balls into one-of-a-kind creations with transparent glass paint. A few quick brush strokes create the lovely Victorian Violets ball, while a dip into green paint makes a striking Two-Tone Ornament.

Victorian Violets

Size

Motif is $1\frac{1}{4}$ inches high

What You Do

1. Clean the ball with the lint-free tack cloth to remove dust.

2. Using the violet paint and referring to the **Violet Diagram,** make two brush strokes on the ball in a "V" shape for the upper petals. Paint one petal on each side of the upper petals and one wider petal at the bottom.

Violet Diagram

3. Repeat Step 2 twice more, evenly spacing three violets around the ball.

4. Hang the ball to dry before painting the leaves.

5. Using the dark green paint and referring to the

Leaf Diagram, paint two overlapping leaves between each violet.

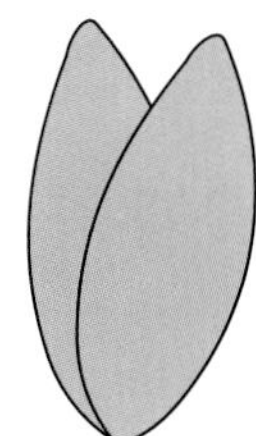

Leaf Diagram

6. Hang the painted glass ball to dry.

Two-Tone Ornament

SIZE

Dipped area is 1¼ inches high

WHAT YOU DO

1. Clean the ball with the lint-free tack cloth to remove dust.

2. Pour the paint into the plastic container, stirring it thoroughly.

3. Holding the ball firmly by the hanger, dip the ball into the paint, allowing it to cover the lower portion of the ball at an angle. Hold the ball over the container to let the excess paint run off, then hang the ball to drip-dry over newspaper.

WHAT YOU NEED

VICTORIAN VIOLETS

- 2½-inch-diameter gold glass Christmas ball
- Lint-free tack cloth
- Violet and dark green translucent glass paint*
- ¼-inch-wide sable or synthetic paintbrush

** See the "Buyer's Guide" on page 244 for ordering information.*

TWO-TONE ORNAMENT

- 2½-inch-diameter gold glass Christmas ball
- Lint-free tack cloth
- Dark green translucent glass paint*
- Plastic container at least 3 inches wide and 2 inches high
- Newspaper

** See the "Buyer's Guide" on page 244 for ordering information.*

PROJECT POINTERS

Hang a length of string or rope for drying large quantities of the hand-painted balls instead of searching for nooks and crannies to dry individual balls.

I usually string a small clothesline in my craft room, then cover the floor with a plastic drop cloth or newspapers. I clip clothespins to the line in groups of two so that the painted balls won't slide together. After painting or dipping each ball, I hang it between two clothespins, and it will dry undisturbed.

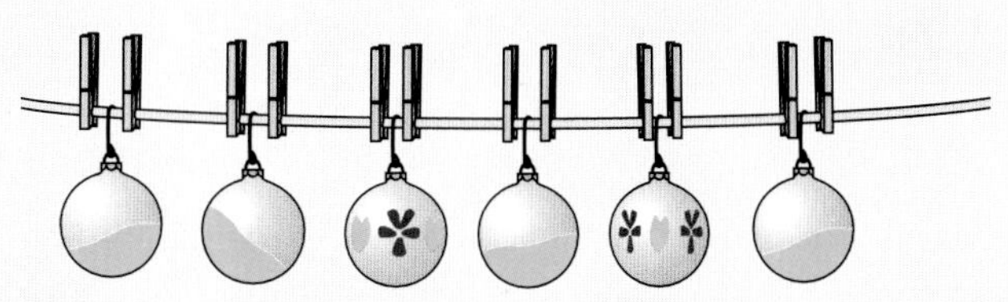

For Kids of All Ages

Here's a parcel of projects that will catch the eye of both the young and young at heart. There's a bevy of creative characters to cuddle and snuggle and hand puppets to entice anyone's imagination, as well as heirloom-quality needlepoint pillows and last-minute tree trims, decorations, and gifts.

Candy Delights

Turn Christmas into a sugarplum fantasy with nonedible holiday trims like a Red Licorice Star, colorful Lollipop Star, Gumdrop Wreath, and beribboned and painted Lollipop Ornament. Let the kids join in the fun, if you can keep them from snacking on all the supplies!

Red Licorice Star

Size

6 inches across

What You Do

1. Referring to **Diagram 1,** glue two of the licorice pieces into an upside-down "V" shape to create the top of the star, laying the right piece on top of the left piece. Glue a third piece to the lower right end of the "V," laying it underneath the right piece and on top of the left piece.

Diagram 1

2. Glue the fourth piece of candy to the top end of the third piece, weaving it under, then over the licorice pieces. Finish by gluing the fifth piece in place, weaving it under, then over the licorice pieces; see **Diagram 2.**

Diagram 2

Lollipop Star

Size

6 inches across

What You Do

1. Unwrap each of the lollipops and lay them on a clean, flat work surface.

2. Referring to the **Lollipop Diagram,** glue the stick end of one lollipop to the candy end of another so that the sticks make a "V" shape. Glue a third lollipop to the second in the same manner. Continue to glue the lollipops together so that the sticks create a star shape and the candies form the points.

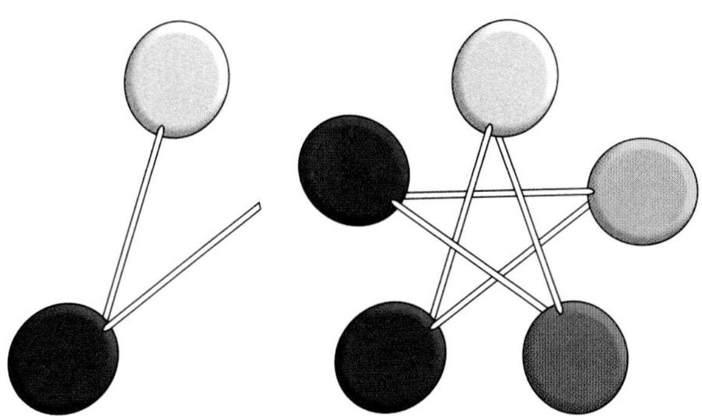

Lollipop Diagram

3. Fold the ribbon in half and loop it around one of the points for a hanger.

What You Need

Red Licorice Star

- Five 6-inch-long pieces of red licorice
- Hot glue gun and glue sticks

Lollipop Star

- Five 1½-inch-diameter flat lollipops in a variety of colors
- Hot glue gun and glue sticks
- ⅜ yard of ¼-inch-wide red satin ribbon for the hanger

Gumdrop Wreath

- About thirty-six ⅜-inch-long candy gumdrops in assorted colors
- ½ yard of 24-gauge aluminum wire
- ½ yard of 1-inch-wide green polka-dot ribbon for the bow

Gumdrop Wreath

Size

4 inches in diameter

What You Do

1. Thread the gumdrops one at a time onto the wire, alternating the colors in a random fashion. You should clean the wire frequently since it will collect the sugary residue of the candy.

2. Coil the wire into a two-coil circle about 4 inches in diameter. Twist the wire ends and clip away any excess wire.

3. Tie a ribbon bow to cover the wire ends.

WHAT YOU NEED

LOLLIPOP ORNAMENT

- Stencil Mylar
- 4-inch square of glass with masked or filed edges
- Masking tape
- Craft knife with extra blades
- Multicolored candy lollipop about 4 inches in diameter
- White artist's tape
- Green acrylic paint
- Saucer or palette
- ¼-inch-diameter stencil brush
- Paper towels
- Multicolored candy sprinkles
- Clear, waterproof polyurethane
- ½-inch-wide paintbrush
- ¼ yard of ¼-inch-wide grosgrain ribbon for the hanger
- Hot glue gun and glue sticks
- ½ yard of 1½-inch-wide grosgrain ribbon for the bow

Lollipop Ornament

SIZE

4 inches in diameter

WHAT YOU DO

1. Trace the **Full-Size Tree Pattern** onto the stencil Mylar. To cut the stencil, place the Mylar on the glass and tape it to secure, using masking tape. Holding the craft knife like a pencil, carefully cut out the tree on the tracing line. Cut toward you, turning the glass as you cut; change blades often. If your knife should slip, mend both sides of the cut with masking tape.

2. Position the stencil in the middle of the lollipop, taping it in place with artist's tape. Place 1 tablespoon of paint on the saucer or palette. Dip the tip of the stencil brush into the paint, then dab it on the paper towels until the brush is almost dry. Holding the brush perpendicular to the surface of the lollipop, brush over the cutout area with a circular motion, working over the stencil edges. While the paint is still wet, sprinkle the candy sprinkles on the tree, as shown in the **Sprinkles Diagram.** Wash the saucer and brush with soap and water before the paint dries.

Sprinkles Diagram

3. Using the paintbrush, coat the lollipop and stick with polyurethane, following the manufacturer's directions. Allow the lollipop to dry.

4. Fold the narrow ribbon in half and glue it to the back of the lollipop for the hanger.

5. Using the wide ribbon, tie a bow at the top of the stick. Cut the ribbon ends in a "V" shape.

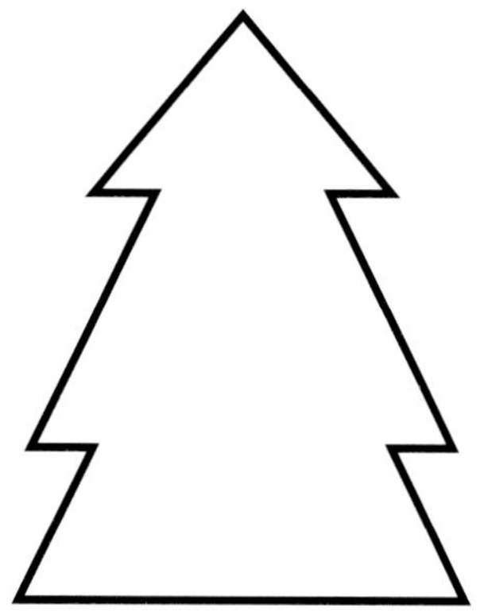

FULL-SIZE TREE PATTERN

Fabulous Felt Felines

These cute kitties are crafted from simple felt shapes and colorful cutouts and emblazoned with vibrant embroidery. Their quizzical expressions and unique patterning will capture the hearts of both cat collectors and kitty-loving kids. Use felt scraps and short lengths of embroidery floss to create the markings and mismatched buttons for the eyes to save money on supplies.

Fabulous Felt Felines

WHAT YOU NEED

- Two 9 × 12-inch pieces of black felt for each cat
- Scraps of turquoise, lime, blue, pink, and gold felt for the markings
- Pink, red, black, gold, and other assorted colors of embroidery floss
- Matching sewing thread
- Polyester fiberfill
- Two ⅜-inch-diameter green or yellow buttons for each cat's eyes
- Fabric glue

SIZE

10½ inches tall

WHAT YOU DO

Note: All seam allowances are ¼ inch.

1. Enlarge the **Fabulous Felt Felines Patterns** as directed in "Enlarging Patterns" on page 238.

2. From the black, cut two bodies, two heads, four legs, and one tail for each cat. For the striped cat, cut three large triangles from the turquoise and three small triangles from the lime. For the spotted cat, cut one 4½-inch-diameter half circle from the blue, one 3½-inch-diameter half circle from the pink, one 3-inch-diameter circle from the gold, one 2½-inch-diameter circle from the turquoise, one 2-inch-diameter circle from the lime, and one 1-inch-diameter circle from the blue.

3. Using six strands of pink or red embroidery floss, work satin and straight stitches for the nose and mouth on the head front where indicated on the pattern; see "Stitch Details" on page 243.

4. Using matching thread, topstitch the head pieces together, leaving an opening between the ears for stuffing. Do not turn the head to the other side. Very lightly stuff the head with fiberfill, being sure to insert a small amount into each ear. Topstitch the opening closed. Set the head aside.

5. Place the body pieces together, then insert the tail and legs between the body front and back, as shown in **Diagram 1.** Topstitch around the body, catching the tail and legs in the seam; leave an opening at the head end of the body. Do not turn the body to the other side. Lightly stuff the body with fiberfill, then topstitch the opening closed.

Diagram 1

6. Referring to **Diagram 2** for placement and using six strands of black floss, attach the head to the body by sewing on the button eyes.

Diagram 2

7. Referring to the **Placement Diagrams,** position the large triangles on the back of the striped cat and the 4½-inch-diameter blue half circle on the back, the 3-inch-diameter gold circle on the hindquarters, and the 2-inch-diameter lime circle on the face of the spotted cat. Glue them in place.

Placement Diagrams

8. Using six strands of a contrasting color floss, work blanket stitches around each triangle or circle; see "Stitch Details" on page 243. Position the small triangles on top of the larger ones, the pink half circle on the blue half circle, the turquoise circle on the gold circle, and the blue circle on the lime circle. Glue them in place. Work blanket stitches around the smaller pieces with contrasting floss.

9. Using six strands of gold embroidery floss, work three blanket stitches at the bottom of each leg to represent the cat's claws.

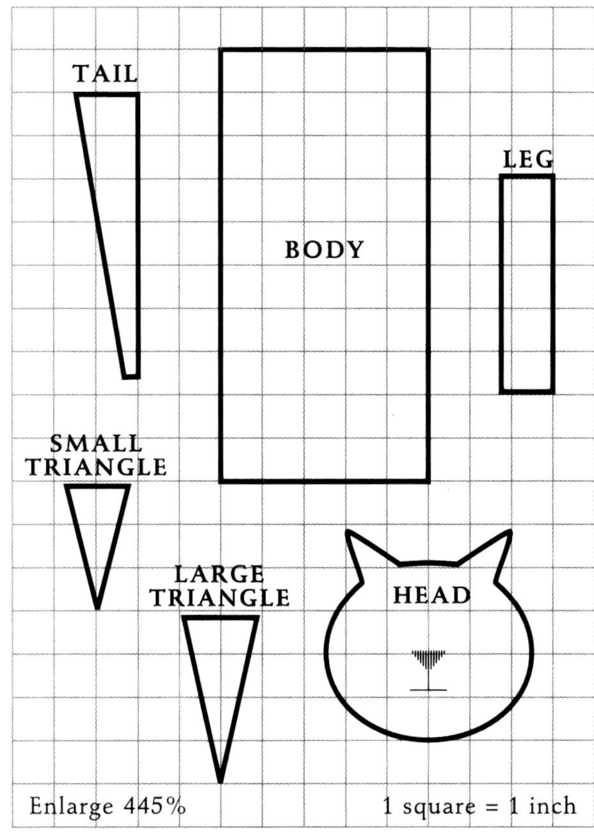

FABULOUS FELT FELINES PATTERNS

Project Pointers

Be sure to make the felt cats in a variety of colors since kids will want a cat that looks like their Fluffy! Use gray, tan, rust, white, and cream felt to create a whole litter of kitty look-alikes! Create cats that are spotted, striped, and plain. Use green, blue, brown, gray, and yellow buttons for the eyes. Add monofilament whiskers to some, but shy away from selling those species to younger children. For fun, add a curly chenille tail to a handful of felines or a stuffed felt fish hanging from the mouths of others. Use brightly colored pom-poms for the noses and chenille stems for the mouths. This is a quickie project where the possibilities are endless! Have fun and keep your fingers crossed for a purr-fectly successful bazaar!

Penny Rug Doily

This colorful accent for table or chest takes its inspiration from embroidered antique penny rugs seen in colonial America. The frugal needlewomen of the time used coins to create the circle patterns and reached into their scrap bag for pieces of colorful wool or felt. In this reproduction, the bright felt and floss are set against traditional black to attract both staunch country enthusiasts and savvy fans of contemporary decor.

Size

9 × 11½ inches

What You Do

1. Enlarge the **Penny Rug Doily Pattern** as directed in "Enlarging Patterns" on page 238.

2. From the black felt, cut one doily.

3. From the colored scraps of felt, cut twelve 1-inch-diameter circles and twelve 2-inch-diameter circles.

4. Referring to the **Placement Diagram,** position the large circles on the felt doily so they are centered within the scallops around the perimeter and in the center. Glue them in place.

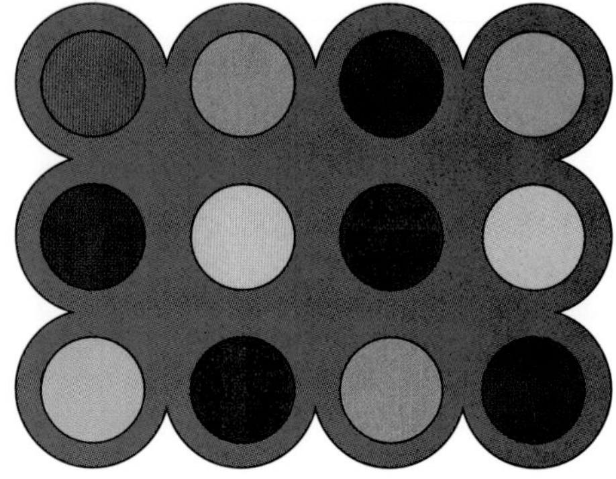

Placement Diagram

5. Using six strands of a contrasting color floss, work blanket stitches around each large circle; see "Stitch Details" on page 243.

6. Position the small circles on top of the large ones, rearranging them until you have a pleasing color combination; glue the small circles in place. Work blanket stitches around the small circles with contrasting floss.

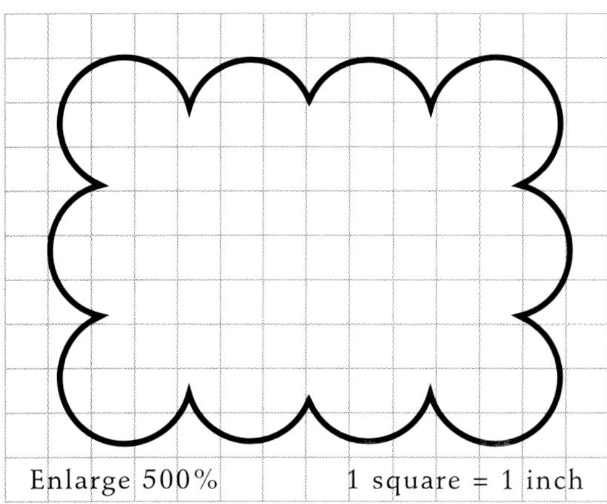

PENNY RUG DOILY PATTERN

What You Need

- 9 × 12-inch piece of black felt for the doily
- Scraps of felt in assorted bright colors for the accents
- Fabric glue
- 12 to 16 skeins of embroidery floss in assorted colors

Project Pointers

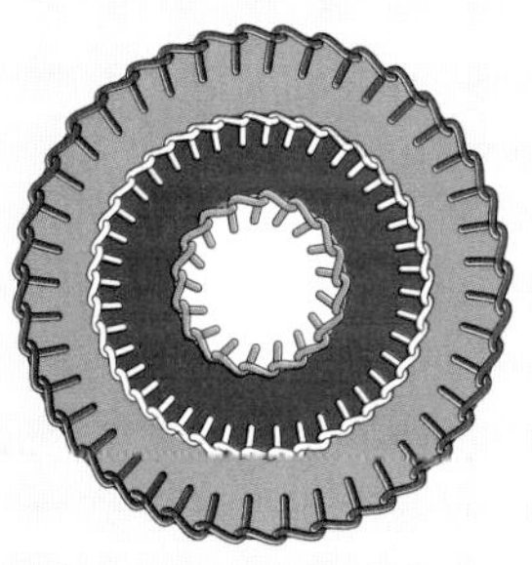

If traditional American folk crafts won't attract buyers to your booth, change the colors in this doily to seasonal green, red, and white. Cut the doily from Christmas green, the large circles from Santa Claus red, and the small ones from snowy white. Accent the circles with green, red, and white floss blanket stitches.

Holiday coasters always sell well at bazaars. Instead of a penny rug doily, cut a 3-inch-diameter circle for the coaster base, then add the 2- and 1-inch-diameter circles in the same manner as for the doily. Use a waterproof glue to glue the felt coaster to a cork circle for absorbency. Package the coasters in sets of four or eight and tie them with a coordinating color satin ribbon.

Freddy the Teddy

Who can resist this sad, little face and woolly, warm body? Freddy the forlorn teddy looks as though he's in need of lots of love. Children of all ages will scurry right up to your booth to cuddle with him and give him a happy home.

Size

About 22 inches tall

What You Do

Note: All seam allowances are ¼ inch unless otherwise indicated.

1. Enlarge the **Freddy the Teddy Patterns** on page 150 as directed in "Enlarging Patterns" on page 238.

2. From the mohair, cut two bodies, two heads, two ears, two legs and two legs reverse, and two arms and two arms reverse. From the scrap of tan felt, cut two inner ears. From the black felt, cut one vest.

3. With the right sides together, sew one inner ear to each ear, leaving the straight edge open. Grade the seam allowance and clip the curves. Turn the ears to the right side and press. Do not stuff.

4. Using the brown floss, sew the button eyes to the right side of one head where indicated on the pattern. Pinch the nose slightly, then make six straight stitches using the red tapestry wool; make three straight stitches for the mouth, referring to the pattern for placement.

5. With the felt side of the inner ear facing the right side of the head and matching the raw edges, baste the ears in place where indicated by the dots on the pattern; see the **Ear Diagram.**

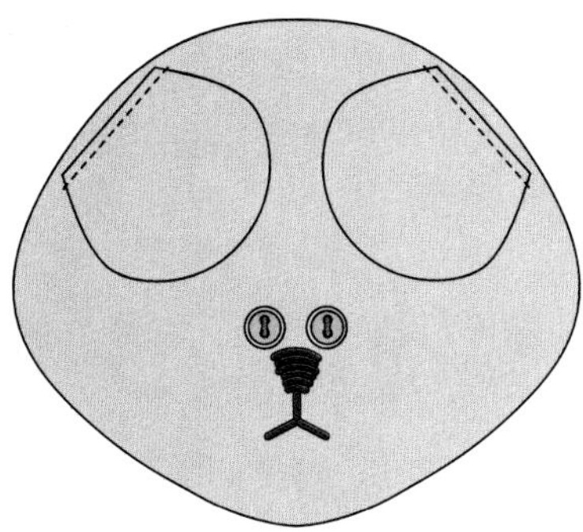

Ear Diagram

WHAT YOU NEED

- ½ yard of plush tan mohair fabric for the teddy
- Scrap of tan felt for the inner ears
- 9 × 12-inch piece of black felt for the vest
- Matching sewing thread
- Brown, turquoise, pink, green, and orange embroidery floss for sewing on the eyes and the vest accents
- Two ½-inch-diameter yellow buttons for the eyes
- One strand of red tapestry wool for the nose
- Size 22 tapestry needle
- Polyester fiberfill

MONEY-SAVING TIP

Instead of purchasing expensive mohair fabric for Freddy, use an inexpensive faux fur fabric. The pile will be a bit higher and you'll need to use a straight pin to lift the fur from the seams, but the savings will be worth the few extra minutes of your time. Or do you have a large collection of country plaid fabrics? If so, give Freddy an antique look by combining various plaids for his body pieces. Toss the fabrics into the washing machine when you're doing other laundry, then tumble dry to "age" the fabric for an authentic look.

If you're also a quilter, you may have large quantities of solid-color cottons. Solid fabrics cost less than prints, so sticking to the basics for Freddy's body will save money. Make his vest out of a finer print fabric since you'll need just ⅜ yard. Be sure to spend your money wisely—on the trims and embellishments—and fall back on the lower-priced basics when you need a large quantity.

6. With the right sides together, sew the head front and back together, leaving an opening. Grade the seam allowance and clip the curves. Turn to the right side and press. Stuff the head, then slip-stitch the opening closed. Set the head aside.

7. With the right sides together, sew the arm pieces together in pairs, leaving the straight edges open. Grade the seam allowances and clip the curves. Turn the arms to the right side and press lightly. Stuff the arms to desired fullness; do not slip-stitch the openings closed.

8. Repeat Step 7 for the legs.

9. With the right side of one body piece facing the arms and legs and matching the raw edges, position and baste the legs and arms in place where indicated by the dots on the pattern. With right sides together and the arms and legs pulled to the center of the body, place and sew the body pieces together, leaving an opening for turning. Turn the body right side out and stuff; slip-stitch the opening closed.

10. Hand tack the head to the body, placing the bear's chin at the dotted line indicated on the body pattern.

11. With the right sides together, sew the front sections of the vest to the back section at the shoulders. Turn the vest to the right side. Using the turquoise, pink, green, and orange floss, work blanket stitches around all edges of the vest; see "Stitch Details" on page 243. Place the vest on the bear.

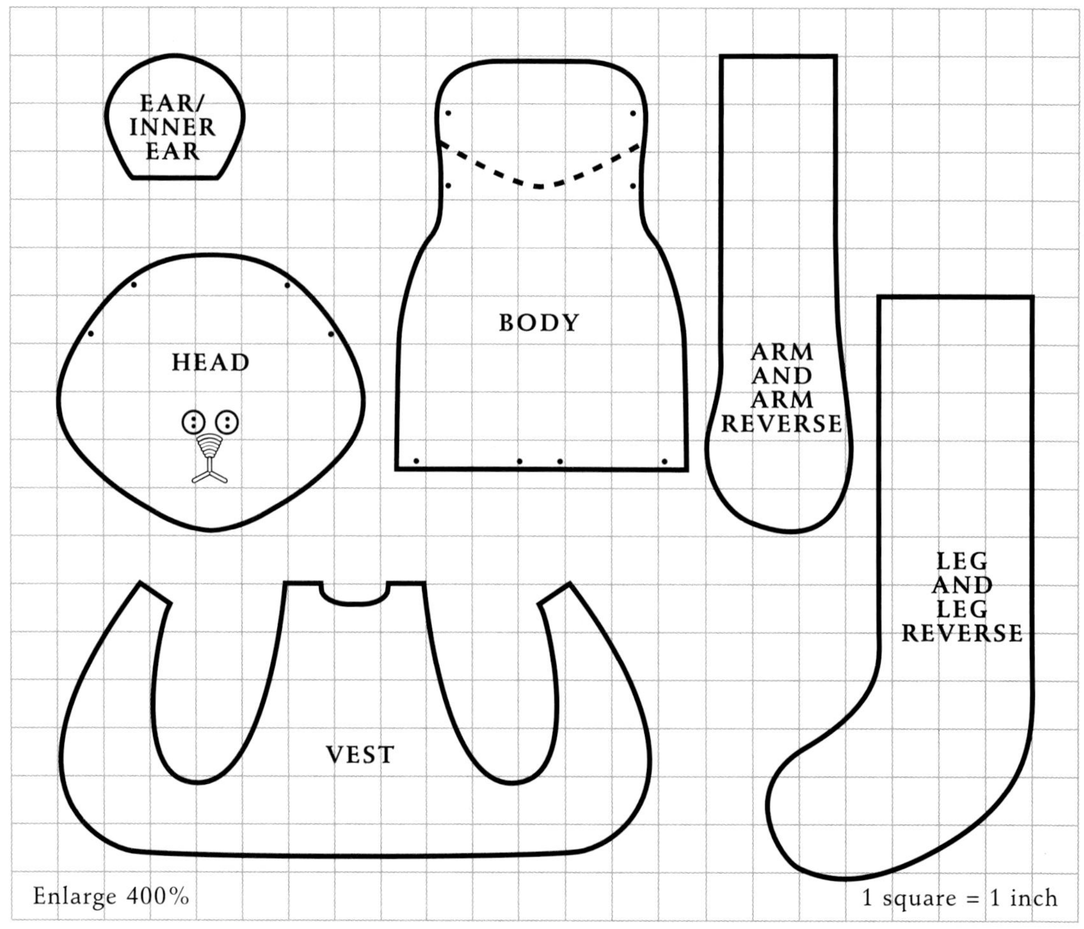

FREDDY THE TEDDY PATTERNS

Stoic Cat Pillows

These stylized kitties sit on different rug backgrounds that consist of quick-to-work needlepoint stitches and broad areas of color. While slightly more involved, this feline duo has a folk-art quality that's hard for sophisticated customers and art connoisseurs to ignore.

Size

About 18½ × 22½ inches, including the ruffle

What You Do

Note: Feel free to adapt each cat's marking or background rug as you desire. Each cat shape is the same, allowing for easy substitution of one rug background for the other. Work the rugs as charted or change the colors and rug patterns to suit your taste or your customer's taste.

1. Machine zigzag or overcast the edges of the canvas to prevent raveling.

2. Using the marker, draw a 16 × 20-inch rectangle in the center of the needlepoint canvas. Draw the design outlines on the **Gray Cat Pillow Chart** on pages 154 and 155 or **Black Cat Pillow Chart** on pages 156 and 157 to the canvas as charted.

3. Read "Needlepoint" on page 241 for general information on needlepoint and the basketweave stitch. Find the center of the marked rectangle and mark it with the marker. Find the center of the chart by connecting the arrows. Matching the centers of the rectangle and chart, work the cat in a basketweave stitch, using three plies of the yarn.

What You Need

- 22 × 26-inch piece of 10-count needlepoint canvas for each pillow
- Permanent black felt-tip marker
- 3-ply Persian yarns in the colors and yardages listed in the specific **Color Key***
- Tapestry needle
- One skein of white or light gray embroidery floss for the whiskers
- ½ yard of olive green solid or black floral fabric to coordinate with the rug colors for the piping
- Matching sewing thread
- 2⅛ yards of ¼-inch-diameter white upholstery cord for each pillow
- ⅞ yard of black fabric for the ruffle and backing for each pillow
- Polyester fiberfill

* *See the "Buyer's Guide" on page 244 for ordering information.*

4. For the gray cat's Navajo rug, work stitches horizontally over two canvas threads, using three plies of yarn. When the background is complete, work blanket stitches with gold to create the rug binding; see "Stitch Details" on page 243.

5. For the black cat's kilim rug, work the stitches vertically over three canvas threads, using three plies of yarn.

6. Following the individual chart and using a couching stitch, add light gray whiskers to the gray cat and white whiskers to the black cat with four strands of floss; see "Stitch Details" on page 243.

7. When stitching is completed, block the canvas if necessary for a rectangular shape, referring to "Blocking" on page 242.

8. From the piping fabric, cut one 1½ × 74-inch bias strip, piecing as necessary; see "Cutting Bias Strips" on page 238. With the wrong sides together, fold the bias strip in half lengthwise and insert the cord close to the fold. Using a zipper foot, machine baste the cord inside the bias strip, stitching as close as possible to the cord; see **Diagram 1.**

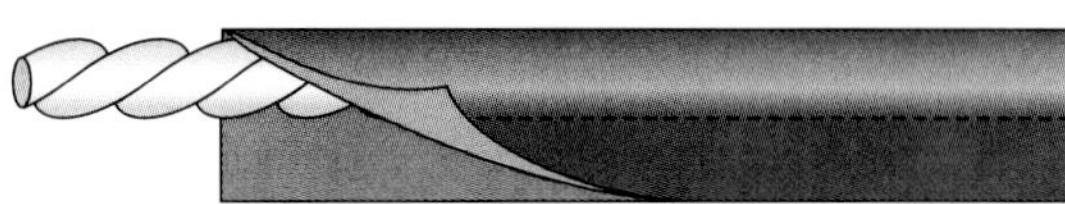

Diagram 1

9. Trim the canvas to within ½ inch of the stitching. Beginning in the middle of the bottom edge, pin the corded piping to the right side of the pillow top, aligning the raw edges; do not sew yet. At the corners, clip the seam allowance of the piping perpendicular to the seam to ease it around the curves. Leaving about 2 inches free at the beginning and end, sew the piping to the pillow top along the basting line. To join the piping ends, pull back the fabric from one end of the piping. Trim the extra length off the cord so the raw ends butt; see **Diagram 2.** Turn ½ inch to the wrong side on one strip end and pull the fabric back over to cover the cord and the other bias strip end, as shown. Finish sewing the seam.

Diagram 2

10. From the green or black fabric, cut one 16 × 20-inch rectangle for the backing and four 3½ × 42-inch strips for the ruffle for each pillow. With the right sides together and the raw edges even, sew the short ends of the four strips together to form one continuous loop. With the wrong sides together, fold the loop in half lengthwise and press. Sew a line of gathering stitches ⅜ inch from the raw edges. Fold the ruffle in half to find the midpoints and place pins at these points.

Match the midpoints of the ruffle and mark the quarterpoints with pins. Gather the ruffle to fit the perimeter of the pillow. With the right sides together, pin the ruffle evenly around the pillow, using the pins as quarterpoint guides. Sew the ruffle to the pillow top, using a ½-inch seam allowance; see **Diagram 3.**

11. With right sides together, place the pillow top and back together. Sew around the outer edge, using a ½-inch seam allowance. Leave an opening at the bottom for turning. Grade the seam allowance.

12. Turn the pillow to the right side and stuff firmly with fiberfill. Slip-stitch the opening closed.

Diagram 3

MONEY-SAVING TIP

Even if you're able to use up scrap skeins of tapestry wool for the rug backgrounds, the cost of the materials may be prohibitive. However, if your bazaar buyers appreciate higher-end handwork, you can make the cats into doorstops, saving you the cost of additional wool, canvas, piping, and ruffle fabric.

Following the chart and color key, needlepoint just the cat. Extend the tail on the left side to create a flat base. Cut out the cat one canvas row beyond the stitching. From the backing fabric, cut a same-size piece for the back of the doorstop. To figure the size of the oval base, measure the lower edge of the cat, multiply the measurement by two, then minus two from that figure; this will be the perimeter measurement of the oval base. For example, if your cat measures 9 inches along the lower edge, the equation should be 9 × 2 = 18 – 2 = 16. Your oval's perimeter should measure 16 inches; see the ***Oval Diagram.*** *From the backing fabric, cut one oval for the base.*

With the right sides together and using a ½-inch seam allowance, sew the cat front and back together, leaving the bottom edge open. Clip the curves and grade the seam allowance to reduce bulk. With the right sides together, pin the base to the bottom edge of the cat. Sew the seam, leaving a 3-inch opening. Turn the cat right side out and press the fabric if necessary. Firmly stuff the top three-quarters of the cat with fiberfill. Fill a 1-quart plastic bag about one-third full of sand, then twist-tie it closed. Insert the sand bag into the bottom of the cat, then slip-stitch the opening closed.

16"

Oval Diagram

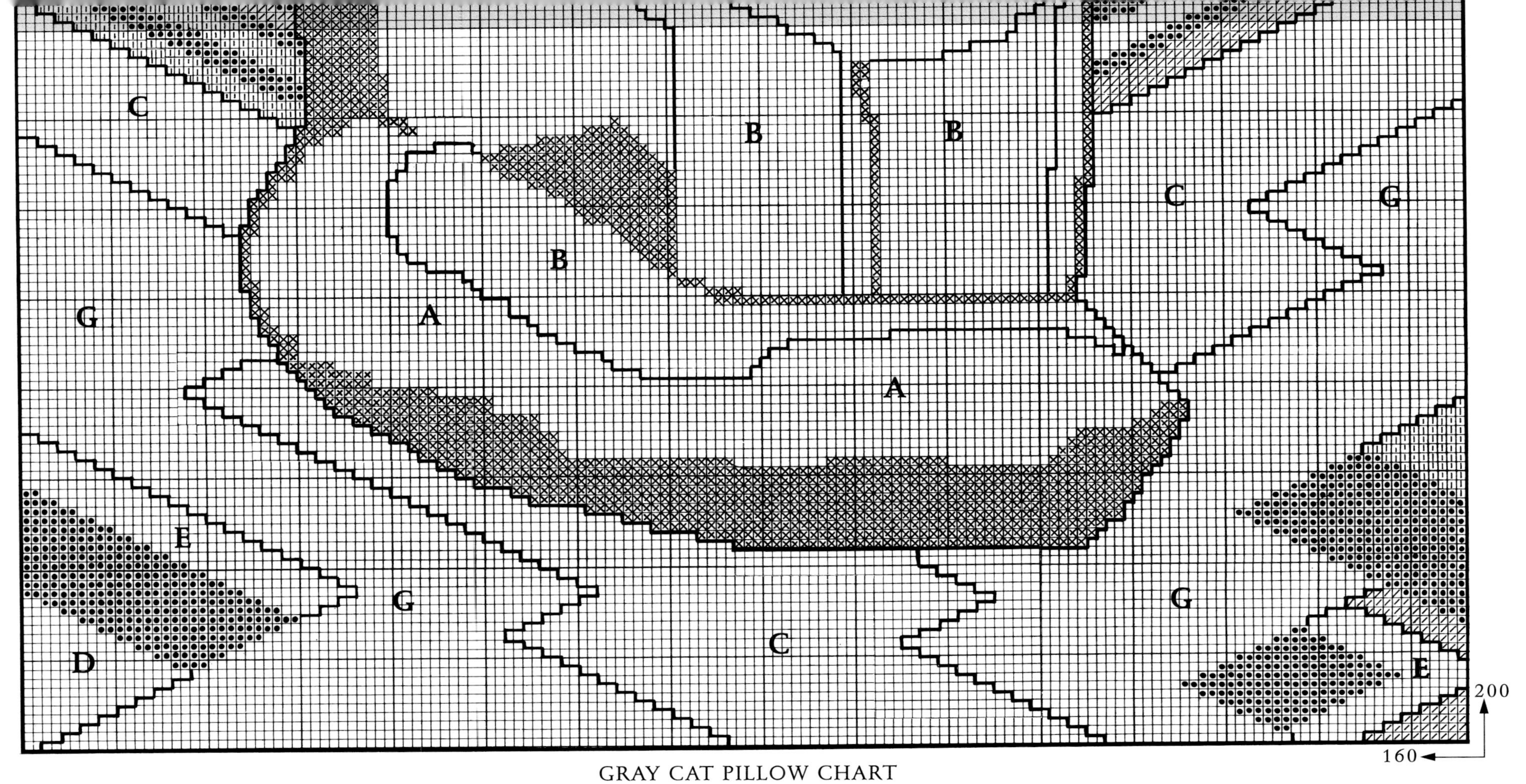

GRAY CAT PILLOW CHART

COLOR KEY

		DMC Floralia			
C ◪	Black	Black (22 yards)	F	7355	Dk. Olive (72 yards)
G ◪	Ecru	Ecru (20 yards)	•	7566	Med. Coral (25 yards)
=	7069	Moss Green (1 yard)		7578	Gold (2 yards)
E	7106	Lt. Coral (25 yards)	B ‖	7647	Lt. Gray (30 yards)
D /	7107	Dk. Coral (25 yards)	–	7713	Steel Gray (2 yards)
I	7113	Chartreuse (1 yard)	×	7843	Dk. Gray (33 yards)
·	7164	Flesh (2 yards)	A	7844	Med. Gray (102 yards)

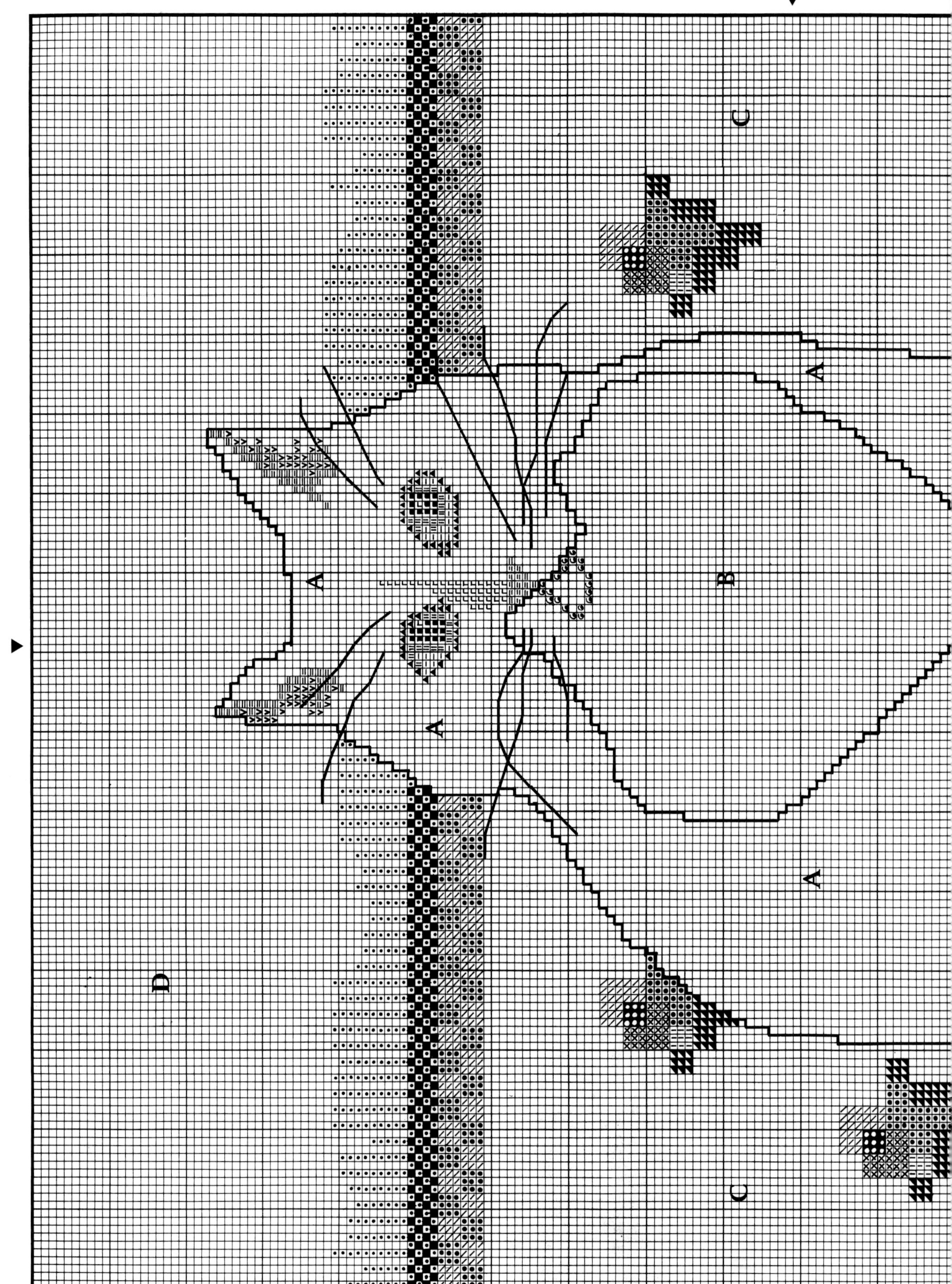

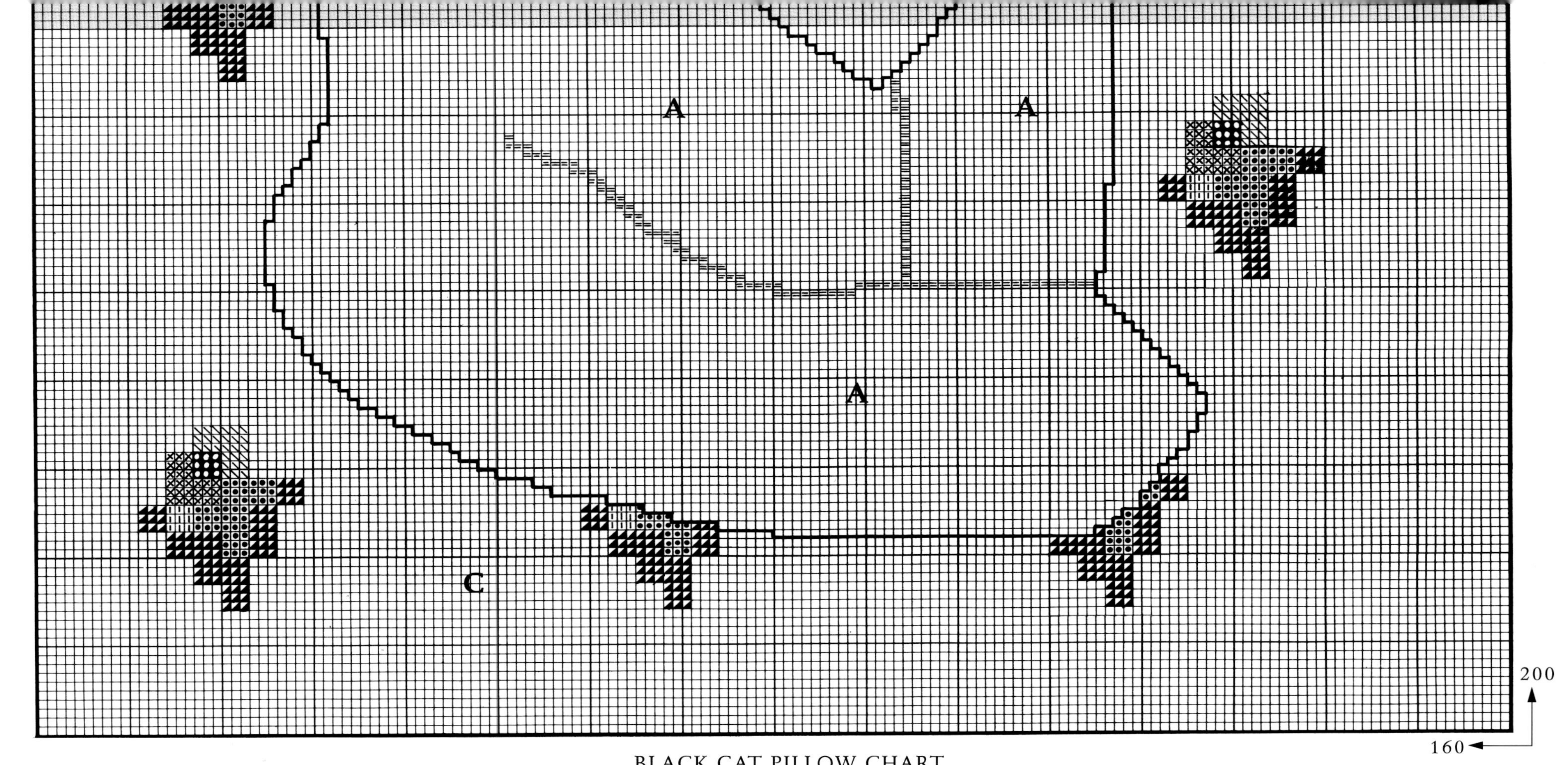

BLACK CAT PILLOW CHART

COLOR KEY

DMC Floralia

Symbol	DMC	Color	Symbol	DMC	Color
B ◪	White	White (45 yards)	■	7501	Dirty Gold (5 yards)
◪ A	Black	Black (98 yards)	◢	7540	Dk. Green (7 yards)
॥	7042	Yellow (1 yard)	I C	7542	Green (90 yards)
\	7107	Red (6 yards)	▲	7713	Steel Gray (2 yards)
×	7205	Rose (2 yards)	–	7744	Bright Yellow (1 yard)
□	7210	Maroon (1 yard)	=	7843	Dk. Gray (5 yards)
D	7355	Brown (72 yards)	V	7844	Med. Gray (3 yards)
6	7381	Pale Gray (3 yards)	•	7894	Pink (7 yards)
•	7388	Tan (5 yards)			

Felt Baby Bunny

These huggable baby rabbits are easy to craft from scraps of felt. Whether you sew by hand or machine, these bunnies require just two seams! In no time, you can stitch up a whole warren in a variety of colors—and they'll hop right out of your booth into the adoring arms of shoppers.

Size

About 3½ inches tall

What You Do

Note: All seam allowances are ¼ inch.

1. Enlarge the **Baby Bunny Patterns** as directed in "Enlarging Patterns" on page 238.

2. From the felt, cut two bodies, two ears, and one belly.

3. Place the body pieces together and sew from the small dot at the tip of the nose over the bunny back to the large dot at the tail area, as shown in **Diagram 1.** Clip the curve. Do not turn the bunny to the right side.

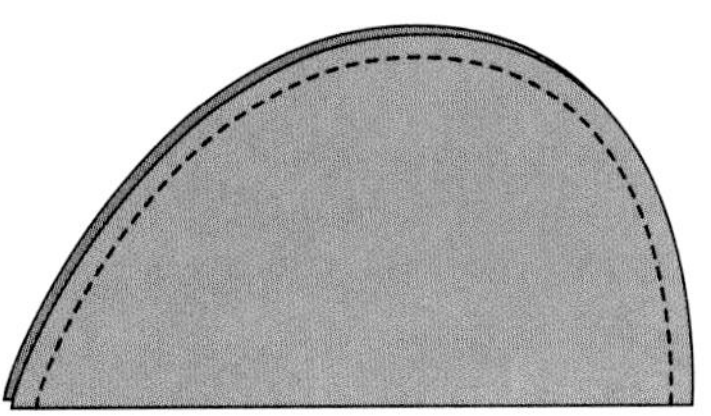

Diagram 1

4. Matching the raw edges, pin and sew the belly piece to the lower edge of the body, easing in any fullness and leaving an opening for turning; see **Diagram 2.** Clip the curves.

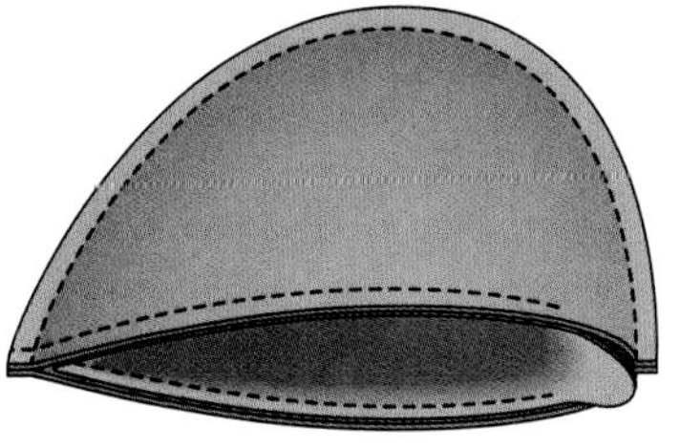

Diagram 2

5. Turn the bunny to the right side and stuff. Slip-stitch the opening closed.

6. Slip-stitch the ears to the body where indicated on the pattern.

7. Using 12 strands of floss and the soft-sculpture doll needle, sew the button eyes securely in place.

What You Need

- 9 × 12-inch piece of felt in desired color for the bunny
- Matching sewing thread
- Polyester fiberfill
- Two ½-inch-diameter buttons for the eyes
- Yellow embroidery floss
- Soft-sculpture doll needle

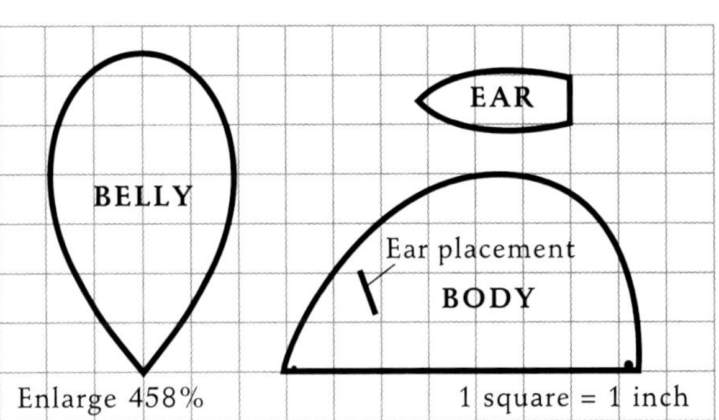

BABY BUNNY PATTERNS

Project Pointers

Projects like the baby bunnies are perfect imagination crafts. You can get creative with embellishments and use up the supplies you have on hand as well. Use floral chintzes for the bunny and cotton solids for the ears. Add a flippy tassel for a whimsical tail and flower buttons for the eyes. Blush the cheeks with pink colored pencil for a more feminine appearance. Or make a plaid gentlemanly bunny with a sisal tail, burlap ears, carpet thread whiskers—with dark-colored antique buttons for the eyes.

Holiday Hand Towels

Quick tricks with fabric scraps, snippets of ribbon, and cross-stitch can dress up plain-Jane hand towels for inexpensive hostess gifts for shoppers to buy. The Ribbon-Trimmed Towel, Red Bird Towel, and Cross-Stitch Greeting Towel make great accents in the kitchen for the holidays.

Ribbon-Trimmed Towel

Size

Ribbon is 1½ inches wide

What You Do

1. Cut the ribbon in half, making sure each piece is 1 inch wider than the width of the towel.

2. Center and pin each ribbon length about 2 inches from the towel's ends; turn under the raw ends of the ribbon ½ inch.

3. Using matching thread, sew along all edges of the ribbon to secure it in place, as shown in the **Ribbon Diagram.**

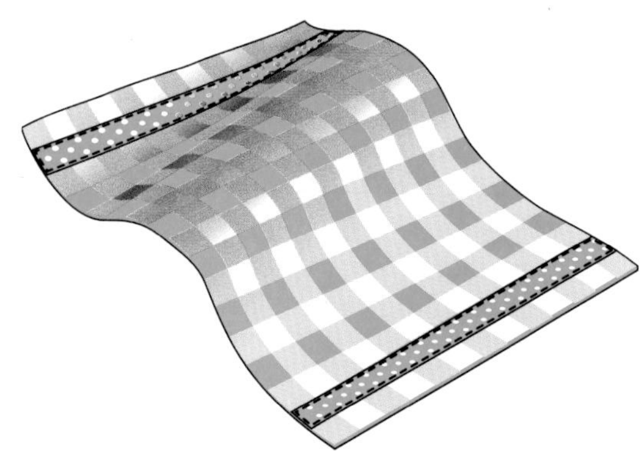

Ribbon Diagram

Red Bird Towel

Size

Motif is 4¼ inches across

What You Do

1. Fuse the fusible web to the pindot fabric, following the manufacturer's directions.

2. Enlarge the **Red Bird Pattern** as directed in "Enlarging Patterns" on page 238.

3. Trace six birds onto the paper side of the fabric. Cut out the birds and remove the paper backing. Position three birds, equally spaced, at each towel end. Fuse each bird in place.

4. Using the tapestry needle and following the **Embroidery Diagram,** make a yellow French knot for the eye. Use the green yarn to work the branch in stem stitch and the leaves in lazy daisy stitches, referring to "Stitch Details" on page 243.

Embroidery Diagram

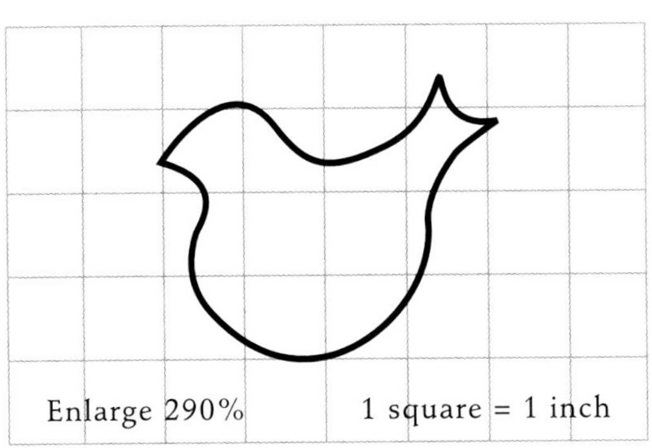

RED BIRD PATTERN

What You Need

Ribbon-Trimmed Towel

- 1½-inch-wide green polka-dot grosgrain ribbon, at least twice the width of the towel plus 2 inches
- Green check hand towel
- Matching sewing thread

Red Bird Towel

- ⅛ yard of fusible web
- ⅛ yard of red pindot fabric
- Red plaid hand towel
- 2 yards each of yellow and green tapestry wool
- Sharp-point tapestry needle

Cross-Stitch Greeting Towel

- Tan linen hand towel with a 14-count Aida band
- One skein of embroidery floss for the color in the **Color Key**
- Size 22 or 24 tapestry needle

Cross-Stitch Greeting Towel

Size

Motif is ⅞ × 10 inches

What You Do

1. Find the center of the Aida band and mark it with a pin. Find the center of the **Cross-Stitch Greeting Towel Chart** on page 162 by connecting the arrows.

2. Matching the centers of the Aida band and the chart, and using two strands of floss, work the design in cross-stitch. Repeat for the other Aida band, if desired.

3. Wash and press the completed towel as directed in "Washing and Pressing" on page 241.

MONEY-SAVING TIP

Buy hand towels for crafting in bulk to get a lower price. Many factories will sell you odd colors and off sizes direct from the manufacturing plant. Other manufacturers have outlet stores for their overruns and seconds.

Adapt your designs to these hand towels by changing the placement of the appliqué or ribbon. You can get great deals on second-quality towels at department or "dollar" stores; if the towels have noticeable flaws, you may be able to disguise them with trims or accents. If the flaws are minor, you're one step ahead of the game since you may not have to change your design at all.

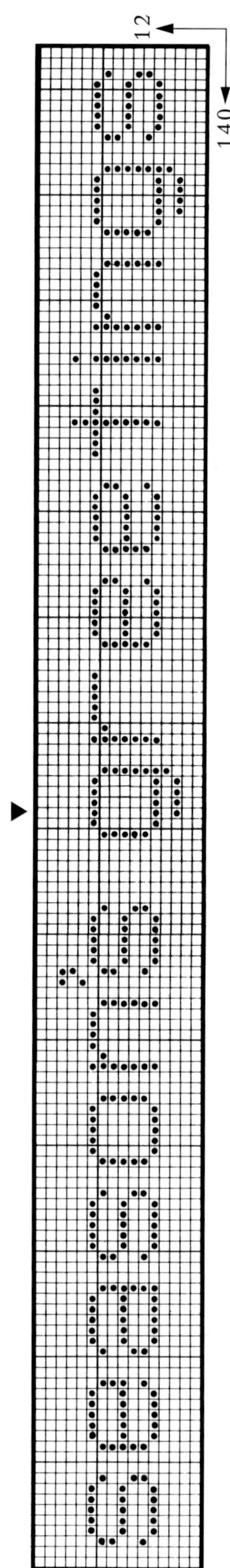

CROSS-STITCH GREETING TOWEL CHART

COLOR KEY

	DMC	Anchor	J. & P. Coats	Color
●	561	212	6211	Very Dk. Jade

So-Soft Baby Toys

The Bright Baby Block and Patchwork Beanbags are great bazaar toys for newborns and toddlers. Their eye-catching hues and fuzzy felt textures will stimulate the senses and provide plenty of happy playtime.

Bright Baby Block

Size

4½ inches high

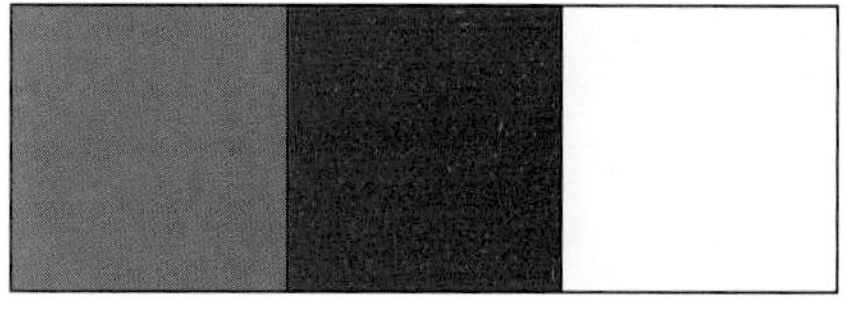

Diagram 1

What You Do

1. Using ¼-inch seam allowances, sew three squares together in a row; see **Diagram 1.** When sewing, be sure to use a small stitch length so a child cannot pull fiberfill through the seams, since it may be a choking hazard.

2. Sew two squares to the top of the center square of the row and one square to the bottom of the center square to create a cross formation that is three squares wide and four squares long, as shown in **Diagram 2** on page 164.

What You Need

Bright Baby Block

- Six 5-inch squares of colored felt
- Matching sewing thread
- Polyester fiberfill

Patchwork Beanbags

- Large scraps of felt in four contrasting colors for each beanbag top
- Matching sewing thread
- Pinking shears
- 8-inch square of coordinating felt for each beanbag back
- Plastic pellets for stuffing

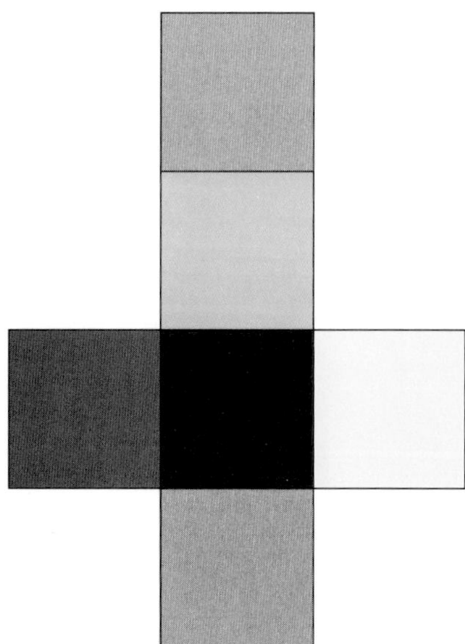

Diagram 2

3. With the wrong sides facing out, fold up, then sew the seams of the squares on each side of the center square to create an open-lid block; see **Diagram 3.**

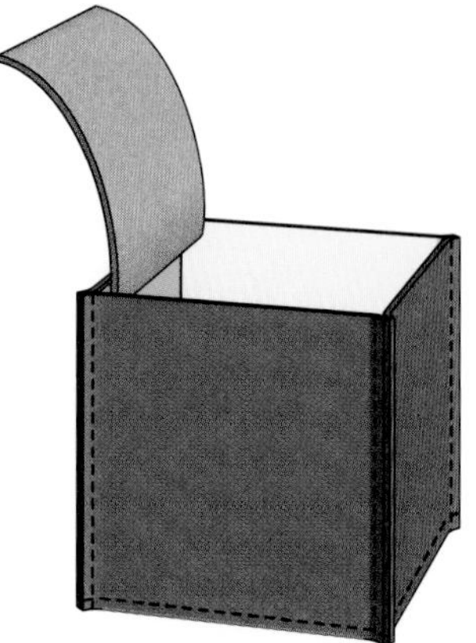

Diagram 3

4. Fold the lid over the block opening, then sew it to the adjoining squares, leaving one side open for turning; see **Diagram 4.**

Diagram 4

5. Turn the block to the right side. Stuff it lightly with polyester fiberfill, then securely slip-stitch the opening closed.

Patchwork Beanbags

Size

8 inches square

What You Do

Note: All seam allowances are 1/4 inch unless otherwise directed. When sewing, be sure to use a small stitch length so pellets cannot slip through the seams, since they may be choking hazards.

1. For each striped beanbag, cut four $1\frac{1}{4}$- to $2\frac{1}{2}$-inch-wide × 7-inch-long strips of felt; the strip widths must total $7\frac{3}{4}$ inches, including the seam allowances. For the patchwork beanbag, cut four $3\frac{3}{4}$-inch squares.

2. For each striped beanbag, sew the strips together along the long edges, varying the placement of the wide and narrow strips; see the **Striped Beanbag Diagrams.** Using pinking shears, cut around the perimeter of the beanbag top to create a decorative edge.

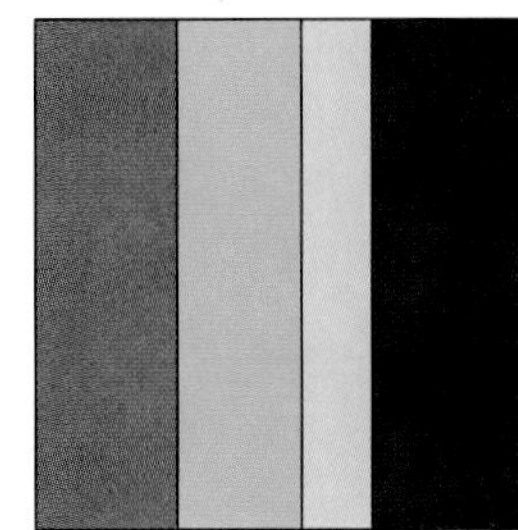

Striped Beanbag Diagrams

3. For the patchwork beanbag, sew the squares together in two rows of two squares each, then sew the rows together; see the **Patchwork Beanbag Diagram.** Using pinking shears, cut around the perimeter of the beanbag top.

Patchwork Beanbag Diagram

4. Using pinking shears, cut around the perimeter of each beanbag back to create a decorative edge. Center the striped or patchwork beanbag top right side up on the beanbag back. Topstitch around the perimeter of the beanbag about 1 inch from the outer edge; leave an opening for filling; see the **Topstitching Diagrams.** Do not turn.

Topstitching Diagrams

5. Fill each beanbag with plastic pellets, then topstitch the opening closed.

TIME-SAVING TIP

Save a whole bundle of time by cutting layers of felt squares and rectangles with a rotary cutter. If you've never used a rotary cutter before, visit your local craft shop for a demonstration. The rotary cutter blade is a round razor that can cut through many layers of fabric at once. It is useful when cutting straight-edged shapes since your cuts will be perfectly straight.

Farmyard Friends Puppets

This playful pair is fresh from farm country. The Barnyard Bull Puppet and the saucy Old Gray Mare Puppet will greet excited youngsters at your holiday display. The gray wool horse will gallop into their little hearts, and the staunch black and white cow is definitely not a bully!

Barnyard Bull Puppet

Size
13 inches tall

What You Need

Barnyard Bull Puppet

- 3/8 yard of white fabric for the body and head
- 1/8 yard of black fabric for the ears, horn center, and spots
- Scrap of tan fabric for the horns
- Scrap of black felt for the hooves
- 1/8 yard of fusible web
- Matching sewing thread
- Polyester fiberfill
- Cardboard toilet tissue tube
- Hot glue gun and glue sticks
- 1-inch-high copper cow bell
- 7-inch length of 1/4-inch-wide red satin ribbon for the bell
- One skein of yellow embroidery floss
- Soft-sculpture doll needle
- Two 3/8-inch-diameter green buttons for the eyes
- 1/2-inch-diameter silver hoop earring for the nose ring

What You Do

Note: All seam allowances are 1/4 inch unless otherwise directed.

1. Enlarge the **Barnyard Bull Puppet Patterns** on page 168 as directed in "Enlarging Patterns" on page 238.

2. From the white fabric, cut two bodies and two heads. From the black fabric, cut four ears and two horn centers. From the tan fabric, cut four horns. From the black felt, cut two hooves.

3. Fuse the fusible web to the remaining black fabric, following the manufacturer's directions. Using the "spot" lines on the body and head patterns, cut two spots for each pattern from the black fabric. Fuse the spots onto the two body and two head pieces. Set the head pieces aside.

4. With the points facing in and raw edges aligned, sew one hoof to each "arm." See **Diagram 1.**

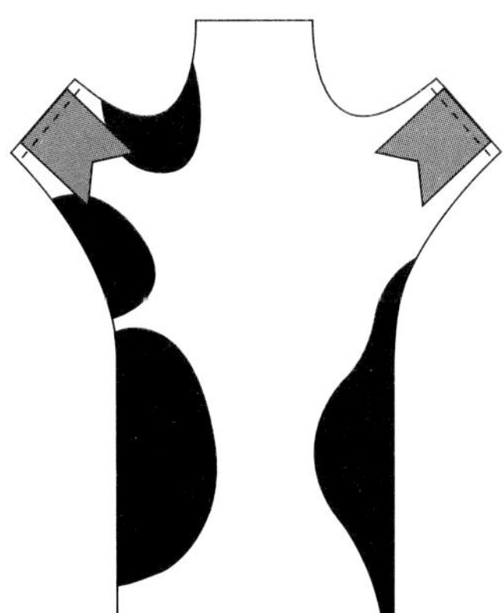

Diagram 1

5. With the right sides together, sew the bodies together, taking care not to catch the hooves in the seams; leave the neck and bottom edges open for turning. See **Diagram 2.** Clip the curves and turn to the right side. Turn under 1/2 inch around the lower edge of the bull's body and slip-stitch the hem in place. Set the body aside.

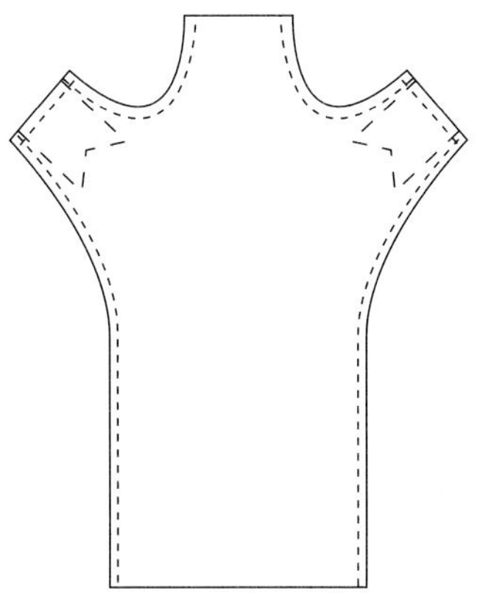

Diagram 2

6. With the right sides together, sew the heads together, leaving the neck edge open. Clip the curves, trim the seam allowance, and turn to the right side. Stuff the head firmly with fiberfill, then insert the cardboard tube about halfway into the neck opening. Hot-glue the tube in place.

7. Insert the other half of the cardboard tube into the neck opening of the body. Turn under ⅛ inch on each raw neck edge, then overlap and securely slip-stitch them to each other.

8. With the right sides together, sew the ears together in pairs, leaving the straight edge open. Clip the curves, trim the seam allowances, and turn each ear to the right side. Turn under ⅛ inch along the raw edges and press. Slip-stitch the ears to the head where indicated on the pattern.

9. With the right sides together, sew the horn centers together, leaving both ends open. Clip the curves, trim the seam allowances, and turn to the right side. Lightly stuff the horn center, but do not slip-stitch it closed. With right sides together, sew the horns together in pairs, leaving the straight edge open. Clip the curves, trim the seam allowances, and turn each horn to the right side. Turn under ⅛ inch along the raw edges and press. Stuff each horn, then slip each one over one end of the horn center and slip-stitch it in place, referring to **Diagram 3.** Slip-stitch the horn center in place on top of the bull's head.

Diagram 3

10. Thread the bell onto the ribbon, placing it in the center of the ribbon; tie a half-knot to keep it from slipping. Wrap the ribbon around the bull's neck so the ends meet at the back. Turn under the ends and slip-stitch them together.

11. Knot an 18-inch length of six-strand yellow floss and thread it through the doll needle. Insert the needle into the head at the eye dot, then pass through the head and out through the other eye dot. Run the needle up through a hole of one button and down through the opposite hole, then back through the head and out the first eye dot. Thread the other button on the floss and pass the needle back through the head and the other button. Pass back through the head and the button, pulling the floss tightly to indent the eye area. Knot tightly.

12. Insert the earring into the nose area on the bull's face for the nose ring.

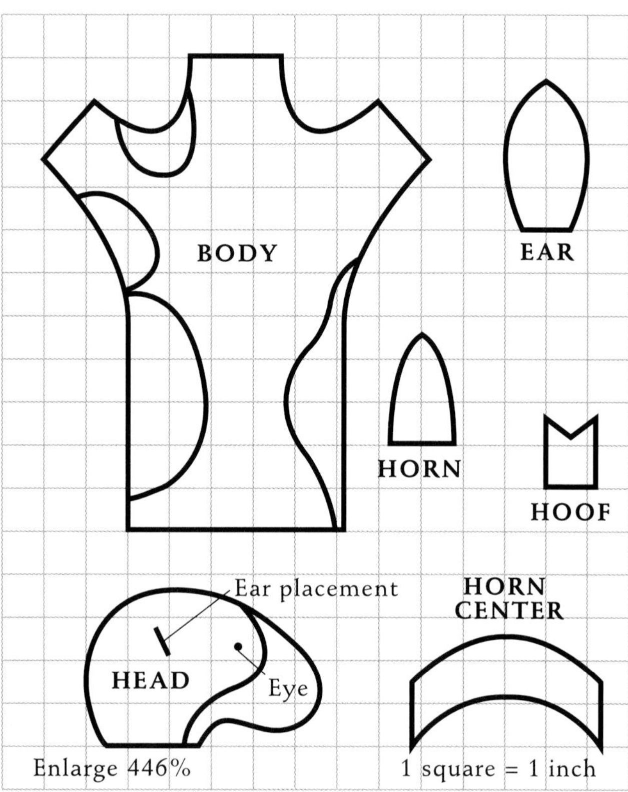

BARNYARD BULL PUPPET PATTERNS

Old Gray Mare Puppet

Size

13 inches tall

What You Need

Old Gray Mare Puppet

- 3/8 yard of loosely woven gray wool fabric for the puppet
- Scrap of black felt for the hooves
- Matching sewing thread
- Polyester fiberfill
- Cardboard toilet tissue tube
- Hot glue gun and glue sticks
- One skein of black embroidery floss
- Soft-sculpture doll needle
- Two 1/2-inch-diameter black buttons for the eyes
- 50-yard skein of gray tweed yarn for the mane
- 1 1/8 yards of twine for the bridle

What You Do

Note: All seam allowances are 1/4 inch unless otherwise directed.

1. Enlarge the **Old Gray Mare Puppet Patterns** on page 171 as directed in "Enlarging Patterns" on page 238.

2. From the gray, cut two bodies, two heads, four ears, and one 1 × 9-inch strip for the mane base, cutting them on the fabric's straight grain. From the black, cut two 1 1/4-inch squares for the hooves.

3. If using loosely woven fabric, machine zigzag all edges of each piece to prevent raveling.

4. With the raw edges aligned and the right side of the fabric facing the hoof, sew one hoof to each "arm," as shown in **Diagram 1.**

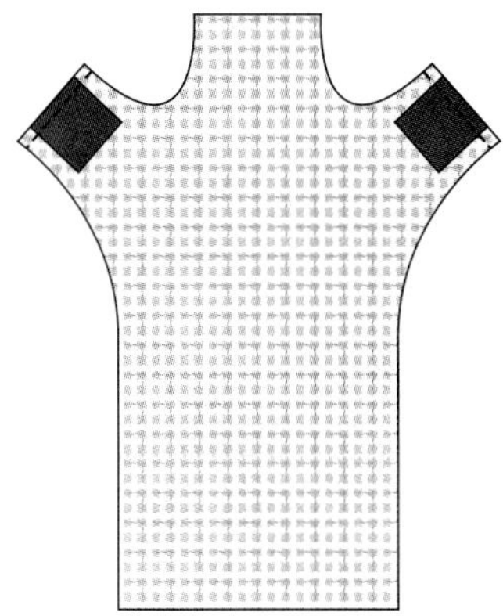

Diagram 1

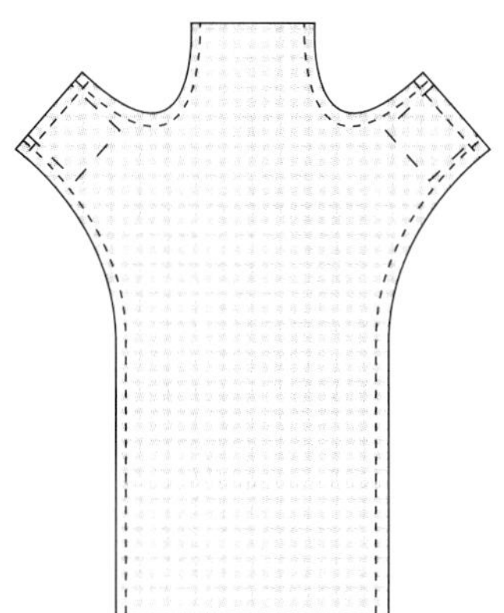

Diagram 2

5. With the right sides together, sew the bodies together, taking care not to catch the hooves in the seams; leave the neck and bottom edges open for turning, referring to **Diagram 2.** Clip the curves and trim the seam allowances to reduce bulk. Turn the body to the right side. Turn under 1/2 inch around the lower edge and slipstitch the hem in place. Set the body aside.

6. With the right sides together, sew the heads together, leaving the neck edge open. Clip the curves, trim the seam allowance, and turn to the right side. Stuff the head firmly with fiberfill, then insert the cardboard tube about halfway into the neck opening. Hot-glue the tube in place.

7. Insert the other half of the cardboard tube into the neck opening of the body. Turn under 1/8 inch on each raw neck edge, then overlap and securely slip-stitch them to each other.

8. With the right sides together, sew the ears together in pairs, leaving the straight edge open. Clip the curves and turn to the right side. Turn under 1/8 inch along the raw edges and press. Slip-stitch the ears to the head where indicated on the pattern.

9. Knot an 18-inch length of six-strand black floss and thread it through the doll needle. Insert the needle into the head at the eye dot, through the head, and out through the other eye dot. Run the needle up through a hole of one button and down through the opposite hole, then back through the head and out the first eye dot. Thread the other button on the floss and pass the needle back through the head and the other button. Pass back through the head and the button, pulling the floss tightly to indent the eye area. Knot tightly.

10. For the nostrils, make two straight stitches where indicated on the pattern to indent the nose area, using the black embroidery floss.

11. For the mane, cut about 300 strands of yarn, each 6 inches long. Lay the 9-inch mane strip on a flat surface with the right side up. Leaving about 1/4 inch free at the top and bottom, lay the strands of yarn crosswise along the length of the mane strip, then machine sew up the center of the yarn to secure the strands in place; see **Diagram 3.**

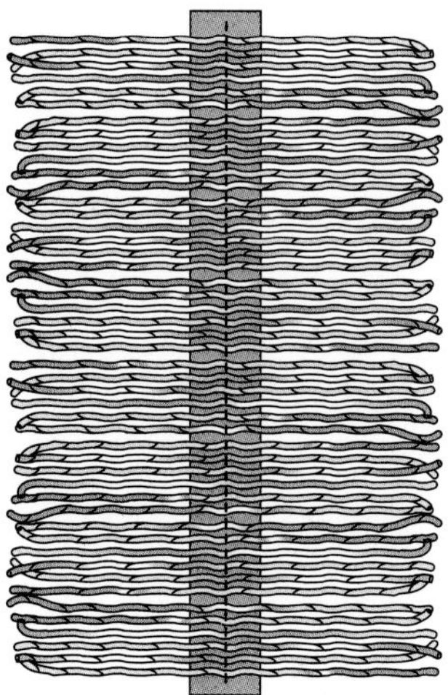

Diagram 3

12. Pull the yarn strands to one side and machine sew the full length of the mane about 1/8 inch from the mane strip; see **Diagram 4.** Fold under 1/8 inch along the raw edges of the mane strip and press. Slip-stitch the strip to the mare's head, starting at the top of the head between the ears and continuing down the neck. Trim the yarn at the top of the mane to about 2 inches, then trim the remainder of the mane in increasingly longer lengths.

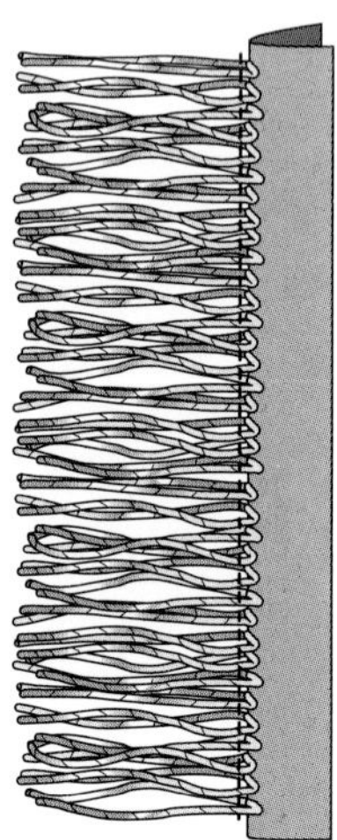

Diagram 4

13. For the bridle, cut one 8-inch, one 10-inch, and one 20-inch length of twine. Referring to **Diagram 5,** wrap the 8-inch length around the nose and knot it; trim any excess. Wrap the 10-inch length around the head, knotting it just behind the ears; trim any excess. Slip the 20-inch length under the tied 10-inch length, then tie each end of the 20-inch length to the nose bridle to form the mare's reins.

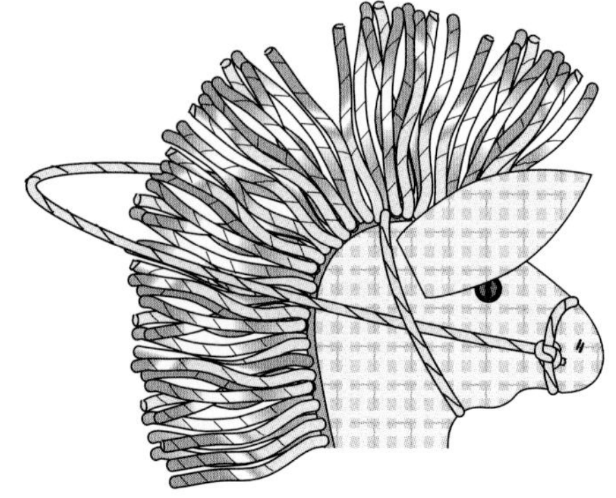

Diagram 5

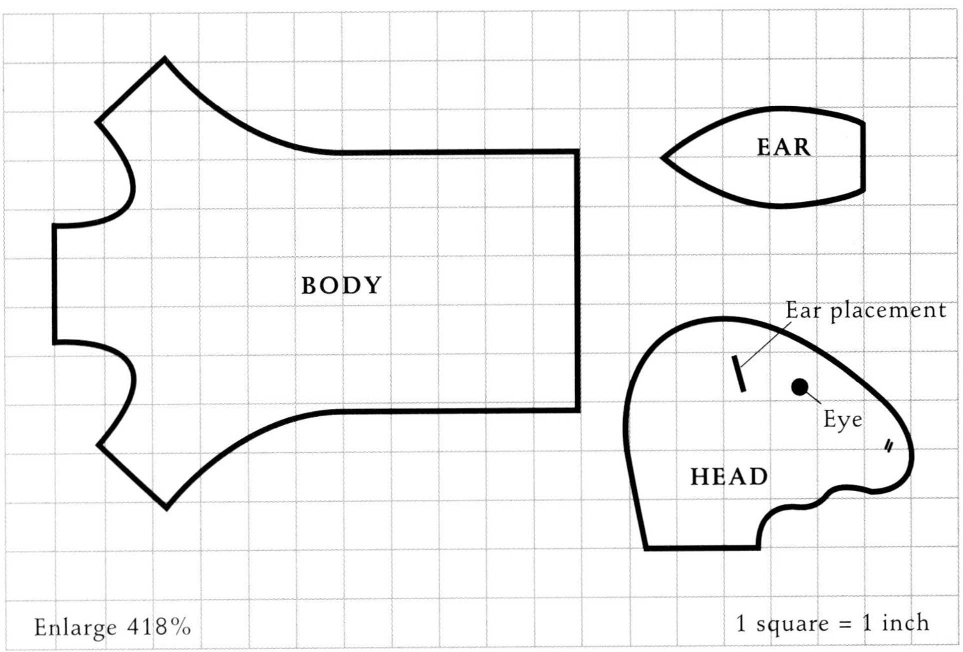

OLD GRAY MARE PUPPET PATTERNS

TIME-SAVING TIP

There's a simple way to save a half hour if you're making the bull puppet. Buy cow-spotted fabric if you can find it so you can skip the fusing of the black spots to the bull's body and head. Or you can paint the spots on the fabric with black acrylic paint. Just use fabric medium as a base coat for the spots so the paint stays put.

You can also save time by changing the design of the bull's horns. Instead of crafting both horns and horn center, just sew and stuff two horns and slip-stitch each one to one side of the bull's head.

For the mane on the horse puppet, you may be able to find strands of yarn bound into fabric in your local craft store. Check the doll-making or stuffed toy department. If you can find it, you won't need to take the time to sew the strands onto the mane strip, saving you at least 15 minutes. You could also substitute a strip of faux fur for the yarn mane. The edges of faux fur don't ravel, so you won't need to turn them under.

If you dread the time-consuming task of slip-stitching, save minutes by fabric gluing the hem, ears, and horn of each puppet in place. Just be sure the glue you use provides a kid-proof bond.

Browse through your local craft store whenever you start a project. There are dozens of time-savers hidden on the shelves in the form of products and tools. It's up to you to find the shortcuts to bazaar crafting, since less time per project means more projects completed in time for the show.

Old-Time Tree Ornaments

Cookie-cutter shapes highlighted with brightly colored balls fashion these country-style ornaments for the tree. Inexpensive felt and rustic embroidery make this an ideal money-making project for crafting kids.

Size

$8\frac{1}{2}$ inches high

What You Do

1. Enlarge the **Old-Time Tree Pattern** as directed in "Enlarging Patterns" on page 238.

2. From each felt rectangle, cut one tree.

3. For each tree, cut five or six 1-inch-diameter circles from assorted colors of felt for the balls. Position the balls on each tree, referring to the **Ball Placement Diagrams** for ideas. Glue them in place.

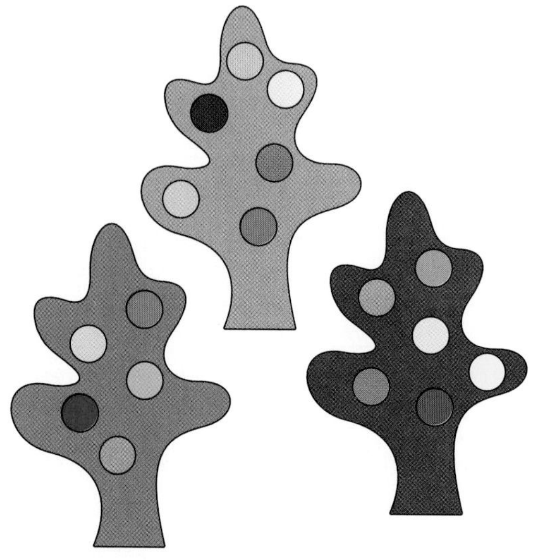

Ball Placement Diagrams

4. Using six strands of a contrasting color floss, work blanket stitches around each ball; see "Stitch Details" on page 243.

5. With contrasting floss, work blanket stitches around the edge of the tree shape.

6. Cut the ribbon in three equal lengths. Fold each ribbon in half and glue one to the back of each ornament for a hanger.

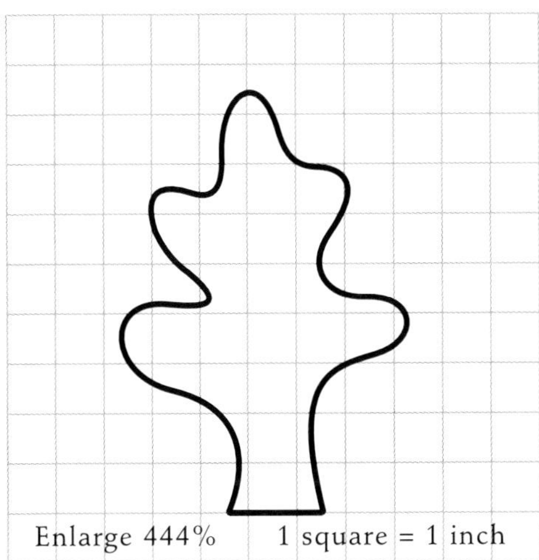

OLD-TIME TREE PATTERN

What You Need

- 6 × 9-inch pieces of green, dark green, and black felt for the trees
- Scraps of felt in assorted colors for the balls
- Fabric glue
- Six to eight colors of embroidery floss
- ½ yard of ¼-inch-wide red satin ribbon for the hanger

Time-Saving Tip

Working blanket stitches is time-consuming but is a nice touch for old-fashioned crafts like the felt tree ornaments. However, if time is of utmost concern as your bazaar nears, consider a quick machine-stitched edging for the balls and trees.

Mark the trees and balls on your felt pieces. Machine zigzag or decorative stitch on the marked lines. Then cut out the pieces just outside the marked lines, being careful not to cut into the thread. And voilà—an instant blanket-stitch substitute! You could even serge a decorative edging on the trees and balls. Use fabric glue to attach the balls and ribbon hanger to the tree ornaments. Saving time is easy when you do machine work instead of handwork, resulting in a modern variation on a traditional design.

Bazaar Gifts with a Natural Touch

Subtle in color, yet packed with texture and personality, these nature-inspired crafts will charm your customers into a yuletide spirit, au naturel.

Country Twig Stars

With a variety of branches or cut grains, there's a galaxy of stars that you can create for a bazaar display. The Sycamore Twig Star, Gathered Wheat Star, Folk Art Twig Star, and Woven Branch Star are perfect for sprinkling on a tree. Take your cue from these rustic twigs and whip up a celestial batch of starry ornaments.

Sycamore Twig Star

SIZE
9 inches across

WHAT YOU DO
Note: When selecting twigs, choose ones that are relatively straight and have interesting bark. Also choose twigs that have more than one offshoot for added interest. It is best to use still-green twigs because of their flexibility.

1. Arrange the twigs into a star shape, moving and adjusting them until you have a pleasing composition; see **Diagram 1.**

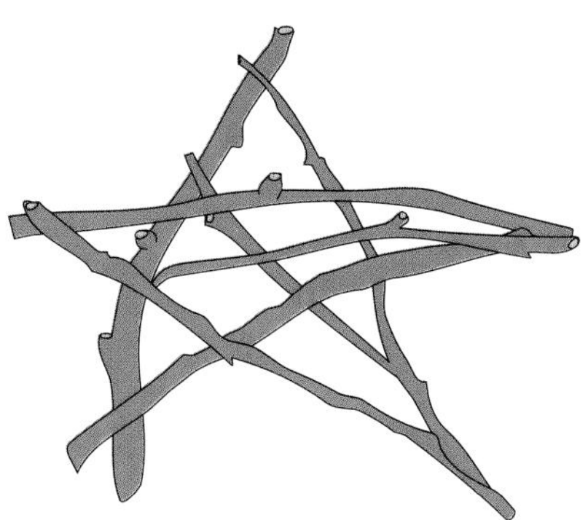
Diagram 1

2. Referring to **Diagram 2** and using the wire, wrap each intersection where the star points meet, overlapping the twigs as desired. Twist the wire ends to secure them. Insert the stem of the seedpod between the twigs of the upper left point of the star.

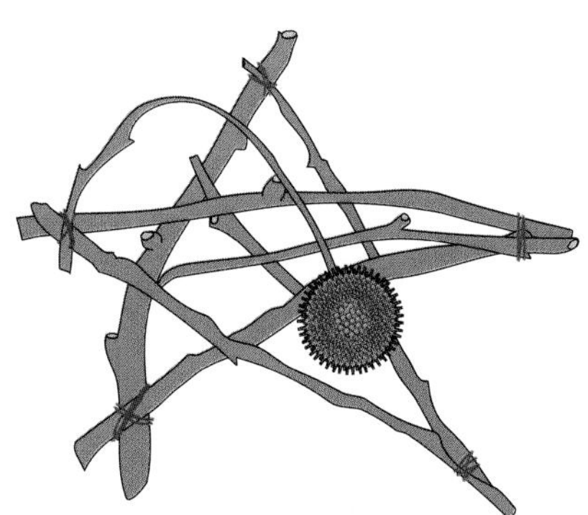
Diagram 2

WHAT YOU NEED

SYCAMORE TWIG STAR

- 5 sycamore twigs, each measuring about ½ inch in diameter and 9 to 10 inches in length
- 24-gauge floral wire
- Dried sycamore seedpod cluster with attached stem

GATHERED WHEAT STAR

- 60 dried wheat stalks, each measuring 8 inches in length
- 2 yards of sisal
- 3 heads of bearded wheat

Gathered Wheat Star

SIZE
8 inches across

WHAT YOU DO

1. Divide the wheat stalks into 5 bunches with 12 stalks in each bunch.

2. Using the sisal, tie two bunches together in an "A" shape by wrapping the sisal around the intersection where the star points meet, as shown in **Diagram 1;** knot the sisal ends.

Diagram 1

3. Using the sisal, tie a third bunch to the loose end of one of the bunches to begin the star shape. Add the fourth and fifth bunches in the same manner to complete the star, interweaving the bunches as necessary for strength.

4. Insert the stems of the bearded wheat between the stalks of the upper left point of the star, letting the wheat heads point toward the center of the star; see **Diagram 2.**

Diagram 2

Project Pointers

When you are nature crafting, be certain that the plants or plant materials you are collecting—twigs, branches, grasses, leaves, stems, flowers, fruits, seeds, and roots—are very common in your area, or over a wide geographic area. If they are not, please do not collect them.

And do not disturb or collect any plants or plant materials from parks, natural areas, or private lands without the permission of the owner. In this way, we can all enjoy our crafting while preserving nature's beauty.

Folk Art Twig Star

Size

8 inches across

What You Do

1. Enlarge the **Star Pattern** as directed in "Enlarging Patterns" on page 238. Trace the pattern onto the mat board and cut it out with the craft knife, changing blades as necessary.

2. Measure and mark a twig to fit the vertical center of the star, angling the marks as necessary to duplicate the star's outline. Cut the twig with the pruning shears, then hot-glue it into position, as shown in **Diagram 1.**

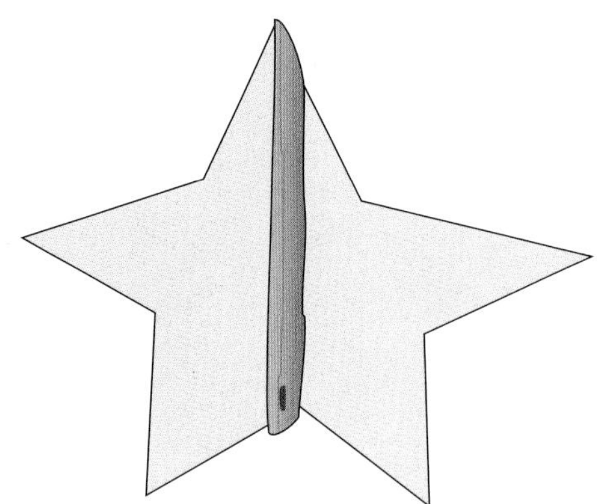

Diagram 1

3. Repeat Step 2 for each twig, working toward the outside edges to cover the entire star; see **Diagram 2.**

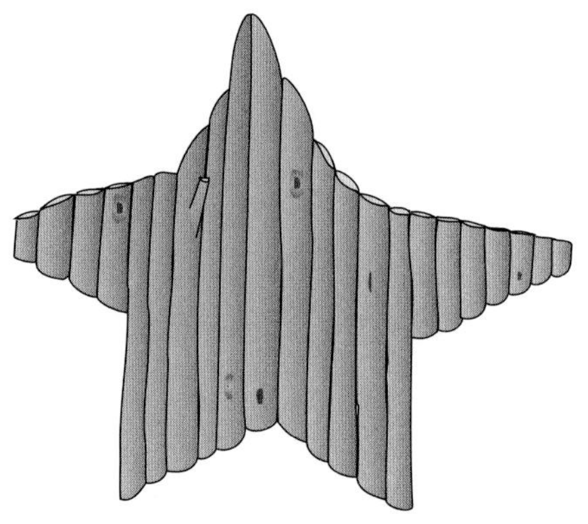

Diagram 2

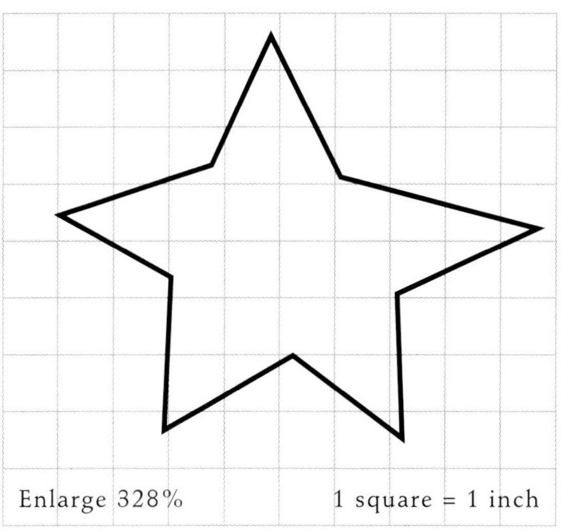

STAR PATTERN

What You Need

Folk Art Twig Star

- 8 × 11-inch piece of mat board
- Craft knife with extra blades
- 25 to 30 smooth twigs, each measuring about 1/4 inch in diameter and 6 to 8 inches in length
- Pruning shears
- Hot glue gun and glue sticks

Woven Branch Star

- Five 8-inch lengths of straight branches
- 8 to 10 pliable branches, each measuring about 1/8 inch in diameter and 8 inches in length
- Heavy-duty sewing thread

Woven Branch Star

Size

8 inches across

What You Do

1. Arrange the five straight branches in a star shape, overlapping them as necessary for stability; see **Diagram 1.** You may need to temporarily secure the shape by tying thread around the branch intersections.

Diagram 1

2. Cut the pliable branches into 8-inch lengths. Weave one branch at a time into each arm of the star shape, as shown in **Diagram 2,** securing the ends with thread if necessary.

Diagram 2

3. Continue weaving the branches until the star has an asymmetrical, rounded appearance, then remove the securing threads. Add additional branches as necessary to fill the gaps and strengthen the shape.

Natural Bath Accessories

Small luxuries are always welcome items at a bazaar. The Sisal Bath Mitt, Beaded Hand Towel, and Terry Cloth Teddies are designed to pamper. Crafted from natural fabrics, they'll scrub and dry and tickle your fancy!

Sisal Bath Mitt

What You Need

Sisal Bath Mitt

- Ball of lightweight sisal cord
- Size 11 knitting needles or size for gauge
- 5 stitch markers
- Large-eye yarn needle

Beaded Hand Towel

- 20 × 30-inch linen hand towel or 21 × 31-inch piece of linen fabric
- 225-yard ball of cream Knit-Cro-Sheen crochet cotton for the fringe
- 9-inch square of cardboard
- Large-eye tapestry needle
- Thirty-nine 13 mm natural wooden beads

Size

Directions are for child's size (5 × 8 inches). Changes for the featured adult size (6 × 9 inches) follow in parentheses.

What You Do

1. Gauge: Knitting every row for garter st, 5 sts and 5 rows = 2 inches.

2. Cast on 26 (30) sts.

3. Work 4 rows of k 1, p 1 ribbing.

4. K 18 (24) rows.

5. To decrease: K 1, place marker (pm), k 2 tog, k 7 (9), k 2 tog, pm, k 2, pm, k 2 tog, k 7 (9), k 2 tog, pm, k 1—22 (26) sts. Slipping markers for remainder of mitt, k 1 row. K 1, k 2 tog, k 5 (7), k 2 tog, k 2, k 2 tog, k 5 (7), k 2 tog, k 1—18 (22) sts. Having 2 less sts bet markers on each dec row, rep last 2 rows until 10 total sts rem.

6. K 1 row and remove markers. K 1, k 2 tog, k 4, k 2 tog, k 1—8 sts. K 1 row.

7. Leaving about a 24-inch tail, cut the sisal cord. Thread the tail through the yarn needle and back through the rem 8 sts; pull up to close the top opening. Make a backstitch to secure it. With the same tail, sew the side seam. Trim the tail and weave it in along the wrong side of the mitt.

Beaded Hand Towel

Size

20 × 30 inches

What You Do

1. If using linen fabric, turn under ¼ inch, then another ¼ inch and hem to form the towel.

2. Wind the crochet cotton around the cardboard 240 times, cutting at one edge to create 18-inch lengths of fringe. Arrange the lengths into 40 groups of six strands each.

3. Fold one six-strand group in half and thread the cut ends through the tapestry needle. Insert the needle into the back of the hand towel on one short end just above the hem and about ½ inch from the towel edge; pull the fringe through, leaving about a ½ inch of loop free, as shown in **Diagram 1.**

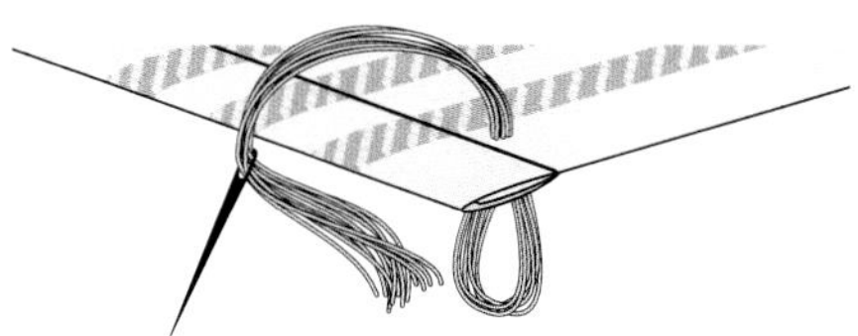

Diagram 1

4. Insert the needle into the fringe loop and pull the fringe to tighten; see **Diagram 2** on page 182.

Repeat across the width of the towel, leaving ½ inch between each fringe.

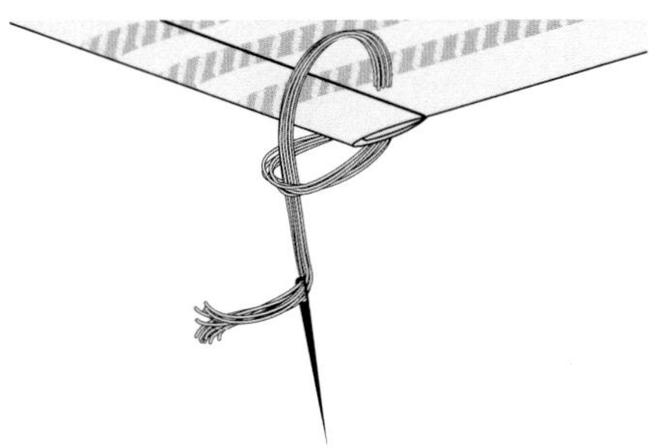

Diagram 2

5. To begin beading, separate the first fringe tassel into two six-strand groups. Pull one group to the side. Holding the remaining six-strand group and a six-strand group from the second fringe together, thread these 12 strands through a wooden bead. Repeat across the towel, leaving the last group of 6 strands free.

6. For the end beads, gather the loose 6-strand group with the first beaded 12-strand group. Make an overhand knot just below the bead; see **Diagram 3.**

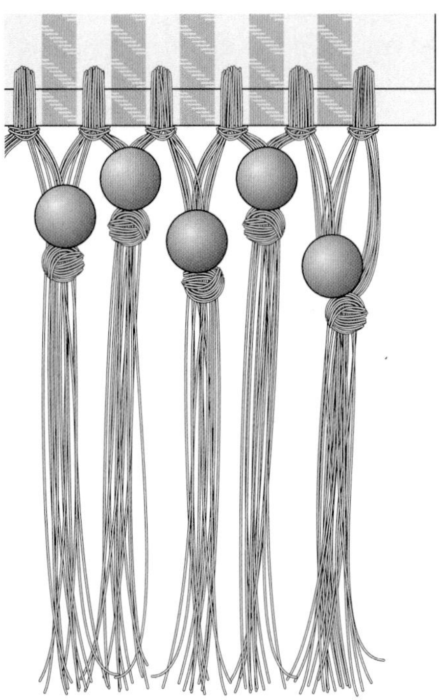

Diagram 3

7. Make an overhand knot below each bead for the remaining beads, alternating the knots from ¾ to 1½ inches from the edge of the fabric.

8. Repeat Steps 3 through 7 to fringe and bead the remaining short end of the towel.

Terry Cloth Teddy

Size

9 inches tall

What You Do

1. Enlarge the **Terry Cloth Teddy Pattern** as directed in "Enlarging Patterns" on page 238.

2. Cut the terry cloth into two 9 × 11-inch pieces. Trace around the pattern onto the wrong side of one terry cloth piece.

3. With the right sides of the two terry cloth pieces together, sew around the teddy on the outline, leaving an opening for turning on one leg.

4. Cut out the teddy ¼ inch outside the stitching line. Clip the curves and turn it to the right side.

5. Stuff the teddy with the fiberfill or foam. If the bear is intended to be a bath toy, then a shredded foam stuffing is best. Slip-stitch the opening closed.

6. Referring to the **Face Embroidery Diagram,** sew on the button eyes using 6 strands of gold floss. Referring to "Stitch Details" on page 243 and using 12 strands of brown floss, satin stitch the nose, pinching the terry cloth slightly to create a raised surface. Work long stitches for the mouth with 12 strands of brown floss.

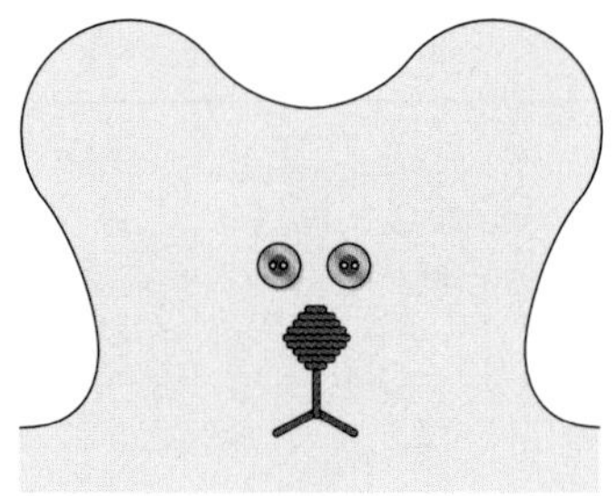

Face Embroidery Diagram

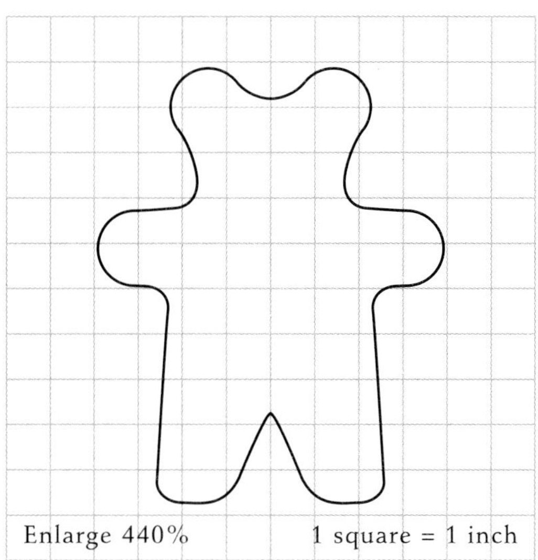

TERRY CLOTH TEDDY PATTERN

WHAT YOU NEED

TERRY CLOTH TEDDY

- Tan or cream terry cloth hand towel or 1/4 yard of woven terry cloth for the body
- Matching sewing thread
- Polyester fiberfill or shredded foam
- Two 3/8-inch-diameter buttons for the eyes
- Gold and brown embroidery floss for the facial features
- Large-eye tapestry needle

PROJECT POINTERS

You can easily change Terry Cloth Teddy's expression with a few quick stitches. Instead of round button eyes, use oval shank buttons. Or satin stitch the eyes and leave off the buttons altogether. Use an outline stitch for embroidering a curved line and French knots for the pupils and the small dots on the faces; refer to "Stitch Details" on page 243.

Feel free to experiment with your stitches. If you place teddy's eyes close together, you'll have a sweet-looking bear. Large eyes, whether they are buttons or embroidered stitches, yield an innocent-looking young teddy. Set the eyes high on the head and far apart to give teddy a wiser, more serious look.

Add French knot freckles and wispy eyelashes for a cute girl teddy.

*Use the **Teddy's Many Faces Diagram** as a guide and personalize each bear you make. If you will be selling your teddies to children, be sure to leave off the buttons since they are choking hazards; stitch each facial feature instead.*

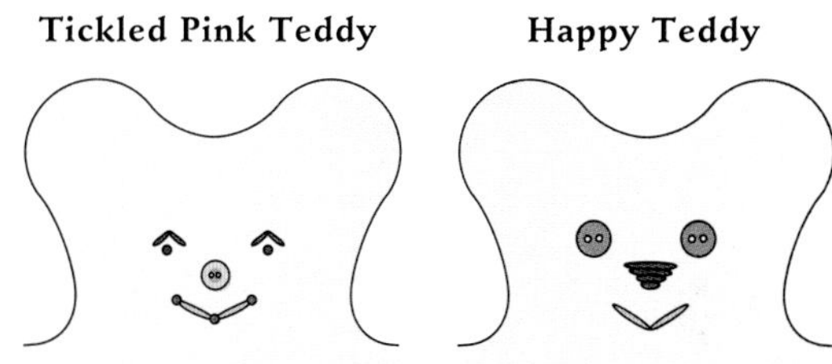

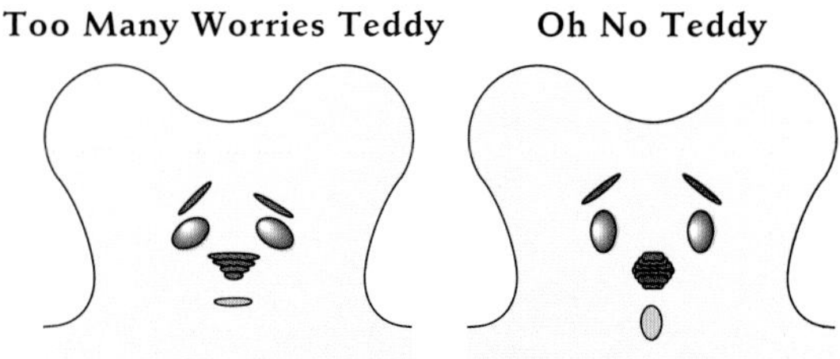

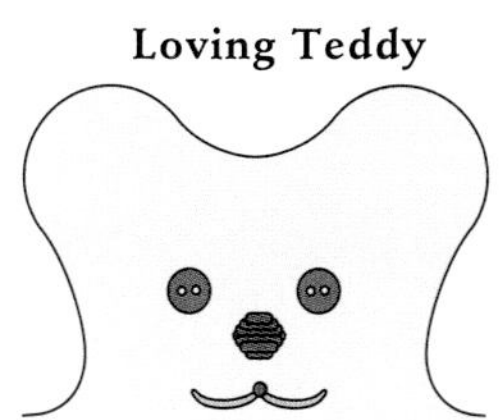

Teddy's Many Faces Diagram

Scented Citrus Trims

The aromatic Clove-Studded Pomander and the Dried Kumquat Wreath are refreshingly different ornaments to make for a holiday bazaar. Because the citrus is naturally air-dried, you have to get an early start on crafting these elegant tree trims, but they're well worth the effort.

Clove-Studded Pomander

Size

About 2 inches in diameter

What You Do

Note: Directions are given for the pomander ball with the attached tassel. If you prefer, you may omit the tassel and the bottom bead.

1. Cover the entire surface of the orange with the cloves by piercing the skin of the orange with the clove stem and inserting it into the flesh of the fruit. If the skin is tough, you may want to start a hole with the tapestry needle; after the skin has been pierced, push the clove into the orange. Leave a ½-inch space at the top of the orange for one gold bead; leave another space at the bottom if you are making the tasseled pomander ball.

2. Air-dry the pomander in a cool, dry place. When the pomander is partially dried, use the tapestry needle to poke a ½-inch-deep hole in the top for the ribbon hanger.

3. Once the pomander has dried, hot-glue the ends of the ribbon hanger into the top hole.

4. Thread one gold bead onto the loop of the folded ribbon hanger and hot-glue it in place at the top of the pomander. Glue the second bead to the bottom.

5. For the tassel, cut twelve 8-inch lengths of floss and knot one end of each length. Thread 30 to 40 seed beads onto each length of floss. Gather the lengths and knot them together at the top. Trim the excess floss, then glue the knotted end into the hole of the bottom bead.

Dried Kumquat Wreath

Size

About 4¼ inches in diameter

What You Do

1. Partially air-dry the fresh kumquats in a cool, dry place.

2. Thread the partially dried kumquats onto the wire, adding a gold bead after every two kumquats.

3. After threading, bend the wire around to create a circle. Twist the ends of the wire together, then snip away any excess wire with the scissors.

What You Need

Clove-Studded Pomander

- Clementine orange
- About 400 whole cloves or enough to cover the surface of the orange
- Size 22 tapestry needle
- 8-inch length of ⅛-inch-wide cream satin ribbon for the hanger
- Hot glue gun and glue sticks
- Two 25 mm metallic gold beads
- Gold embroidery floss
- About 480 gold seed beads for the tassel

Dried Kumquat Wreath

- 10 kumquats
- 15-inch length of 24-gauge wire
- Five 13 mm metallic gold beads
- Craft scissors

Project Pointers

Citrus fruit is best dried the natural way—slowly and in a cool, dry place. Moisture of any sort is considered an enemy and will counteract the drying process. For best results, set the fruit to be dried on a large, flat surface and leave for four to six weeks. Check and turn the fruit periodically for even drying. The drying process will also harden the often squishy nature of citrus, making it easy to use these fruits in craft projects. It is always best to start with more fruit than you need since several pieces will fall prey to rotting or spoiling while drying.

Sew-Simple Pillows

This Woven Rag Pillow and Soft Chamois Pillow are quick and easy accents for the home that you can whip up in practically no time at all! Crafted from scraps of coordinating fabrics or buttery-soft auto supply store chamois, they're perfect for first apartments, summer camps, or rustic country homes.

Woven Rag Pillow

Size

14½ inches square

What You Do

1. Wash all the fabrics to preshrink them. Tear the print fabrics into 2½-inch-wide strips, then cut them into 15-inch lengths. Remove any loose threads from the strips. You may want to fray the long edges to create a more rustic look. Choose 24 lengths for the pillow top and back, being sure to have a nice variety of print patterns and color variances for best effect. From the solid, cut two 15-inch squares for the base fabric.

2. Lay one 15-inch base square right side up on a flat surface. Varying the colors, lay six strips vertically on top of the 15-inch square with right sides up to form the warp; do not overlap the torn edges. See the **Warp Diagram.**

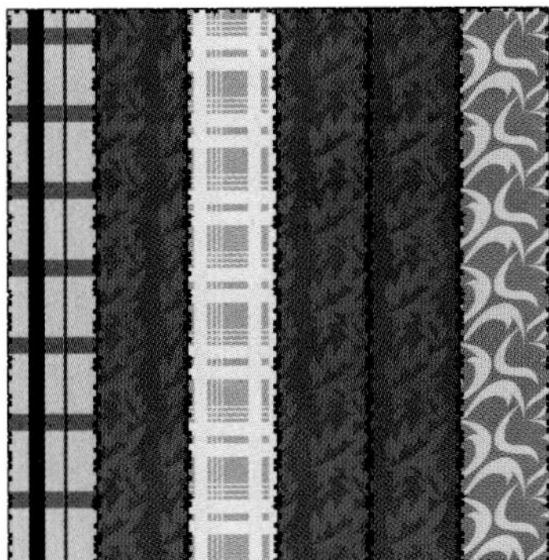

Warp Diagram

3. Starting at the lower left corner, weave one strip over and under the warp strips to form the weft, as shown in the **Weft Diagram.** Continue weaving strips over and under until the pillow front is complete.

Weft Diagram

4. Pin, then baste around all four edges to secure the woven pillow front to the base fabric, using a ¼-inch seam allowance.

5. Repeat Steps 2 through 4 for the pillow back.

6. With the right sides together, sew the pillow front and back together, using a ¼-inch seam allowance and leaving a 10-inch opening along one side for turning. Grade the seam allowance to reduce bulk.

7. Turn the pillow right side out and press, taking care not to flatten the weaves. Insert the pillow form, adding fiberfill to the corners; slip-stitch the opening closed.

What You Need

Woven Rag Pillow

- Assorted rust, brown, and olive print fabrics equal to 1 yard of fabric for the woven strips
- ½ yard rust solid fabric for the pillow base
- Matching sewing thread
- 14-inch square pillow form
- Polyester fiberfill

Soft Chamois Pillow

- Two 13 × 15-inch chamois cloths or available size
- White dressmaker's chalk pencil
- Metal ruler
- Matching sewing thread
- Polyester fiberfill

Soft Chamois Pillow

Size

About 13 × 15 inches

What You Do

1. Study and position your chamois cloths back to back to determine the best possible placement of the raw and cut edges. Most cloths have at least two irregular edges and, for best effect, these should be layered to form a pleasing free-form hem.

2. Very lightly mark a 7 × 9-inch rectangle in the center of one chamois cloth with the chalk and ruler; adjust the rectangle size if necessary to fit your cloth size, leaving at least 2 to 4 inches all around to create a flange edge.

3. With wrong sides facing, sew along the marked rectangle line, leaving a 2-inch opening along one side for stuffing. You may want to round the corners of the rectangle to soften the look.

4. Stuff the pillow to desired firmness, then finish sewing the seam.

MONEY-SAVING TIP

If the chamois you've chosen for the pillow project is very irregularly shaped, you may want to trim some of the excess cloth for other bazaar projects. One of the easiest things you could make is a decorative lapel pin. Since chamois doesn't ravel, you won't need to use fancy and time-consuming seams or seam finishes. I've included a few ideas to get you started.

For a ***Victorian Heart Pin,*** *cut two same-size hearts from the leftover chamois, then accent one heart with white, royal blue, and green lazy daisy stitches and a green French knot. Place the two hearts together with wrong sides facing and work traditional blanket stitches around the edge, leaving a small opening for stuffing. Stuff the heart very lightly with fiberfill, then finish the blanket-stitch edge around the pin. Sew on a pin clasp. If you'd like to give the pin a romantic look, you may even color the small bits of chamois with red dye before you start.*

Victorian Heart Pin

For the ***Country Star Pin,*** *cut two stars from chamois. Using a running stitch, sew the two stars together, leaving an opening for stuffing. Stuff very lightly with fiberfill, then finish the seam. Sew on a pin clasp, then sew or glue tiny shirt buttons in a random pattern on the front of the star pin to give it a mismatched country feel.*

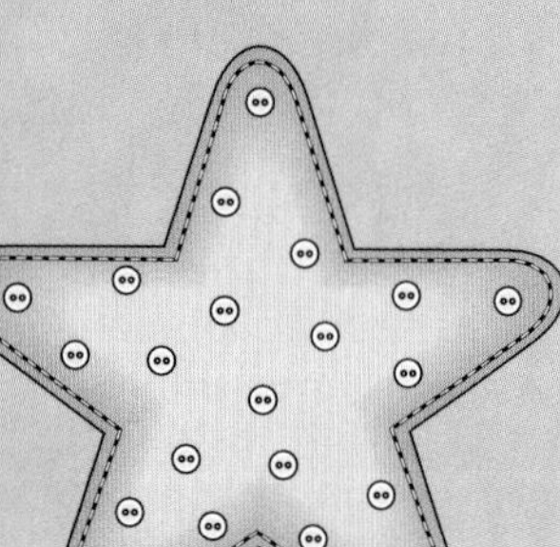

Country Star Pin

You could also make bunny or cat pins, accenting them with glass seed beads, ribbons, and buttons. If you'd rather not draw shapes, consider square or round pins. Dress up the simple lines with spatters of acrylic paint, lace appliqués, feathers, charms, and easy embroidery. Use found items for your embellishments or check your button box for interesting accents. You may be able to find antique safety pins, tarnished lockets, or even diary keys. These pins are very inexpensive to make since you use leftovers from other projects. And they're a great way to get more mileage out of each craft supply purchase.

Country-Style Lamp Shades

Hand-decorated lamp shades are popular bazaar items since they can give a refreshing look to a tired room. The Pierced Oak Leaf Shade and the Sponged Shade will brighten any corner in your home. The Country Quote Shade proclaims that "In the country we forget to count the hours."

Pierced Oak Leaf Shade

Size

8 inches in diameter at the base

What You Do

1. Enlarge the **Oak Leaf Pattern** on page 190 as directed in "Enlarging Patterns" on page 238. Trace the pattern onto tracing paper.

2. Position and tape the pattern on the lamp shade for the center leaf; see the **Oak Leaf Placement Diagram.**

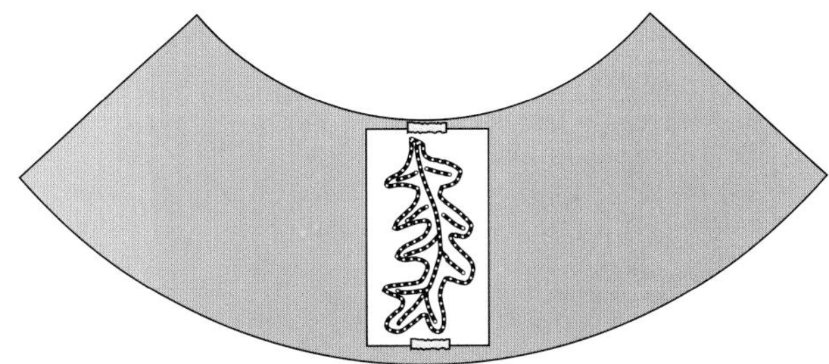

Oak Leaf Placement Diagram

3. Using the tapestry needle, pierce each dot on the pattern.

What You Need

Pierced Oak Leaf Shade

- Tracing paper
- 8-inch-diameter brown paper lamp shade
- Artist's tape
- Sharp-point tapestry needle

Sponged Shade

- White acrylic paint
- Saucer or palette
- Piece of natural sponge
- 8-inch-diameter brown paper lamp shade
- White household string
- Sharp-point tapestry needle

4. Reposition the pattern on the shade, then pierce each of the four remaining oak leaves.

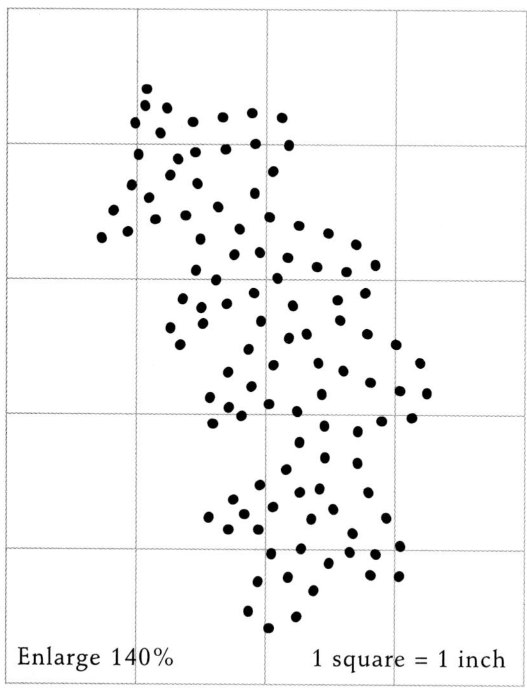

OAK LEAF PATTERN

Sponged Shade

Size

8 inches in diameter at the base

What You Do

1. Squeeze the paint onto the saucer or palette, adding water to create a creamy consistency. Be sure the paint is not too watery, or the shade will ripple as it dries.

2. Sponge the paint lightly onto the shade in a random pattern; let it dry thoroughly. Wash the saucer or palette with soap and water before the paint dries.

3. Using the string and the tapestry needle, embroider a row of blanket stitches about ⅝ inch deep around the top and bottom rims of the lamp shade; see "Stitch Details" on page 243. If you have difficulty pulling the string through the shade, you may need to punch holes with a paper punch or large needle.

Country Quote Shade

Size

14 inches in diameter at the base

What You Do

1. Using the stylus or pen and unneeded letters, practice rubbing the letters onto the paper bag before you begin accenting the shade. Experiment with the amount of rubbing pressure you apply, being sure the entire letter has been transferred to the paper bag. You should also practice aligning the bottoms of the letters, since this is important to the success of the shade project.

2. When you feel confident with the technique, you can decorate the lamp shade. Press each letter of the quote onto the lamp shade about 1 inch from the bottom edge, taking care to align the letters evenly; refer to the **Quote Placement Diagram.**

Quote Placement Diagram

WHAT YOU NEED

COUNTRY QUOTE SHADE

- Stylus or dry ballpoint pen
- White instant rub-on letters (typeface shown: 144-point Futura Medium)
- Brown paper bag for practicing the technique
- 14-inch-diameter brown paper lamp shade

PROJECT POINTERS

If you would prefer to make a more durable Country Quote Shade, consider stenciling the letters onto the shade. You'll need to have the following supplies: three sheets of stencil Mylar, 8½ × 11-inch sheet of glass with masked or filed edges, a craft knife with extra blades, masking tape, white artist's tape, white acrylic paint, a saucer or palette, a stencil brush, and paper towels.

Enlarge the ***Country Quote Stencil Letters*** *as directed in "Enlarging Patterns" on page 238, then trace one line of letters onto each sheet of Mylar, taking care to accurately align the bottoms of the letters for ease in stenciling. To cut the stencil letters, place the Mylar on the glass and tape it to secure. Holding the craft knife like a pencil, carefully cut out the letters on the tracing line. Cut toward you, turning the glass as you cut. If your knife should slip, mend both sides of the cut with masking tape.*

Position the stencil about 1 inch above the bottom edge of the lamp shade, referring to the ***Quote Placement Diagram.*** *Secure the stencil with artist's tape. Place 2 tablespoons of paint on the saucer or palette. Dip the tip of the stencil brush into the paint, then dab it on the paper towels until the brush is almost dry. Holding the brush perpendicular to the surface, brush over the cutout areas with a circular motion, working over the stencil edges. Allow the paint to dry on one section before moving on to avoid smearing the paint. After stenciling the entire quote, wash the brushes and saucer with soap and water before the paint dries.*

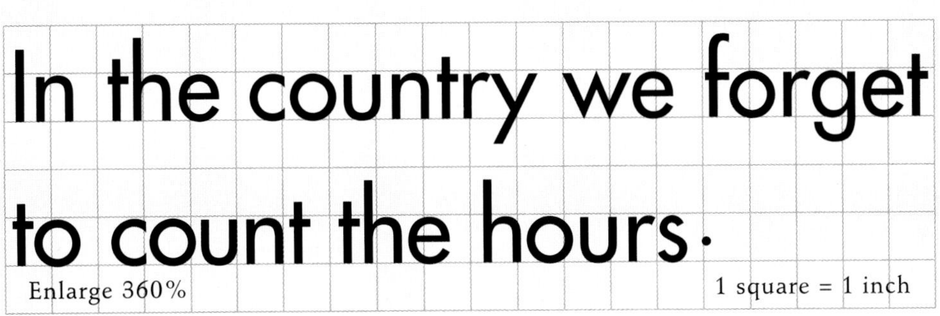

COUNTRY QUOTE STENCIL LETTERS

Decorator Flowerpots

Transform ordinary terra-cotta flowerpots into spectacular containers for holiday flowers and plants. They're easy bazaar projects and will make an unusual addition to your booth or benefit. You can use newly purchased and weathered flowerpots for two different looks. As an added attraction, purchase inexpensive plants, such as primroses or Christmas cacti, in plastic containers to sell in the pots as a ready-made gift for your customer.

Touch-of-Gold Flowerpot

SIZE

About 6 inches high

WHAT YOU DO

1. If you're using a weathered or used flowerpot, clean off any excess dirt, taking care not to remove or damage any of the weathered natural patina on the surface of the pot.

2. Working a section at a time, apply a smooth, even coat of acrylic decoupage medium to the pot's exterior with one of the paintbrushes. While the decoupage medium is still wet, "float" a torn section of the gold leaf onto the wet surface by placing it gently onto the pot. Using the dry paintbrush, press the leaf in place. Continue until the desired result is achieved, placing as little or as much gold leaf onto the surface as desired. If you're using a weathered pot, take advantage of worn and weathered spots and place the gold leaf to best advantage for character. Allow the gold leaf to dry thoroughly.

3. Cover the entire pot with a second coat of decoupage medium for protection.

WHAT YOU NEED

TOUCH-OF-GOLD FLOWERPOT

- New or used clay flowerpot, 4 to 6 inches in diameter
- Acrylic decoupage medium*
- Two 1-inch-wide paintbrushes
- 5 to 8 sheets of imitation gold leaf

* *See the "Buyer's Guide" on page 244 for ordering information.*

STAR-STUDDED FLOWERPOT

- New or used clay flowerpot, 4 to 6 inches in diameter
- Star-printed tissue paper or another motif-printed gift tissue
- Acrylic decoupage medium*
- 1-inch-wide paintbrush

* *See the "Buyer's Guide" on page 244 for ordering information.*

Star-Studded Flowerpot

SIZE

About 6 inches high

WHAT YOU DO

1. If you're using a weathered or used flowerpot, clean off any excess dirt, taking care not to remove or damage any of the weathered natural patina on the surface of the pot.

2. Tear the tissue paper into small irregular pieces.

3. Working one section at a time and using the paintbrush, apply a smooth, even coat of acrylic decoupage medium to the flowerpot's exterior. While the decoupage medium is still wet, place a torn piece of tissue paper onto the surface of the pot, overlapping and arranging as desired. Continue arranging tissue paper pieces until the desired result is achieved, placing as little or as much of the tissue onto the surface of the pot as you want. If you're using a weathered pot, take advantage of worn and weathered spots and place the tissue paper to best advantage for character. Allow the tissue paper to dry thoroughly.

4. Cover the entire pot with a second coat of decoupage medium for protection.

Natural Nut Tree Trims

Imagine a profusion of these imaginative nut ornaments hanging on a fragrant fir tree. These Pistachio Balls and Pecan Star Ornaments will dazzle country and nature enthusiasts alike. They are easy enough to make that the kids can get involved in the fun of crafting and selling handmade ornaments.

Pistachio Ball

Size

About 4 inches in diameter

What You Do

1. If you're using natural-colored pistachios, work in a well-ventilated area and spray paint the foam ball tan to disguise areas that might show between the nuts; if using red-dyed nuts, spray paint the ball red.

2. Poke a small hole into the foam ball using the point of a pencil. Glue the ends of the ribbon into the hole to form a loop for hanging.

3. Starting at the ribbon and working a small section at a time, glue the pistachios to the ball. Continue gluing small sections at a time until the ball is completely covered.

Pecan Star Ornament

Size

About 3½ inches in diameter

WHAT YOU DO

1. Glue the pointed ends of the pecans together to create a star shape, as shown in **Diagram 1.**

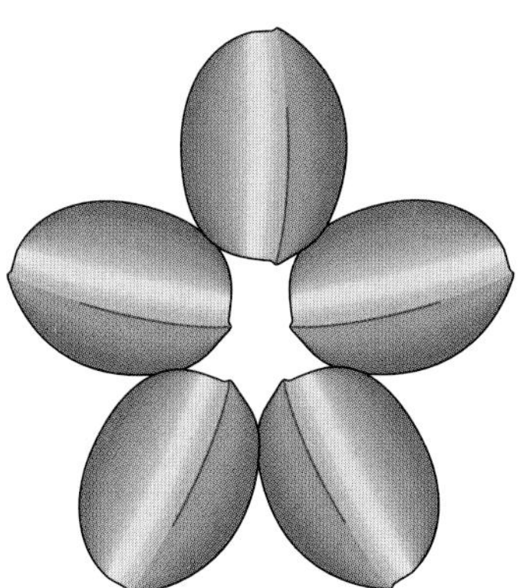

Diagram 1

2. For the dried flower center, glue the blossom to the center of the star, being sure to completely cover the center hole.

3. For the knotted-cord center, tape the ends of the upholstery cord with cellophane tape to prevent raveling, then glue one end of the cord into the hole of the star. Twist the cord tightly around itself in a clockwise motion to create the knot, trimming and tucking the remaining end under the knot to hide the raw ends; see **Diagram 2.**

Diagram 2

4. Glue the ends of the hanger cord to the back of one pecan.

WHAT YOU NEED

PISTACHIO BALL

- 3-inch-diameter Styrofoam ball
- Tan or red spray paint
- 8-inch length of 1/8-inch-wide cream satin ribbon for the hanger
- Hot glue gun and glue sticks
- About 125 natural or red-dyed pistachios

PECAN STAR ORNAMENT

- 5 equally sized pecans
- Hot glue gun and glue sticks
- Dried rosebud, dried strawflower, or 3-inch length of 3/8-inch-diameter gold upholstery cord for the ornament center
- Cellophane tape
- 6-inch length of 1/8-inch-diameter gold cord for the hanger

PROJECT POINTERS

Upholstery cords are made of tightly twisted threads that resemble rope. When cut, the cord ends unwrap and fray very rapidly. To prevent this, wrap a small piece of cellophane tape around the area where you'll be cutting; this will hold the twisted threads together and prevent raveling. Simply cut the cord at the center of the taped area and glue or stitch the cord in place, being careful to hide any taped ends.

Maple Leaf Pot Holders

These leafy-shaped pot holders will rake in the buyers at your holiday-time crafts bazaar. They are terrific items to sell as inexpensive gifts—their subtle autumn hues and simple top stitching give them enough character for any shopper's country kitchen.

SIZE

$8\frac{1}{2} \times 10$ inches

WHAT YOU DO

1. Enlarge the **Maple Leaf Pot Holder Pattern** as directed in "Enlarging Patterns" on page 238. Transfer all top-stitching lines as directed in "Transferring Markings" on page 238.

2. From each calico print and the batting, cut one maple leaf. Transfer the top-stitching lines to one fabric maple leaf.

3. Layer the batting, one leaf right side up, then the remaining leaf wrong side up. Pin all three layers together. Using a ¼-inch seam allowance, sew around the outer edge of the leaf shape, leaving a 2-inch opening along one straight section. Grade the seam allowance to reduce bulk and clip all points for ease in turning. Turn the pot holder right side out and slip-stitch the opening closed. Press well.

4. Topstitch ¼ inch in from the pot holder edge, then topstitch on the marked lines to define the leaf's veins.

WHAT YOU NEED

- Two 11-inch squares of coordinating calico prints
- 11-inch square of insulated quilt batting
- Matching sewing thread

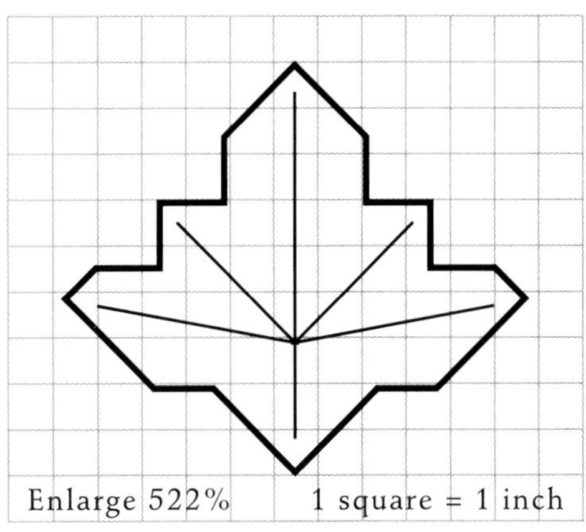

MAPLE LEAF
POT HOLDER PATTERN

PROJECT POINTERS

If you want to incorporate a hanging loop into your pot holder, cut a $1\frac{1}{4} \times 3\frac{1}{2}$-inch piece from one of the calico prints. Press under ¼ inch along each long edge. With wrong sides together, fold the hanging loop in half lengthwise. Topstitch along the long open edge. Fold the loop in half crosswise and baste across the raw edges. With the raw edges even, pin the loop to one calico print leaf, as shown in the ***Hanging Loop Diagram.*** *Then layer the batting and fabric leaves and assemble the pot holder as directed.*

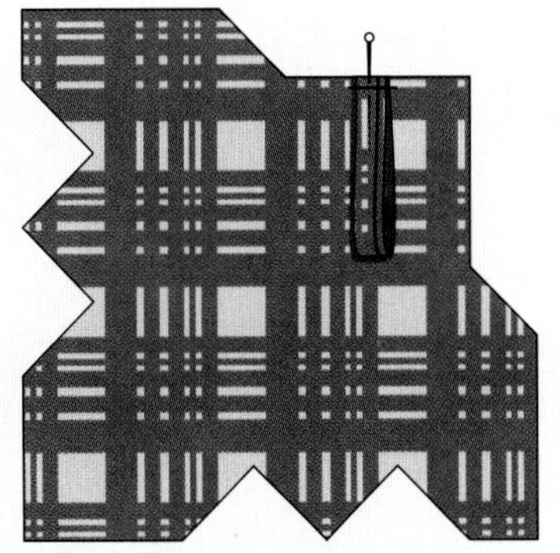

Hanging Loop Diagram

Many cooks use dime-store pot holders when preparing meals and save fancier ones as decorative kitchen accents. To attract these decorator types, sell four coordinating-color pot holders tied with paper ribbon; accent them with a mini wooden spoon or whisk ornament to add a touch of whimsy.

Seashell Ornaments

Whether gathered while walking along the beach or purchased from a souvenir shop, seashells are popular collectibles. Take advantage of this, and craft these elegant Christmas ornaments to sell at your holiday bazaar. The scallop ornament, starfish ornaments, shell icicles, and adorable shell angel are perfect additions to an ornament collection. Who could resist hanging each and every one of these on their tree?

Miniature Scallop

Size
2 inches across

What You Do

1. Fold the ribbon in half to make a hanger. Glue the ends to the inside of one scallop shell.

2. Run a line of hot glue around the edge of the shell, then press the two shells together to form a closed shell.

Starfish on a Starfish

Size
4 inches across

What You Do

1. Glue the small starfish to the center of the large starfish and one pearl to the tip of each point of the starfish.

2. Fold the cord in half, then glue it to one arm of the starfish for a hanger.

Golden-Wrapped Starfish

Size
6 inches across

What You Do

1. Glue the scallop shell to the center of the large starfish.

2. Fold the ⅛-inch-diameter cord in half, then glue it to the top arm of the starfish, having one cord end centered on the front and the other end centered on the back of the starfish for the hanger, as shown in the **Hanger Diagram.**

What You Need

Miniature Scallop

- 6-inch length of ¼-inch-wide white satin ribbon for the hanger
- Hot glue gun and glue sticks
- Two 2-inch-wide scallop shells

Starfish on a Starfish

- One ¾-inch and one 4-inch starfish
- Hot glue gun and glue sticks
- Five 6 mm light green craft pearls
- 6-inch length of 1/32-inch-diameter metallic gold cord for the hanger

Golden-Wrapped Starfish

- 6-inch starfish
- ¾-inch-wide scallop shell
- Hot glue gun and glue sticks
- 6-inch length of ⅛-inch-diameter metallic gold cord for the hanger
- 6¼ yards of 1/32-inch-diameter metallic gold cord for the arm wraps

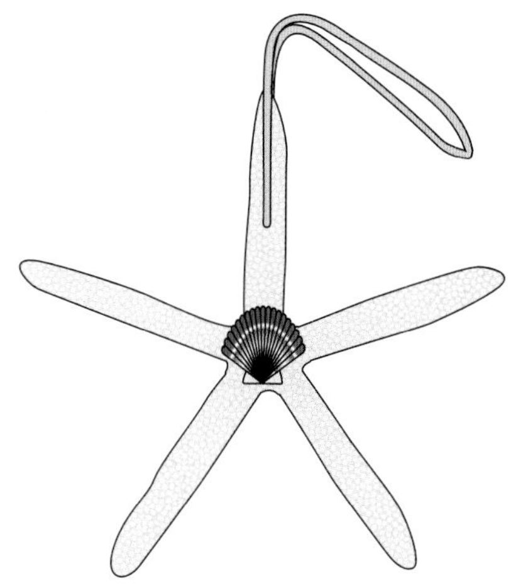

Hanger Diagram

WHAT YOU NEED

ELEGANT SHELL ICICLES

- 5/8 yard of 1/8-inch-wide white satin ribbon for the hangers
- Three 3½- to 4½-inch-long cone-shaped shells
- Hot glue gun and glue sticks
- 3/4-yard strand of white pearls-by-the-yard
- 3/4-inch-diameter gold glass Christmas ball
- ½-inch-diameter white craft pearl
- 1-inch-wide scallop shell

SEASHELL ANGEL

- Two 1½-inch-wide light-colored scallop shells for the wings
- 4-inch-wide flat scallop shell*
- Hot glue gun and glue sticks
- 1½-inch-wide dark-colored scallop shell for the head
- 1-inch-diameter wooden ball for the head
- 6-inch length of 1/8-inch-diameter metallic gold cord for the hair
- Extra-hold hair spray
- 3-inch length of 1/8-inch-wide metallic gold braid for the halo
- Permanent black felt-tip marker
- 2½-inch starfish
- 8-inch length of 1/4-inch-wide white satin ribbon for the hanger

* *Also available from kitchen and baking shops.*

3. Cut the remaining cord into five 45-inch lengths. Wrap one length around each arm of the starfish, covering the ends of the hanging loop on the top arm. Glue all cord ends in place at the back of the starfish.

Elegant Shell Icicles

SIZE

3½ to 4½ inches long

WHAT YOU DO

1. Cut the ribbon into three equal lengths. Fold each length in half to make a hanger. Glue the ends of each hanger inside the top opening of one cone-shaped shell.

2. For the pearl-wrapped shell, wrap, then glue the pearl strand around the shell, using the natural spirals of the shell as a guide. For the gold-tipped shell, remove the plastic cap from the Christmas ball and glue the ball to the point of the shell. For the scallop-accented shell, glue the pearl to the top opening and the scallop shell to the front of the shell.

Seashell Angel

SIZE

4 inches tall

WHAT YOU DO

1. Referring to the **Placement Diagram,** glue the two light-colored scallop shells to the back of the flat scallop shell for the wings, having the rounded edge of the flat shell form the hem of the dress. Glue the dark shell to the center front of the flat shell between the wings to hold the head. Glue the ball to the center shell for the head.

Placement Diagram

2. Wrap the gold cord tightly around a pencil and spray it with hair spray. Allow the hair spray to dry thoroughly. Repeat with a second coat if necessary. Remove the sprayed coil from the pencil and glue it in place around the wooden ball for hair, tucking in the ends and keeping the loops flush to the head; see the **Hair Diagram.**

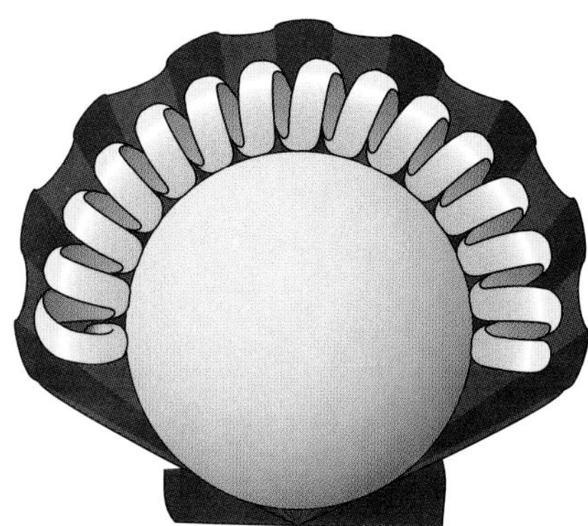

Hair Diagram

3. Using the metallic gold braid, make a circle for the halo and glue it in place at the back of the dark-colored shell.

4. Using the marker, make small dots for eyes, as shown in the photograph on page 198.

5. Glue the starfish to the upper right of the angel's dress.

6. Fold the ribbon in half to make the hanger. Glue the ends of the hanger to the back of the angel between the wings.

Project Pointers

If you are lucky enough to live close to the beach, you may be able to collect shells for your projects. You will need to spend a little time, however, preparing found materials for crafting.

Clean each shell to remove any residue. If it still contains the remains of the animal that made the shell its home, boil the shell for up to a half hour, then remove the animal with a fork or ice pick; use a steady twisting action so that the animal is removed in one piece. If some of the animal breaks off, place a few drops of alcohol in the shell and set it on end. The remaining residue can be removed in about two days. To remove any remaining odor, soak the shell overnight in a bleach-and-water solution.

If the shell contains grains of sand or small pebbles, rinse the shell under warm running water to flush out the particles. Some shells may be covered with barnacles or lime deposits and should be cleaned. Apply a small amount of hydrogen peroxide to the shell and scrub with a soft-bristle brush. Once clean, brush baby oil on the shell to help preserve the color and sheen.

To add a touch of elegance to your seashell ornaments, lightly spray the shells with metallic gold or silver paint. Or brush paint on the edges for a gleaming effect.

You could also glue teeny starfish in a random pattern on the Seashell Angel's dress to create the look of calico. Add a delicate pearl garland at the hem to duplicate the look of lace.

Copper-Edged Glass Frame

"Suspend" vintage doilies, treasured fabrics, pressed flowers, postcards, greeting cards, postage stamps, or even baseball cards between glass and sell them in your bazaar booth as decorative items for the home.

SIZE

As desired

WHAT YOU DO

1. Carefully measure the item to be framed to determine its size. Add 4 inches to each measurement to get the size needed for the glass pieces; this will allow for a 2-inch margin of clear glass around the object. For example, if the object you're framing is 3 × 5 inches, the glass measurements should be 7 × 9 inches.

2. Purchase the appropriate-size glass or cut it yourself using a glass cutter. If you've never cut glass before, it's a good idea to have your glass cut to size by a professional.

3. Lay the glass on a smooth, clean surface and clean all sides thoroughly with glass cleaner. Allow both sides of the glass to dry completely.

4. Center the item on one sheet of glass, taking care to have a 2-inch margin all around. Place the second sheet of glass on top of the first sheet.

5. To frame the glass, cut strips of the copper foil 1½ inches longer than the length of each glass side.

6. Peel back the paper backing and center the adhesive strip over the outside edge of the glass, working from the top of the glass to the bottom, as shown in **Diagram 1.**

Diagram 1

WHAT YOU NEED

- Selected item to be framed such as a doily, photograph, or vintage correspondence
- 2 sheets of glass cut to the appropriate size*
- Glass cleaner
- ½-inch-wide adhesive copper foil†

* *Available at a glass and mirror supply store or hardware store.*

† *Available at a stained-glass supply store.*

7. Fold both sides of the foil down onto the glass surface and press them lightly to adhere, but do not rub; see **Diagram 2.** Take care to keep the glass sheets in the same position so they do not shift.

8. Fold the ends over and around the corners, trimming the foil if necessary to reduce bulk. Repeat for the remaining three sides.

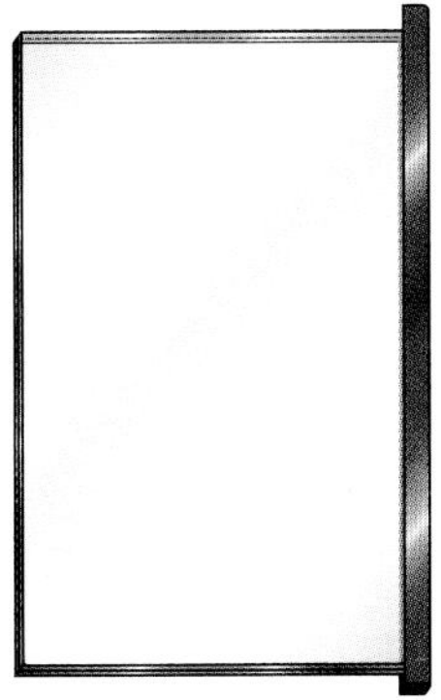

Diagram 2

PROJECT POINTERS

Since handcrafted jewelry is always a hot seller at bazaars, why not use this technique to make high-fashion brooches? Find interesting bits and snips of old-world ribbon, crocheted lace, fabric swatches, pressed meadow flowers, small antique photographs, or what-have-you, as shown in the examples here. Assemble the brooches in the same manner as the frames, then hot-glue a pin clasp to the back of the brooch.

Meadow Flower Brooch

Crocheted Lace Brooch

Festive Wreaths and Trims

These glittery pinecone ornaments offer a twist on the traditional look. The pinecone and artichoke wreaths are super simple to make.

Decorated Pinecones

Size

About 2½ inches across

What You Do

1. For the golden pinecone, work in a well-ventilated area and spray paint the entire cone gold, taking care to paint between each scale. For the pearl-accented cone, glue one pearl to the tip of each scale to create a dewdrop effect. Leave the natural pinecone unembellished.

2. Cut the ribbon in thirds for the hangers. Fold each ribbon in half, forming a loop at the top. Glue one ribbon loop to the top of each pinecone, leaving 3-inch tails, as shown in the **Hanger Diagram.** Clip the ribbon ends diagonally.

Hanger Diagram

Pinecone Wreath

Size

About 16 inches in diameter

What You Do

1. Fold the hanger wire in half. Loop it around the wreath form, twisting the ends to secure it. Clip any excess wire.

2. Select evenly sized pinecones to place around the edges of the wreath form; set the remaining pinecones aside.

3. Lay the wreath form on a flat surface, then glue a row of cones around the outer edge of the form, gluing the base of each pinecone to the form. Repeat for the inner edge of the form.

4. Glue the reserved pinecones on top of the form, taking care to pack them as tightly as possible to cover the surface of the form.

5. Glue the popcorn in circular rows between the pinecones to fill in any holes.

Artichoke Wreath

Size

About 11 inches in diameter

What You Do

1. Cut a 3/8-yard length of wire for the hanger. Fold the length in half and loop it around the twig wreath, twisting the ends to secure it. Clip any excess wire.

2. Cut the remaining wire into 12-inch lengths. Wrap the middle of one wire length around the stem of each artichoke.

3. Using the wire ends, attach each artichoke to the twig wreath, working in a counterclockwise direction.

4. Working in a well-ventilated area, lightly spray paint the finished wreath in order to give it a golden luster.

What You Need

Decorated Pinecones

- Three 2½-inch-diameter pinecones
- Metallic gold spray paint
- About eighty 3 mm seed pearls
- Hot glue gun and glue sticks
- 1 yard of ½-inch-wide red satin ribbon for the hangers

Pinecone Wreath

- 3/8 yard of 24-gauge wire for the hanger
- 12-inch-diameter Styrofoam wreath form
- About one hundred 1½- to 2-inch-diameter pinecones
- Hot glue gun and glue sticks
- About 4 cups of popped popcorn

Artichoke Wreath

- About 4 yards of 24-gauge wire
- 8-inch-diameter twig wreath
- 8 to 10 dried Italian artichokes
- Metallic gold spray paint

Project Pointers

The artichokes used in the Artichoke Wreath are Italian artichokes, a variety that is smaller, pricklier, and more pointed than the typical artichoke. These Italian artichokes are available at specialty and gourmet shops. Because of their size, they dry quite easily. If you cannot find these, regular artichokes can be substituted.

Farm Animal Cutting Boards

Cutting boards are always popular kitchen items at bazaars and craft shows, and these whimsical Brooding Hen, Napping Sheep, and Grazing Cow Cutting Boards are no exception. Packed with personality, their simple shapes are easy for woodworking enthusiasts to cut from a length of 1 × 12 hardwood—and the finishing is a snap.

Size

Brooding Hen is 11 × 12¾ inches
Napping Sheep is 10¾ × 16¾ inches
Grazing Cow is 11 × 15¾ inches

What You Need

- 13-inch length of 1 × 12-inch hardwood (such as ash, maple, or oak) for the hen; 18-inch length for the sheep; or 17-inch length for the cow
- Band, saber, or coping saw and clamps
- Drill and ¼-inch drill bit
- 2-inch length of ¼-inch-diameter dowel for the cow's udders
- Wood glue
- Medium-grit sandpaper
- 2 clean, lint-free cloths
- Behlen Salad Bowl Finish*
- ⅔ yard of sisal for the cow's tail
- Cellophane tape

* *See the "Buyer's Guide" on page 244 for ordering information.*

What You Do

1. Enlarge the **Farm Animal Cutting Board Patterns** on page 208 as directed in "Enlarging Patterns" on page 238.

2. Trace each pattern onto the wood surface, transferring the markings for the eyes.

3. Using a band saw, cut along the lines to create the desired shape. If you do not have a band saw, use clamps to clamp the wood to a worktable and cut with a saber saw. The shapes can also be cut by hand with a coping saw, but it will require considerably more effort. (If you have limited tools or none at all, you may be able to have an employee at your local lumberyard cut the shapes for you for a fee.)

4. For the hen, drill a hole for the eye using the ¼-inch drill bit. For the sheep, drill a hole to start the eye using the ¼-inch drill bit, then cut out the remaining area with a coping saw. For the cow, drill two holes in the underside of the udder for the teats, one in the backside for the tail, and one for the eye, using the ¼-inch drill bit and referring to the **Cow Diagram** for placement of the holes. Cut the dowel into two equal lengths and glue one length into each udder hole, using wood glue.

Cow Diagram

5. Sand all the edges smooth with medium-grit sandpaper. Using a lint-free cloth, wipe away any grit from the cutting board.

6. Using the second lint-free cloth, rub all surfaces with the finishing oil. Allow the cutting board to dry at least 72 hours. Apply a second coat of the oil if necessary.

7. Cut the sisal into three equal lengths for the cow's tail. Tape the top end, then braid the lengths together, knotting the working end. Fray the sisal below the knot. Remove the tape and glue the braid ends into the drilled tail hole, using the wood glue.

FARM ANIMAL
CUTTING BOARD PATTERNS

Project Pointers

Cut hang tags out of brown paper bags using pinking shears. You could even cut out a cow shape to match the cow cutting board. Paper-punch a hole in the upper left corner of each tag, then attach it with a strip of ripped homespun fabric. If you have a child who has nice handwriting, have her or him hand letter tags that give instructions on cleaning and caring for the newly purchased cutting board; see the examples below.

Your country cutting board has been coated with a special nontoxic finish that resists stain. After using, clean your cutting board with a 2:1 water-and-bleach solution and a hard-bristle brush. Lighten badly stained areas with lemon juice.

You have purchased a country cutting board from the workshop of Jim Williams. If treated with care and cleaned after each use, your cutting board should last a lifetime.

Made by Hand
of Vermont Maple
by Jim Williams
Autumn 1995

Decorator Picture Frames

Picture frames are another item that have proven popularity at crafts shows. Everyone is on the lookout for interesting frames to accent their collection of family photographs. These handcrafted fabric-covered frames will stand out with their crisp linen or vintage fabrics and catch the eye of curious buyers.

Decorator Picture Frames

What You Need

Drapery Fabric Frame

- Four 7 × 9-inch pieces of mat board for the frame front, base, back, and stand
- Craft knife with extra blades
- ½ yard of medium green drapery fabric or similar vintage fabric for the frame covering
- Hot glue gun and glue sticks
- Dressmaker's shears
- 5-inch length of ½-inch-wide medium green grosgrain ribbon for the support

Plaid Linen Frame

- Four 8 × 10-inch pieces of mat board
- Craft knife with extra blades
- ½ yard of white and brown plaid linen fabric or similar vintage fabric
- 8 × 10-inch piece of thin fleece
- Hot glue gun and glue sticks
- Dressmaker's shears
- 5-inch length of ¾-inch-wide white grosgrain ribbon for the support

Drapery Fabric Frame

Size

7 × 9-inch frame with 2½ × 4-inch opening

What You Do

1. Mark the photograph opening on one piece of the mat board, as shown in the **Photograph Opening Diagram.** Using a ruler to ensure a straight cut, cut out the opening with the craft knife, changing blades as necessary.

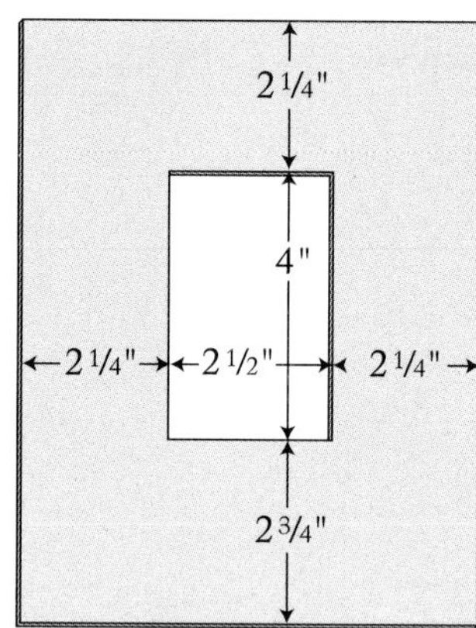

Photograph Opening Diagram

2. Enlarge the **Drapery Fabric Frame Stand Pattern** on page 213 as directed in "Enlarging Patterns" on page 238.

3. From one mat board, cut one frame stand. From the fabric, cut two frame stands, adding a ½-inch seam allowance all around to one stand. Also cut three 9 × 11-inch pieces, using the patterns in the fabric to best advantage. Press all fabric pieces.

4. Lay one piece of fabric, right side down, on a flat, clean surface. Place the mat board with the photograph opening in the center of the fabric.

5. Fold the top edge of the fabric to the back of the mat board, then glue it in place. Fold and glue the opposite edge in the same manner, keeping the tension even. Repeat for the other two sides of the frame, trimming the corners as needed for a smooth fit.

6. Lay the covered mat right side down. Using dressmaker's shears, make a small slit in the center of the fabric that covers the opening, then make mitered cuts to each corner of the opening; see **Diagram 1.** For best results, the cuts must be precise and go directly into the center of each corner.

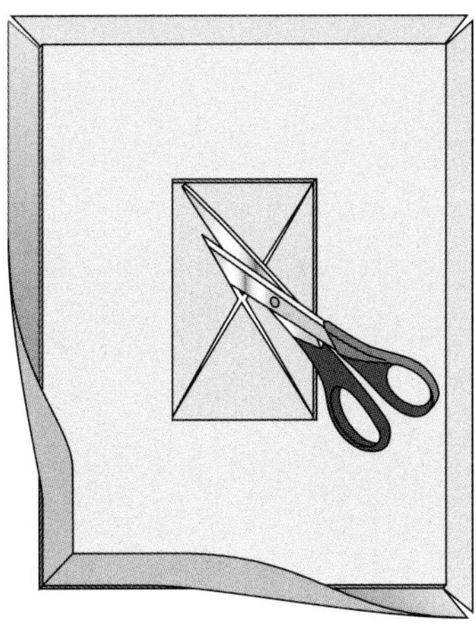

Diagram 1

7. Stretch the fabric flaps of the opening to the back of the frame and glue them in place. You may find it necessary to add a drop of glue at each corner. If you desire, press the clipped fabric corners with a warm iron. This forms the mat for the frame. Set it aside.

8. Repeat Steps 4 and 5 to cover the two remaining 7 x 9-inch pieces of mat board, omitting the opening reference. One covered mat board forms the frame base; the other is part of the frame back.

9. Cover one side of the frame stand with the larger frame stand fabric piece, leaving a 1-inch flap at the top and gluing the edges in place; see **Diagram 2.** Press under ¼ inch along the top edge. Press under ¼ inch around all sides of the remaining piece of stand fabric, then glue it to the underside of the stand to hide the raw edges of the previously glued fabric.

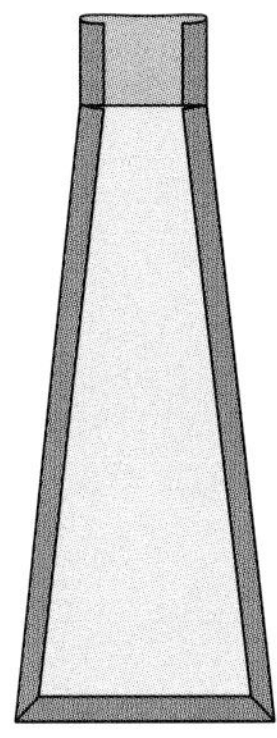

Diagram 2

10. Bend the flap to the wrong side of the frame stand. Center and glue the flap to the frame back, aligning the lower edges of the frame and frame stand. Glue about ¾ inch of one ribbon end to the frame stand and ¾ inch of the other end to the frame back. See **Diagram 3.** Let the glue dry thoroughly. This forms the assembled frame back.

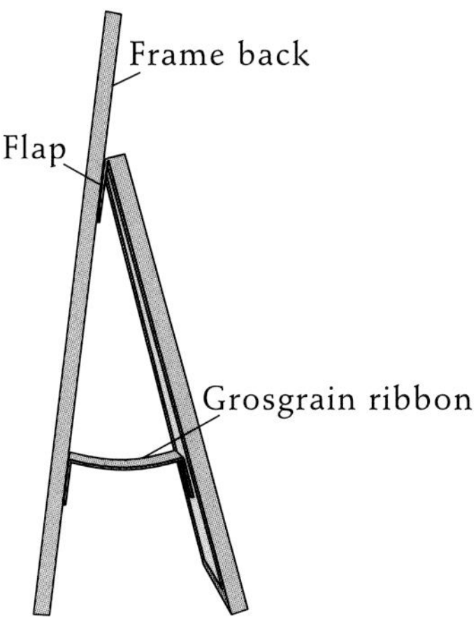

Diagram 3

11. To assemble the frame, glue the wrong side of the covered mat to the front of the frame base, leaving the bottom edge open so that a photograph may be inserted in the frame; do not allow the glue to spread into the window. Press under heavy books to seal, allowing the glue to dry thoroughly before proceeding.

12. Glue the wrong side of the frame base to the wrong side of the assembled frame back, then press under heavy books to seal.

Plaid Linen Frame

Size

8 x 10-inch frame with 3½ x 5½-inch opening

What You Do

1. Mark the photograph opening on one piece of mat board, as shown in the **Plaid Photograph Opening Diagram** on page 212. Using a ruler to ensure a straight cut, cut out the opening with the craft knife, changing blades as necessary.

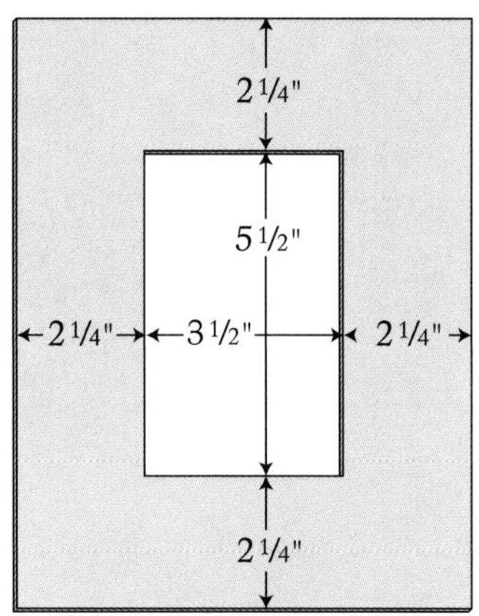

Plaid Photograph
Opening Diagram

2. Enlarge the **Plaid Linen Frame Stand Pattern** as directed in "Enlarging Patterns" on page 238.

3. From one mat board, cut one frame stand. From the fabric, cut two frame stands, adding a ½-inch seam allowance all around to one stand. Also cut three 10 × 12-inch pieces, using the lines in the plaid to best advantage. Press all fabric pieces.

4. Glue the fleece to the mat board with the photograph opening, then cut out the photograph opening by trimming away the fleece in the center.

5. Lay one piece of fabric, right side down, on a flat, clean surface. Place the fleece mat board, fleece side down, in the center of the fabric.

6. Repeat Steps 5 through 12 of the Drapery Fabric Frame on pages 210–211.

Fabric-Covered Frame and Vintage Mat

Size

6 × 8-inch frame with 4½ × 6½-inch opening

What You Do

1. Enlarge the **Fabric-Covered Frame Stand Pattern** as directed in "Enlarging Patterns" on page 238.

2. From one mat board, cut one frame stand. From the tan fabric, cut two 8 × 10-inch pieces for the frame and frame back. Also cut two frame stands, adding a ½-inch seam allowance all around to one stand. From the floral fabric, cut one 8 × 10-inch piece for the covered mat. Press all fabric pieces.

3. Lay one piece of tan fabric, right side down, on a flat, clean surface. Place the round-edged frame, right side down, in the center of the fabric. Fold the top edge of the fabric to the back of the frame, then glue it in place. Cut away any excess fabric. Fold and glue the opposite edge in the same manner, keeping the tension even. Repeat for the other two sides of the frame, trimming the fabric and corners as needed for a smooth fit.

4. Lay the partially finished covered frame right side down on a flat surface. Using the dressmaker's shears, make a small slit in the center of the fabric that covers the opening, then make mitered cuts to each corner of the opening; see the **Photograph Opening Diagram.** For best results, the cuts must be precise and go directly into the center of each corner.

Photograph Opening Diagram

5. Stretch the fabric flaps of the opening to the back of the frame and cut away the excess; glue the flaps in place. Add a drop of glue at each frame corner if necessary. Set the covered frame aside.

6. Lay another piece of tan fabric, right side down, on a flat surface. Place one piece of mat board in the center of the fabric. Fold the top edge of the fabric to the back of the mat board, then glue it in place. Fold and glue the opposite edge in the same manner, keeping the tension even. Repeat for the other two sides of the mat board, trimming the corners as needed. This forms the frame back.

7. Repeat Steps 9 and 10 of the Drapery Fabric Frame on page 211 to cover and attach the frame stand.

8. Trim the remaining piece of mat board to fit inside the covered frame. Repeat Step 6 to cover the mat with the floral fabric.

9. Glue the mat inside the frame. Then glue the wrong side of the frame back to the back of the assembled frame. Press under heavy books to seal, allowing the glue to dry thoroughly.

10. Use spray adhesive to adhere the photograph to the mat.

WHAT YOU NEED

FABRIC-COVERED FRAME AND VINTAGE MAT

- ⅜ yard of loosely woven tan fabric
- 7 × 9-inch piece of floral drapery fabric or similar vintage fabric
- Three 6 × 8-inch pieces of mat board
- 6 × 8-inch round-edged wooden frame without glass
- Hot glue gun and glue sticks
- Dressmaker's shears
- 4-inch length of ½-inch-wide tan grosgrain ribbon for the support
- Spray adhesive

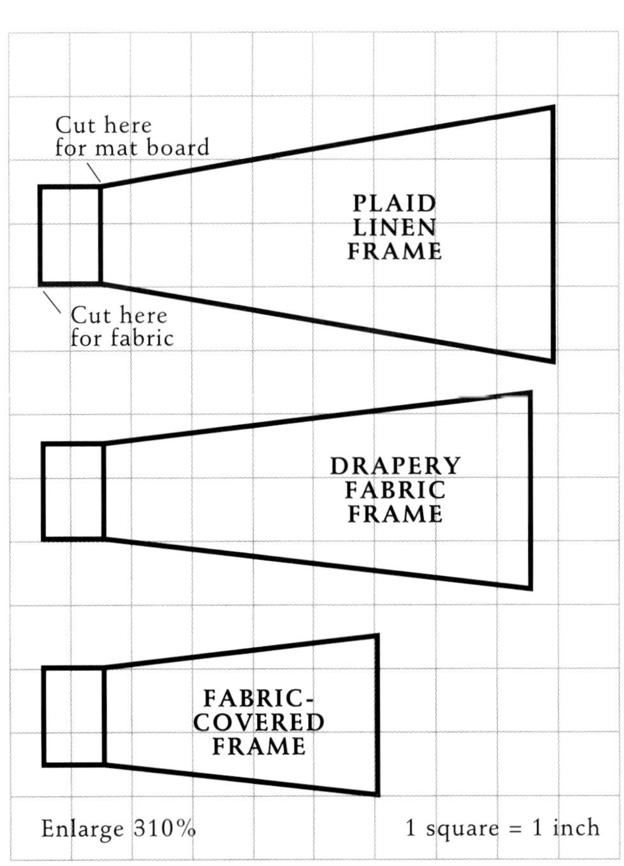

FRAME STAND PATTERNS

PROJECT POINTERS

If you've inherited yard goods or vintage fabrics, you should know how to care for them. Store vintage fabric in a clean, white pillowcase. Never keep fabric, antique or otherwise, in plastic bags since condensation will break down the fibers. Do not store fabrics in cedar chests or cardboard boxes because they cause "wood" burns.

Hand wash soiled vintage fabric in lukewarm water, add a mild detergent, and then gently knead it. Soak it for a short time, then drain the water and rinse until the water runs clear. Gently press the fabric to remove the excess water. Dry the fabric on a clothesline, out of direct sunlight.

Successful Bazaar Secrets

A craft bazaar can be both fun and profitable. And with the proper mix of preplanning and organization, sale days can also be stress-free. While the preparation may be slightly different for the craftsperson or social group, the hoped-for result is the same—big profits, great organization, and lots of fun!

Crafting Your Way to a Successful Bazaar

A Dream Takes Shape

The notion of earning money from your crafts always creates enthusiasm. But, along with the thoughts of profit and blockbuster sales is a dose of reality. It takes energy and a dedicated spirit to follow through with plans for a bazaar. And it requires a large time commitment to purchase supplies for and craft the projects that you plan to sell at your chosen bazaar. You'll need to plan your strategy and organize your crafting time to ensure that your participation is as successful and profitable as possible.

Use this section as your planning guide—follow the suggestions, adapting the information for your own use, and add your own know-how. Then, hitch your wagon to a star and enjoy the excitement of participating in a crafts bazaar.

Know Your Market

If you're just beginning to explore the lucrative possibilities that local bazaars hold, investigate your options before you participate. Search out area bazaars that are best suited to your crafts. Attend shows to decide whether your specialty is

Christmas wouldn't be Christmas without a holiday crafts bazaar. Each year, thousands of shoppers crowd churches, schools, and auxiliary halls, eager to purchase unique handcrafted ornaments, gifts, and decorations.

compatible with the other merchants' items. Is your work too upscale? Are others selling a similar product? Do the people attending look as though they would be your customers? It's acceptable to have similar items, but you'll need to have something different to draw the buyers to your table—an attractive display, an abundance of choices, or an unusual item that only you offer.

Solicit reactions from other crafters and local craft guilds as well. Most will be happy to discuss the customers' response to their work and the pros and cons of any given show. Any research you do is time well spent. Invest your time, effort, and money in shows that look promising; skip ones that have disappointed other crafters.

Bazaars charge a rental fee for the booth or space. Decide whether this fee is affordable by basing your decision on the sales you expect to generate. A more expensive table may mean that you'll be able to display higher-end crafts. A less expensive table with lower-end crafts may net more profits in the long run if the bazaar always attracts a big crowd. Only you can decide whether or not to take that calculated risk. Start small by renting space at a variety of suitable shows in as many markets as possible to learn how your work is received by the shoppers.

Hand-decorated gift bags and boxes add a personal touch to a shopper's purchase.

LOW-COST CRAFTS SOURCES

As you stockpile crafts to sell, you'll inevitably find that you're spending money without seeing an immediate return on your investment. To keep your outlay of cash to a minimum, you need to be creative in finding affordable craft supplies.

To help cut your overhead costs, explore discount markets and wholesale supply sources. Many companies will sell wholesale but only if you have a tax ID number from your state and are incorporated as a small business. To do this, contact your state's taxation department. It will also be necessary for you to purchase materials in volume from manufacturers in order to qualify for wholesale prices; the amount of items will vary from product to product, but be aware that some minimum orders will far exceed what you'll use as a bazaar crafter. Take stock of what you really need and make wise purchasing decisions.

Consult the *Craft & Needlework Age Annual Directory* for a compendium of companies that provide wholesale craft materials; see the "Buyer's Guide" on page 244 for addresses. This directory features alphabetical listings of every craft supply imaginable and a state-by-state listing of manufacturers.

If you're not ready to invest in volumes of felt, fiberfill, beads, or miscellaneous notions to create your products, then consider other ways of gathering inexpensive materials. Watch for seasonal sales at craft supply shops where markdowns run as high as 50 percent. For fabrics, search out remnants from local upholsterers and seamstresses. Contact your local lumberyard for small scraps of wood for toys and ornaments.

If you're adventurous, explore tag sales and secondhand shops for old clothes in interesting fabrics to recycle into vintage-look projects. It takes a dedicated and creative crafter to see that a torn velvet dress can become an elegant Victorian stocking or that a mod '70s disco shirt can become the base fabric for a stuffed toy or tree trim.

Hang delicate ornaments like these Crocheted Choirboys from a branch of a small tabletop tree to add a festive air to your booth.

Attracting the Buyer

Unusual displays, inexpensive-yet-clever projects, and extra-special crafts that double as conversation pieces are all good ways to attract buyers to your booth. Like bees to honey, the devoted crafts aficionado has an eye for projects that are interesting, imaginative, and original. If you can provide these ingredients, then you're sure to find your area swarming with customers.

A theme or an attractive, well-thought-out display is another surefire way to bring potential buyers to your booth. Victorian, country, nifty fifties, romantic florals, bright kid colors, animals, kitchen crafts, and art deco are all good themes. (See the sample booth setups on pages 220–223.) Decide which is best suited to your crafting style, then accent your booth or table with one or two large similarly themed props to enliven your display and set off your assigned area from those around you. You can create interest in front of your booth with props as well. A wicker laundry basket filled with country-style crafts or a small velvet-covered ottoman displaying Victorian-style needlecrafts will add credence to your theme.

To set up an appropriate booth, you will need to know at the outset what is provided by the bazaar organizers in the booth rental fee. Most organizations provide only the space; some, like a church or school, will probably provide tables, chairs, and possibly wall space. You should consider decorative display accents like freestanding screens or hinged walls of painted plywood, fiberboard, Peg-Board, or fabric to block off other vendors; these screens or walls can also serve as hanging displays. For an outdoor show, an awning, canopy, or tent are essential all-weather protectors for crafts and seller alike.

Shelves, cabinets, or artificial Christmas trees will also set a mood. Glass display cases may also be a wise investment for showcasing handmade jewelry or small glass pieces. Calculate the amount of table surface available in your booth and have fabrics to cover the top and front. By having an attractive table covering, you can disguise the storage of crafts, wraps, and bags under the table while still presenting a clean and uncluttered image out front.

Shoppers love freebies, so take advantage of their willingness to approach a booth offering giveaways. Easy stenciled bookmarks or pretty pinecone ornaments can be displayed in a basket on the corner of your table; be sure to make a sign that says "Help Yourself." These freebies cost next to nothing to make but may engage shoppers long enough for them to browse through your craft offerings. A napkin-lined basket filled to the rim with hand-decorated Christmas cookies may entice a hungry craft lover into your booth. It may just result in a nice sale!

If you've themed your booth, get in the spirit and dress in the style you've chosen for your crafts. Victorian projects may dictate a high-collared velvet dress and a pretty brooch, or you may want to model one of your own garments if you have a handcrafted clothing booth. If your specialty is Santa crafts, make or rent a bright red St. Nick ensemble to delight holiday shoppers.

Making the Day Stress-Free

Just prior to the day of the sale, it's wise to have a dry run for setting up and taking down your booth. You should also test-fit the booth supplies and packaged crafts into your car. You'll avoid last-minute problems and aggravations if you know ahead of time that it will take two trips to deliver everything to the bazaar. It would also be helpful to have your crafts in handled boxes or bags to make toting them easier. You may need to enlist the aid of a friend with a roomy vehicle or consider renting a van for sale weekends.

It's a good idea to take along a friend, neighbor, spouse, or teenager on the day of the sale. It often takes more than one pair of hands to set up your booth and arrange your display in the short time you'll have to get everything ready prior to opening. And having someone with you can help out during those busy times or for those necessary breaks. Make a checklist of everything that you need to bring to the bazaar, including lunches, drinks, and snacks for yourself and any of your helpers. Make a return-trip checklist as well so you're sure not to leave behind any of your belongings.

Record keeping can be an important aspect of a successful booth, so plan to have a box or expandable file for your notes. It is also helpful for storing all of your receipts from the day's sales for tax purposes. Keep notes on what sells and what didn't sell and jot down why, if you know.

You should also keep the name and phone number of the bazaar organizer in the event you decide to rent space at next year's bazaar. Write down any other after-sale notes that give insight into your success or shortcomings or any problems that may have arisen during the day—ran out of dollar bills, customers wanted smaller bags, lots of requests for Victorian or baby projects, and the like. Making use of these records can help you to plan for a much more successful bazaar the next time around.

You're bound to be caught off guard with forgotten supplies or demanding customers at your first few bazaars, but, with experience, you'll be able to pinch-hit in any situation.

Incorporate vintage props into your booth to create an eye-catching display. Antique shutters are an ideal backdrop for the assorted Teatime Ornaments.

Setting Up Shoppe with a Victorian Flair

The rich look of Victoriana provides a wealth of possibilities when displaying crafts in a bazaar booth. Drape an elegant cloth over your sales table to create a soft surface, then hang a luscious fabric backdrop to visually separate your booth and the next one.

To add the illusion of height, consider a small tabletop tree or display rack to highlight ornaments or smaller handcrafted objects. Tuck similar projects, like embellished pillows, into a stylish wooden box or elegant woven basket. Display one of each style or color to give customers a wide selection. As soon as a particular item sells, be sure to restock the area to avoid lost sales. If you take special orders for color and size variations, be sure to post a small sign or sandwich board nearby.

Group multiples made in similar fabrics, like the sachets and covered boxes, in different areas of your display so passers-by can distinguish one craft from another.

JOSEPH MÖHR, 1818
Silent Night
(Stille Nacht)
FRANZ
Angels, from the Realms of

Creating a Cozy Country Display

The basic country booth begins with weathered wood and homespun linens. Bring in a distressed or painted cupboard with shelves as a focal point for display. Gather a collection of country baskets and small trunks and fill each to the brim with your crafted ornaments, toys, and trims. For wearables, a country mirror will aid in sales as well as provide atmosphere and charm in your booth.

On a more rustic note, construct shelves from old buckets or bricks and barn wood, or pile bales of straw as a shelving system to show off your wares. Display quick and easy crafts in multiples to let customers know that these items are highly affordable and perfect Secret Santa and coworker gifts.

For your one-of-a-kind designs, take the time to set up a small vignette, like standing the puppets in a wooden case. That way, they'll draw the attention of bazaar buyers. For items that will be handled frequently, have a sample on display and keep your stock below the table. Freshen up the sample after each show and replace frayed ribbons or resew loose buttons to keep it in tip-top shape.

PRICING AND TAGGING YOUR CRAFTS

Once you've decided on which shows to do, you will need to set prices for your work that are fair, competitive, and profitable. Comparison shop at other crafters' booths who produce a similar type of product before you decide. To reach a fair price, you will have to take into account the cost of the materials, your time involved, and a percentage of any overhead you may incur; booth rental fees, car expenses, price tags, and bags are just a few things you'll need to consider. Remember, you are doing this to make money and you'll need to decide how much money you want to make when setting a price.

Almost any crafter will tell you that you cannot base your price on an hourly fee (the real time it took you to make the piece), particularly with a large, time-consuming piece like needlepoint, crochet, or a wood carving. Hourly pricing simply becomes too costly and you'll be left holding your piece at the end of the sale. Often, these pieces are merely a labor of love, but you can also consider them a drawing card; a shopper may purchase other less-expensive items instead of the larger one when browsing in your booth. It might be better to ask yourself what you really need to compensate you for the supplies and still make a profit. A rule of thumb that works for most crafters is to double or triple the cost of the materials, especially if you paid retail for them.

If you're selling simple toys, decorative objects, or ornaments made from scraps, leftovers, and inexpensive materials, you can sometimes increase the charge slightly to compensate for those larger-sale items. Most customers, for instance, won't think anything of spending $3 to $5 for an ornament, depending on its appeal and originality; it may have cost you only pennies and a few minutes to produce it. Remember, too, that an imaginative, simple item like a cut-paper ornament or felt beanbag that's marked for 50¢ or $1 might entice shoppers to your table.

In this era of mass-marketed products and assembly-line decor, bazaar shoppers search for the personal touch when buying holiday crafts.

Forget boring gummed price stickers! Get creative and craft price tags with impact. Cut decorative giftwrap, handmade papers, and posterboard into small shapes and accent with holiday bells, antique buttons, metallic pens, and satin ribbons. Handmade price tags are the crowning touch for the successful bazaar crafter.

Consider a handmade tag for each craft that lists the price, describes its care or use, and/or lets the buyer know where she can purchase more!

For just pennies, you can create a variety of hangtags for your salable items. Experiment with rubber stamps or metallic markers to liven up your tags. Reach into your notions drawer for jingle bells, star studs, and odd buttons to add a crafty touch. Fuse elegant or festive fabrics to posterboard to add an air of prestige to a sophisticated craft, or comb-paint bright price tags that would appeal to the hip, younger buyers. Use up short lengths of ribbon, thread, or yarn to hang the tags from your crafts.

Try to create tags that complement your booth style. If you craft rustic bazaar items, use simple, natural color tags. If your booth set-up features elegant ribbon crafts and one-of-a-kind designs, your price tags should be just as stunning.

"Wrapping" Up a Sale

For your first few bazaars, use newspaper and small bags saved from the grocery store to package the buyer's purchase. Wrap the selected item in white tissue, then newspaper, and add a bright red ribbon to dress up the look. Small paper bags can be tied with two strands of raffia to keep the purchase safe. Spend a little time on the details to make your personal contact with the buyer a memorable experience.

As your bazaar business picks up, you should consider a more decorative approach to your bags and wrappings. Inexpensive brown or white paper bags dressed up with your business name will add a touch of class. Simply print or write the name on the bag with a marker, adding a creative flourish if you like. A purchased stamp or even a potato print with indelible ink is another way to personalize your bags and provide free carry-around advertising for yourself. White or colored tissue paper can be purchased by the ream at paper or school supply stores.

Invest a few dollars in business cards if you are planning to devote a lot of energy to your crafts business. Stack the cards at the edge of your booth so shoppers who are buying or browsing can contact you to order or inquire about your wares. And always remember to stick a business card in with the purchase since it may encourage special orders.

It goes without saying that a friendly crafter is probably a prosperous crafter. Remember that you are your own public relations representative when you're selling crafts at a bazaar. A cheery personality behind the table or in a booth can attract customers, talk up a particular item, and even help cement a sale.

Manpower

If you're part of an organization that has decided to host a benefit crafts bazaar, your first item of business should be to elect a chairperson who will be responsible for overseeing the event. The chairperson should be someone who is well organized, able to designate duties with a friendly authority, and can devote a good deal of time to this undertaking.

Committees are another important element in any successful bazaar. It is helpful to have at least three people on each committee depending on the duties of the committee and the size and scope of the sale. Nominate people who are willing to work together toward a common goal, and elect one person as the head of each committee who will report to and meet with the chairperson. Essential committees may include booth registration, decorations, refreshments, publicity, and, of course, cleanup.

Have the organizing committee begin by researching and choosing a date for the bazaar. Are there any other bazaars or crafts fairs in the area scheduled for that date? Will a competitive event pull buyers and crafts vendors away from your show? Is there a major sports event or concert that would interfere with attendance? What about other smaller local events? Will they take away from or add to the number of potential attendees? Address each concern and choose an alternate date if necessary.

The booth registration committee plays the most important role of all the committees. Its objective is to notify crafts vendors of the upcoming sale; set booth rental fees; design the placement of booths and establish traffic patterns within the school, church, or auxiliary hall; and learn the particular building codes and special parking requirements, if any.

The decorations and refreshments committees are responsible for creating a pleasant holiday atmosphere for shoppers, and it's up to the publicity committee to get the word out to the community about the bazaar. Recruit as many volunteers as possible to help out after the event; you're sure to need "un"decorators, broom sweepers, and trash removers. The cleanup committee may not be the most glamorous committee, but it serves a vital role in determining if your organization will be permitted to use the same facilities for a future event.

Crowd-Pleasing Ideas

Your organization may wish to host special events during the bazaar to attract and amuse shoppers. Consider a kid's crafting or play area, a jewelry-making table, a colonial cut-paper silhouettes booth, a gift wrap booth, and live entertainment.

For a special holiday kid's corner, have volunteers sew simple felt stockings; junior customers can purchase one for a dollar and decorate it with member-donated buttons, trims, ribbons, beads, and puff paints. Another child-oriented possibility is a supervised play area for youngsters to use while parents browse. Get members to donate games and toys, or gather together trunks full of old clothes for dress-up.

It would be best to contain the children's activities in a separate room, making supervision

Keep younger bazaar browsers occupied at a make-it, take-it booth. Stock the booth with simple felt stockings, glittery sequins, colorful pom-poms, tiny gift bows, easy-to-use fabric paints, and cheerful holiday ribbons.

easier; enlisting the help of various professionals, like teachers and youth counselors, would be ideal. It's important for parents to know that their kids are well cared for and that knowledgeable assistance is at hand. Have at least one volunteer who is qualified and experienced in CPR and other safety procedures in the event of an emergency.

A jewelry-making booth would be popular among teens at your bazaar. Have group members donate old costume jewelry that can be unstrung and recycled into new creations. Be sure to have plenty of narrow ribbon or cord on hand for stringing the beads.

All it takes for a silhouettes booth is black paper, sharp scissors, and a bright light. Volunteers with a moderate amount of artistic ability can easily trace and cut out the shadow of the seated model to create a treasured keepsake for buyers.

A gift wrap booth is a great way to earn extra cash for your benefit. Keep your options simple, but offer a tasteful wrap for busy gift-givers. Ordinary white butcher paper can be transformed into smashing gift wraps with narrow satin ribbons or pinecones and twine.

Sign up local musical groups to perform at scheduled intervals; they may even be willing to donate their time. A magician or roving juggler is another source of amusement for your customers. Any added attraction will delight the customers, keep them there longer, and perhaps inspire them to spend more.

A Chance to Raise More Money

A crafts raffle is an excellent way to earn extra money for your organization, if it is legal within your state. A committee member should investigate the legality of such an event by contacting your state tax department. Many times you can follow the example of past exhibits in regard to raffles, but double-checking is worth the time.

Given the go-ahead for the raffle, you will need to decide on the type of prize or craft to offer. The intended project should be something of notable quality, beauty, and general appeal. Perhaps there is a talented crafter in your organization who is willing to donate one of her or his pieces to the cause—a knitted or crocheted afghan, a needlepoint pillow, a cross-stitch sampler, an

intriguing woodworking piece, a patchwork quilt, or an appliquéd wallhanging. The "Bringing in the Tree" Wallhanging, shown here and on page 232, is the perfect raffle prize for a smaller bazaar or craft fair. Another possibility, if there is time, is a group project by several crafters in your organization. This could take the form of an heirloom-quality needlepoint rug, a traditionally patterned quilt, or a basket of handcrafted items.

Once the raffle prize has been selected, determine a value for the piece, set a dollar goal, and price the chances accordingly. Your organization should also decide how to use the money that's raised during the raffle. Ideally, it should be designated for a special project like refurbishing a building, cleaning up an overgrown playground, or assisting a family in need. It's important to let raffle ticket buyers know how the funds will be spent so they can feel like they have had a hand in the success of the project.

The prize should be prominently displayed at the door of the sale or on a platform so it's visible to all shoppers. Volunteer raffle sellers should be posted throughout the room with tickets and a photo of the project. Raffle tickets can be printed professionally in advance or simply be slips of paper with special handwritten raffle numbers and a space for the name, address, and phone number of the purchaser. A corresponding slip with the same information will need to be placed into the raffle drawing box.

Set a time for the drawing and inform ticket buyers so they can be present if they so choose. When the hour arrives, gather the crowd around, and pull the winning ticket!

Publicity

Publicity is perhaps the single most important factor in producing a successful bazaar. Once the date, time, and theme of the event are decided, artistic individuals can begin creating signboards and flyers to distribute and post prior to the sale. Make your announcements eye-catching by adding a holiday motif or by accenting a black-and-white poster with colored markers or paints. Be sure to list all the necessary information on the poster, including the name of the bazaar, date, time, place, name of a contact person who can supply additional details to an interested shopper, and the group or organization that will receive the proceeds.

In addition to flyers, your publicity should encompass newspapers, radio, or possibly even TV exposure. Perhaps someone in your group is affiliated in some way with one of these media and can get free or low-cost advertising for your bazaar. If not, collect what funds you can to invest in a small amount of advertising. The more exposure your event has, the larger the crowds.

You may even be able to attract shoppers by choosing a theme for your organization's bazaar. By combining your craft show with an antiques sale, for instance, you can count on additional traffic through your bazaar; ordinarily, most antique buffs wouldn't attend a craft show, but they'll certainly browse through the aisles of crafts if they're already at the sale. Or you can choose to style your event after an old-fashioned country bazaar or host a juried arts and crafts exhibit as a way to bring shoppers in the front door. Holiday themes are always appropriate and inviting and succeed in getting buyers in the spirit of the season. Consider a White Christmas Crafts Show or a Twelfth Night Bazaar or a blockbuster Red and Green Christmas Bazaar, then decorate the hall or church accordingly. Your decorations committee can coordinate colors and decorations for group-sponsored events as well as assist in providing the appropriately colored supplies for the publicity committee's activities.

Display your raffle prize in a prominent location, such as at the front entrance to the bazaar, close to the refreshment area, or on a stage or riser. Position raffle ticket sellers at small tables throughout the vendor area so long lines of ticket buyers don't discourage others who wish to take a chance.

Home-baked goods are always popular with busy bazaar-goers. "Wrap" breads, pies, and cookies with ribbons and garlands for a prepackaged gift idea.

REFRESHMENTS

Entice holiday shoppers to your organization's refreshment stand by offering a variety of tasty food and drink to enjoy while shopping or as take-along goodies. Recruit some of the fine cooks or bakers in your organization to donate several dozen cookies and brownies, as well as pies, cakes, and pastries. Bars and cookies can be sold by the piece or by the dozen and pies and cakes by the slice or as a whole. If possible, provide tables and chairs for weary buyers to sit, relax, and enjoy their yummy purchases.

If you have access to cooking facilities, then your refreshment committee can expand the menu to include a variety of foods. Consider simple, hearty sandwiches on slices of home-baked bread. In the winter, bazaar shoppers would appreciate piping-hot chowder or chili. Perhaps a member of your group will offer a secret recipe for the event and other members can donate the ingredients; you may want to contact grocery stores in your area to see if they would be willing to donate things, especially if the refreshment money is going to a charitable cause. Keep the menu simple; offer only a few selections to avoid kitchen confusion on the day of the sale.

Today's families are eating healthier, so bazaar shoppers may appreciate low-calorie, low-cholesterol fare as well. Finger sandwiches, vegetable sticks, and a fresh fruit cup may be just as popular as the traditional hot dog or bowl of hearty soup.

Keep the drink selection to a minimum as well. Coffee and tea, sodas, juice, cider, and bottled water are the staples for a well-stocked refreshment bar. You may wish, depending on the theme, to offer nonalcoholic beer and wine to your customers. Contact a local distributor to see if you can purchase beverages at a discount. During the sale, have plenty of plastic glasses, napkins, and trash receptacles on hand.

Keep your offerings affordable since holiday craft bazaars tend to attract families and older folks. Beverages shouldn't be priced higher than retail outlets and treat prices should be low enough to entice hungry buyers into purchasing more than one goodie. While a refreshment stand should see a profit, remember that one of its goals is to provide an additional perk to the shoppers attending the bazaar that day.

LAST-MINUTE PREPARATIONS

A well-organized bazaar committee should have few surprises in the days preceding an event. But, even when plans have been finalized weeks in advance, certain last-minute tasks will need the chairperson's attention.

A checklist of to-do's is always a helpful guide and should include items like obtaining the building's key from the manager or caretaker, arranging for heat or air-conditioning to be turned on a few hours in advance, and picking up change at a local bank for the organization-run booths the day before the bazaar.

Have each committee call its volunteers three days prior to the sale to remind them of the agreed-upon responsibilities and hours of service. Specify a time to meet for last-minute instructions the day of the sale; you'll need some volunteers for crowd control because there are always early birds who want to get a jump on the "best" craft items.

If possible, have the booth registration committee set up the tables (if they are provided) a day or two ahead of the sale and mark the booth perimeters with masking tape. That way, bottlenecks or unclear traffic patterns can be worked out ahead of time, instead of on bazaar day. Number each table clearly so the vendors can easily find their space as they enter to set up their wares.

It is also helpful to have a few eager souls (like husbands and teenagers) on hand to fill the important job of acting as gofers or to pinch-hit as problems arise. Make sure that everyone knows who these important people are and that all volunteers are identifiable in some fashion: a badge or sticker, a bright ribbon, a colorful pin, or a hat.

Remember that bazaar crafting and selling is hard work and that glitches will occur. But, by being prepared and well organized, you can handle most of the unpleasantries and concerns ahead of time. On bazaar day, you'll be able to answer questions and make decisions on the spot—things that vendors and shoppers notice! So get ready to have a busy and profitable day!

Your holiday bazaar's refreshment table should overflow with delectable desserts and soothing beverages. Offer individual items for sale on trays and platters that echo the bazaar's theme.

"Bringing in the Tree" Wallhanging

Let raffle ticket buyers take a fond trip back to a simpler time. As dusk falls, this country family enjoys the annual ritual of a horse-drawn sleigh ride to choose their Christmas tree. Display this stunning raffle prize right inside the bazaar's front door so shoppers can buy tickets on their way in and out!

WHAT YOU NEED

- 2⅛ yards of maroon print fabric for the border, backing, hanging sleeve, and binding
- ⅝ yard of bleached muslin for the appliqué base
- ⅛ yard of white solid fabric for the corner blocks
- ⅛ yard of black solid fabric for the corner blocks
- 3 yards of fusible web
- ⅛ yard of medium blue solid fabric for the upper sky
- ⅛ yard of light blue solid fabric for the lower sky
- ½ yard of white-on-white print fabric for snowbanks #1, #3, and #4
- ¼ yard of white-on-ecru print fabric for snowbanks #2 and #5
- ⅛ yard of dark brown print fabric for trees #1, #3, and #5
- ⅛ yard of medium brown print fabric for trees #2 and #4
- ¼ yard of green-on-green print fabric for the grove of trees, small tree, and tree middle
- ¼ yard of green-on-green print fabric for the treetop and tree bottom
- Scrap of dark gray print fabric for the house
- Scrap of pale yellow solid fabric for the house windows
- Scrap of dark red print fabric for the barn back
- Scrap of dark red plaid fabric for the barn side
- Scrap of dark gray print fabric for the barn roof
- ¼ yard of tan print fabric for the horse front and right front leg
- ¼ yard of medium tan print fabric for the horse derriere
- Scrap of dark brown-and-gold print fabric for the mane, tail, and hooves
- Scrap of dark red print fabric for the sleigh
- Scrap of pale gray print fabric for the hoof prints
- Scrap of dark blue print fabric for the parents' sleigh blanket
- Scrap of medium blue solid fabric for the mother's hat brim
- Scrap of light blue solid fabric for the mother's hat
- Scrap of red print fabric for the father's cap
- Scrap of dark red print fabric for the father's cap brim
- Scrap of dark green print fabric for the father's muffler
- Scrap of red solid fabric for the younger brother's hat
- Scrap of red print fabric for the younger brother's hat brim
- Scrap of green plaid fabric for the younger brother's coat
- Scrap of green print fabric for the older brother's hat
- Scrap of dark green print fabric for the older brother's hat brim
- Scrap of gold solid fabric for the older brother's scarf
- Scrap of red print fabric for the older brother's coat
- Scrap of peach solid fabric for the brothers' faces
- Scrap of dark blue print for the brothers' sleigh blanket
- 20 × 24-inch piece of tear-away stabilizer
- Matching sewing thread for each fabric
- One skein each of black, peach, red, and green embroidery floss for the embroidered accents
- 29½ × 33½-inch piece of fleece

SIZE

28 × 32 inches

WHAT YOU DO

Notes: Wash, dry, and press all your fabrics before beginning this project. All seam allowances are ¼ inch.

1. Enlarge the **"Bringing in the Tree" Wallhanging Patterns** on pages 236–237 as directed in "Enlarging Patterns" on page 238.

2. From the maroon print, cut two 5½ × 22½-inch pieces for the top and bottom border strips, two 5½ × 18½-inch pieces for the side border strips, one 29½ × 33½-inch piece for the backing, and one 4½ × 30-inch piece for the hanging sleeve. Also cut one 2½ × 124-inch bias strip, piecing as necessary and referring to "Cutting Bias Strips" on page 238. Using the bias strip, make bias binding, referring to "Making Bias Binding" on page 239. From the muslin, cut one 18½ × 22½-inch piece for the appliqué base. From the white and black solids, cut eight 3-inch squares each. Set these pieces aside for now.

3. Following the manufacturer's directions, fuse the fusible web to the remaining fabrics. Trace the mirror image, or reverse, of each appliqué onto the paper side of the fusible web and cut it out as follows: From the medium blue solid, cut one upper sky. From the light blue solid, cut one lower sky. From the white-on-white print, cut one snowbank #1, one snowbank #3, and one snowbank #4. From the white-on-ecru print, cut one snowbank #2 and one snowbank #5.

From the dark brown print, cut one tree #1, one tree #3, and one tree #5. From the medium brown print, cut one tree #2 and one tree #4. From the first green-on-green print, cut one tree bottom, one treetop, and one small tree. From the second green-on-green print, cut one tree middle and one grove of trees. From the dark gray print, cut one house.

From the pale yellow solid, cut four house windows. From the dark red print, cut one barn back. From the dark red plaid, cut one barn side. From the dark gray print, cut one barn roof. From the tan print, cut one horse front and right front leg. From the medium tan print, cut one horse derriere. From the dark brown-and-gold print, cut one mane, one tail, one left front hoof, one left rear hoof, and one right rear hoof. From the dark red print, cut one sleigh. From the pale gray print, cut one of each hoof print. From the dark blue print, cut one parents' sleigh blanket.

From the medium blue solid, cut one mother's hat brim. From the light blue solid, cut one mother's hat. From the red print, cut one father's cap. From the dark red print, cut one father's cap brim. From the dark green print, cut one father's muffler. From the red solid fabric, cut one younger brother's hat. From the red print, cut one younger brother's hat brim. From the green plaid, cut one younger brother's coat. From the green print, cut one older brother's hat. From the dark green print, cut one older brother's hat brim.

From the gold solid, cut one older brother's scarf. From the red print, cut one older brother's coat. From the peach solid, cut one younger brother's face and one older brother's face. From the dark blue print, cut one brothers' sleigh blanket. Remove the paper backing from the appliqué pieces.

4. Center the appliqué pieces on the appliqué base, referring to the **Appliqué Placement Diagram,** layering as indicated by the dashed lines on the pattern pieces. Fuse in place, following the manufacturer's directions.

Appliqué Placement Diagram

5. Center and pin the tear-away stabilizer to the back of the appliqué base. Using matching thread and a closely spaced zigzag stitch, machine appliqué all edges of the appliqués.

6. Refer to the **Accent Stitching Diagram** and "Stitch Details" on page 243. Using two strands of black floss, work the reins in stem stitch and the horse's eye in satin stitch. Using two strands of peach floss, work straight stitches for the brothers' eyes and mouths. Using two strands of red floss, work straight stitch tassels on the younger brother's hat and father's cap; use green floss for the older brother's hat tassel. Machine satin stitch the bridle with brown thread, the sleigh runners and tracks with black thread, and the upper window on the house with yellow thread. Remove the stabilizer by tearing it away.

Accent Stitching Diagram

7. With the right sides together and raw edges even, sew one 5½ × 18½-inch border strip to each side of the appliqué base, as shown in **Diagram 1.** Press the seams toward the border.

Diagram 1

8. Referring to **Diagram 2,** sew each white square to a black square. Sew each white/black unit to another white/black unit to create a four-patch checkerboard. Press the seams open.

9. Sew a four-patch checkerboard to each end of the 5½ × 22½-inch top and bottom border strips, as shown in **Diagram 3.** Press the seams open.

Diagram 2

Diagram 3

10. With the right sides together and raw edges even, sew one assembled checkerboard border to the top and bottom of the center panel; see **Diagram 4.** Press the seams toward the border.

Diagram 4

11. Place the backing wrong side up on a flat surface. Place the fleece on top of the backing, then place the appliquéd wallhanging right side up on top of the backing and fleece. Trim away any excess batting and backing. Pin or baste the three layers together.

12. Quilt in the ditch on the border seams.

13. Attach the bias binding as directed in "Attaching Binding" on page 239.

14. With the right sides together, fold the hanging sleeve in half lengthwise and sew along the long edge. Turn under ¼ inch, then another ¼ inch along each end and hem. Turn the sleeve right side out, then pin it to the back of the wallhanging just below the binding. Slip-stitch it in place along both long edges.

PROJECT POINTERS

Since the raffle prize can generate a tremendous amount of income for your organization, take advantage of every opportunity for additional funds. If local ordinances allow, distribute raffle ticket books to members of your organization for prebazaar sales. Give everyone a goal of how many tickets to sell, instead of just handing out books and having them returned unsold.

Try to keep raffle ticket prices at $1 or less since most browsers don't mind parting with that amount.

As a group, decide how the funds raised will be used; for example, people may be more willing to buy if they know the money will buy new books for the school's library or buy groceries for needy families at the holidays.

On bazaar day, don't wait until the last few minutes to pull the winning ticket. Ideally, the winner should be drawn about an hour before the bazaar ends. This way, you can still have a crowd present to share in the excitement of the drawing.

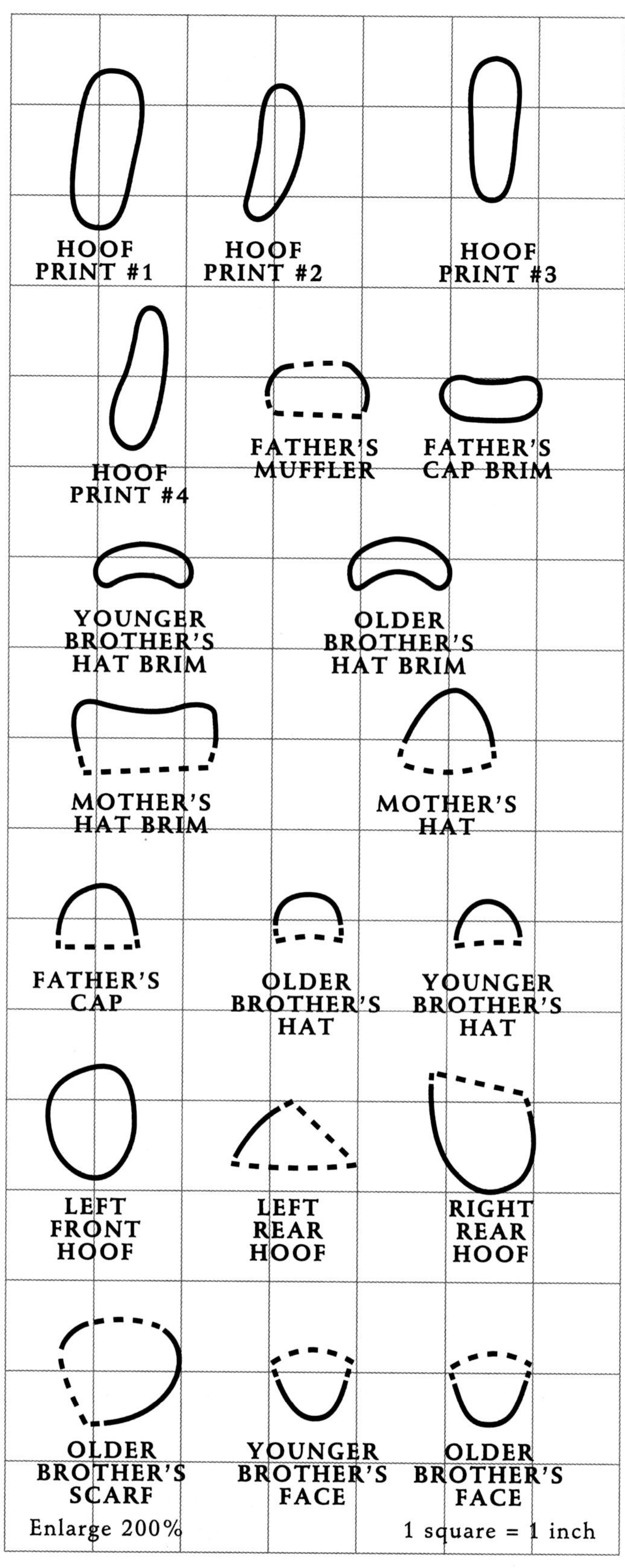

"BRINGING IN THE TREE"
WALLHANGING PATTERNS

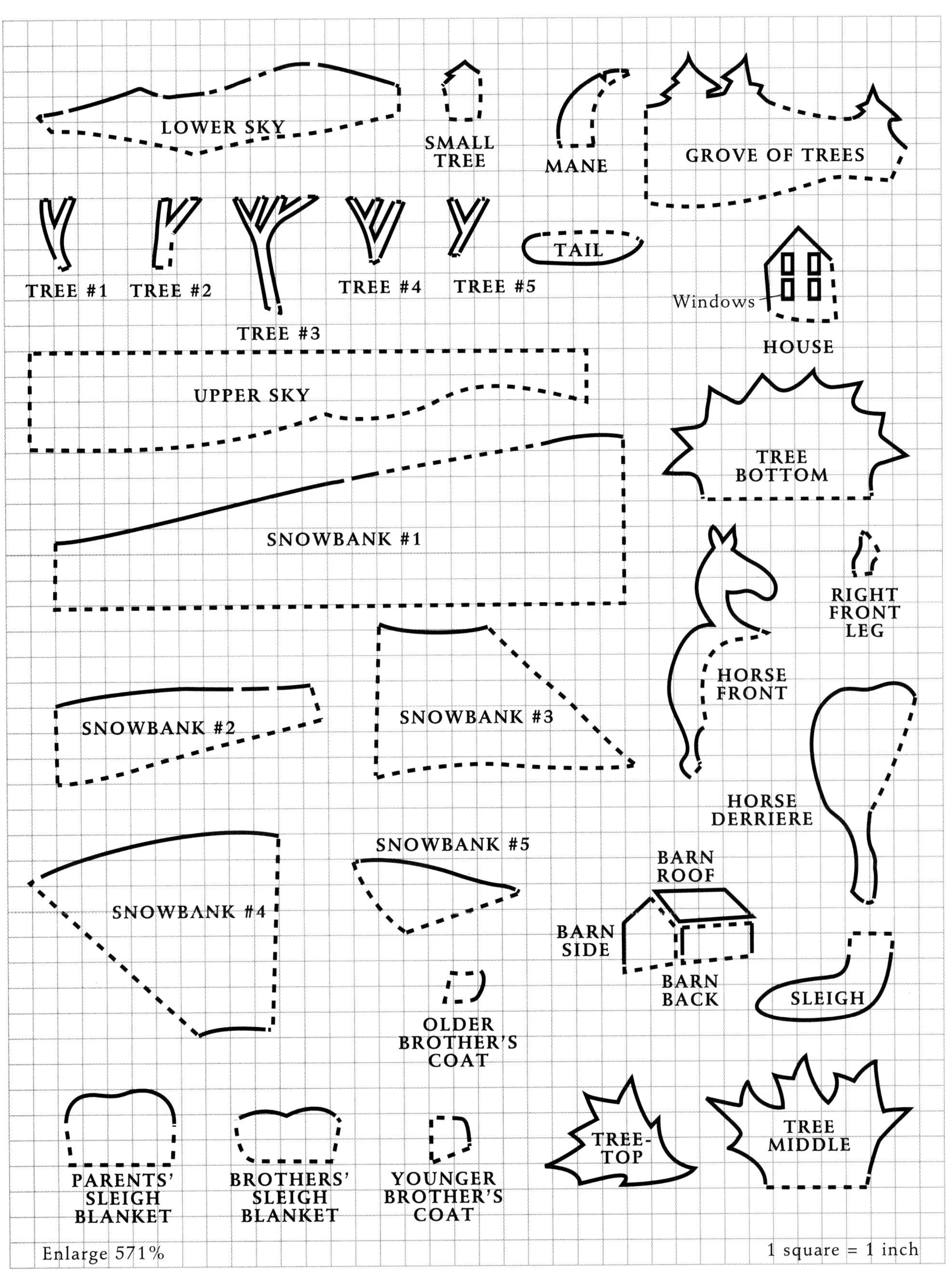

"BRINGING IN THE TREE" WALLHANGING PATTERNS

Needlecraft Basics

Crafting for a church, school, or charitable bazaar should be quick, easy, and inexpensive. These projects were designed to be all three of these things. Experienced crafters can look at the projects in the photographs and reproduce them without a blink. Less-experienced crafters need a few hints and detailed directions to speed them along. This brief, yet handy, resource provides additional information for the crafter who's new to the art of "bazaaring" or for someone who's a little out of practice with their sewing and crafting skills.

Craft Sewing

If you can thread a sewing-machine needle, you're on your way to success with the projects in this book. Bazaar crafts are easy to make and require only basic sewing knowledge, allowing even the beginner or young crafter an opportunity for fun and profits.

Preparing Full-Size Patterns: As space permitted, patterns for some projects are given full size. Simply trace the full-size patterns for use.

Enlarging Patterns: Most projects have patterns reduced on a grid, because of the limitations of the page size. To prepare the patterns that are presented on a grid, enlarge the gridded patterns on a photocopy machine at the percentage given, or until the boxes measure 1 square inch.

Marking Pattern Pieces: Mark around your patterns onto your fabric with a dressmaker's pencil, No. 2 graphite pencil, or water- or air-erasable fabric marker. Mark the needed pieces one at a time on the fabric, leaving a small space between pieces for cutting.

Transferring Markings: Following the manufacturer's directions, use dressmaker's carbon paper or erasable fabric marker to transfer accent lines from a pattern to the fabric.

Sewing Seams: With the right sides placed together (unless otherwise directed) and raw edges aligned, sew the two fabrics to be joined, working backstitches at each seam end to secure the thread. Clip the excess thread.

Clipping Curves and Grading Seams: After sewing a curved seam, it is necessary to clip the seam allowance for ease in turning the piece to the right side. Cut perpendicular from the fabric edge to the seam line, being careful not to cut your stitches. Grade seam allowances to reduce bulk by trimming away one seam allowance so that it is narrower than the other, giving a layered appearance.

Cutting Bias Strips: Some projects feature piping or binding as an accent or a finishing technique. The directions for these crafts include at least 3/8 yard of fabric for cutting the bias strips for the piping or binding. It's easiest to use a rotary cutter, rotary ruler, and rotary mat for precision cutting, but a ruler, protractor, pencil, and dressmaker's shears will work just as well. Square off the end of your fabric before cutting your bias strips so you are working on the straight of grain.

If rotary cutting, align the 45-degree-angle line on your ruler with the bottom edge of your fabric to make your first cut. Trim off the triangular corner along the edge of your ruler; you won't be using this piece. Move the ruler across the fabric, cutting parallel strips in the width stated in the directions, as shown in **Diagram 1.** If using dressmaker's shears, mark a 45-degree angle with a protractor, then mark bias strip lines across the width of your fabric in the same manner as for rotary cutting.

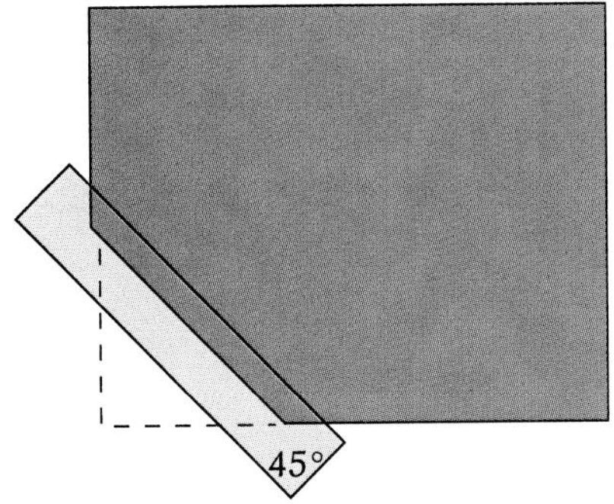

Diagram 1

For both methods, sew the short ends of the bias strips together to make one long bias strip. The project's directions instruct you to prepare piping or binding 2 inches longer than the actual perimeter measurement to allow for ease around corners and joining the ends.

Making Bias Binding: Once your bias strips are joined, fold the strip in half lengthwise with wrong sides together and press.

Attaching Binding: Place the binding on the right side of the project top, aligning the raw edges and having the folded edge of the binding opposite the project's edge. Beginning a few inches from the corner on one side of the project, leave about 3 inches of the binding free and start sewing the binding to the project, using a ¼-inch seam allowance.

For projects with curved edges, sew the binding around the entire project. For projects with four corners, like wallhangings, stop stitching exactly ¼ inch in from the raw edge of the project. Backstitch and remove the project from the sewing machine. Fold the binding up and away from the corner, forming a 45-degree fold, as shown in **Diagram 2.** Then fold the binding strip back down and align the raw edges with the adjacent side. Begin the stitching on the next side ¼ inch in from the corner. This provides the fullness necessary to bring the binding to the back side of the project. Miter all corners in the same manner.

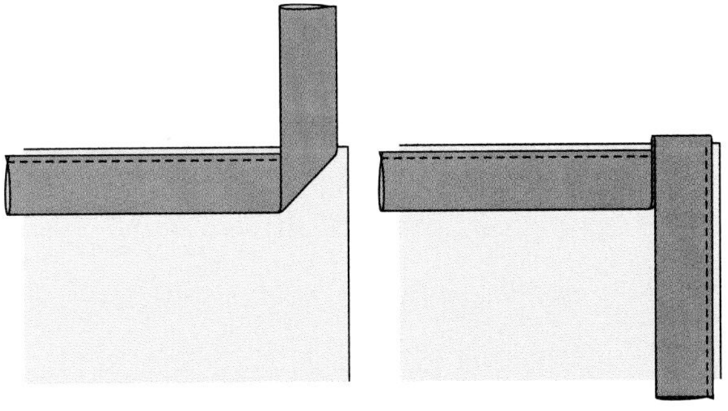

Diagram 2

For both curved projects and projects with corners, stop sewing as you approach the point where you began attaching the binding and backstitch. Overlap the folded beginning of one binding strip with the end of the other binding strip, as shown in **Diagram 3.** Sew across this overlapped section to complete the seam, allowing the end of the binding strip to extend approximately ½ inch beyond the beginning of the binding strip. Trim the excess fabric even with the seam allowance.

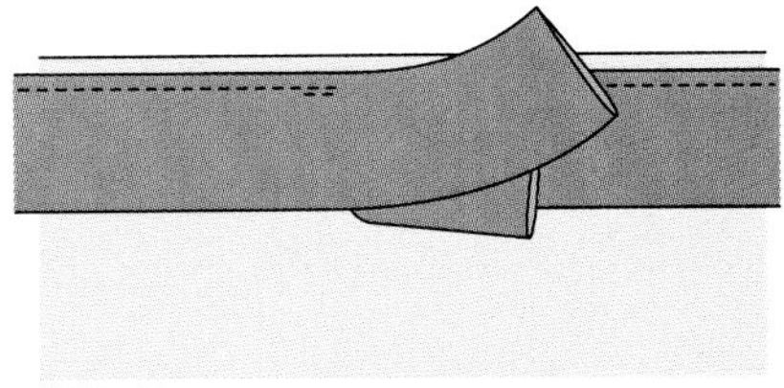

Diagram 3

Bring the binding to the back of the project and slip-stitch the folded edge in place, covering the machine stitches. At each corner, fold in the adjacent sides of the binding and then make several stitches in the miter, as shown in **Diagram 4.** In the same manner, add several stitches to the mitered corners on the front of the project.

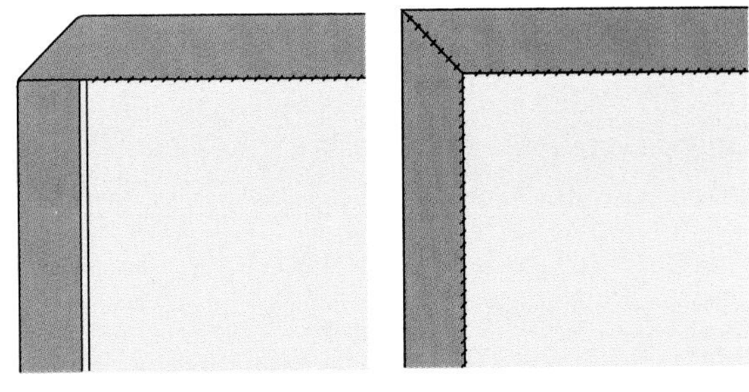

Diagram 4

Attaching Ruffles: Gather the ruffle to fit the pillow top perimeter. With the right sides together and raw edges even, pin the ruffle evenly around the pillow top edges, using the pins as quarter-point guides. Sew the ruffle to the pillow top, using a ¼-inch seam allowance.

Covered Pillow Forms: With the right sides together, sew the two muslin pieces together, leaving an opening along one edge. Clip the corners diagonally. Turn the cover right side out and stuff. Slip-stitch the opening closed.

Assembling a Pillow: With the right sides together, place the pillow top and pillow back together, then sew around the outer edge, leaving an opening along the bottom edge. Grade the seam allowances. Turn the pillow to the right side. Insert the pillow form into the pillow and slip-stitch the opening closed.

CROSS-STITCH

Cross-stitch is a very popular needlework technique and can be sprinkled on numerous bazaar projects to add a handmade touch. It's a good idea to take a few practice stitches before beginning any project to test the number of floss strands in the fabric you're using; since bazaar crafting often allows you to use up scraps, you may have slightly different results from what's shown in the photograph in this book.

Fabric: Evenweave fabrics have been designed especially for embroidery since they are woven with the same number of vertical and horizontal threads per inch. The number of stitches per inch—or count—of any evenweave fabric determines the size of a finished design. The more stitches per inch, the smaller the design.

To prevent the fabric from raveling, overcast the edges by hand or zigzag the edges by machine. Or you may apply liquid ravel preventer (available at fabric stores) along the edges. Do *not* use masking tape; it leaves a very sticky residue.

Embroidery Floss and Tapestry Needles: Any six-strand embroidery floss can be used for cross-stitch. The floss is divided and each project lists the number of strands to use. I list color numbers for the three largest floss manufacturers for each cross-stitch project when applicable. Each brand, however, has its own color range, so these suggestions are not perfect color matches. There are also metallic and specialty flosses available.

Cut your floss into comfortable working lengths of approximately 18 inches. When you stitch, the floss strands tend to twist; allow your needle to hang freely from your work to untwist. Do not carry your floss across the back of your work for more than ¼ inch since it could show through to the front. If you are using dark floss on a light fabric, end your length instead of carrying it across the back.

Cross-stitch should be worked with a blunt-point tapestry needle. Your needle should slip between the fabric threads as you stitch. Use a size 22 or 24 tapestry needle for 8-, 11-, and 14-count fabrics, and a size 24 or 26 for 16-, 18-, and 22-count fabrics.

Charted Designs: Counted cross-stitch designs are worked from charts. Each square on a chart represents one cross-stitch. Each chart also gives the number of horizontal and vertical stitches in the design. The symbol in each square represents the floss color used. Each chart is accompanied by a Color Key that gives the floss color number. If a color name appears without a symbol, the color is only used for decorative stitches or is mentioned in the text because of a special usage.

Starting to Stitch: Unless otherwise directed, center your design on the fabric. Follow the arrows at the bottom and side of a charted design to find the center. Count the fabric threads or fold the fabric in quarters to find its center; mark the center with a straight pin.

Thread your tapestry needle with the number of strands indicated. Bring the threaded needle from the back of the fabric to the front. Hold an inch of the floss end against the back, then anchor it with your first few stitches. To end your thread or begin a new one, weave the floss through the backs of several stitches. Do not knot your floss.

The Stitches: A single cross-stitch is formed in two motions. Following the numbering in the

Cross-Stitch Diagram, bring your threaded needle up at 1, down at 2, up at 3, and down at 4, completing one cross-stitch.

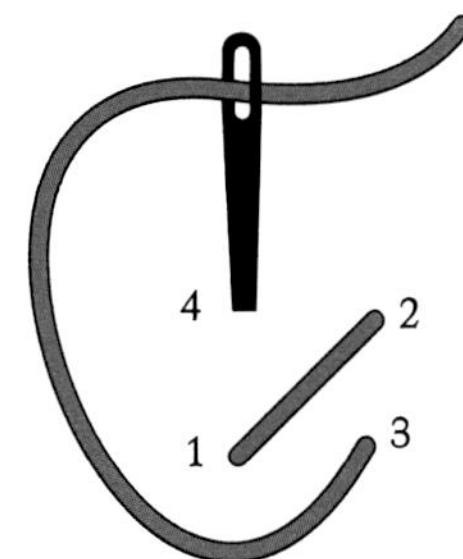

Cross-Stitch Diagram

A backstitch is worked after all other cross-stitches are completed. Each project's directions will state which floss colors to use for back-stitching. The chart will indicate where to place backstitches and how long each backstitch should be. The **Backstitch Diagram** shows how to make a series of backstitches. Bring your needle up at the odd numbers and down at the even numbers.

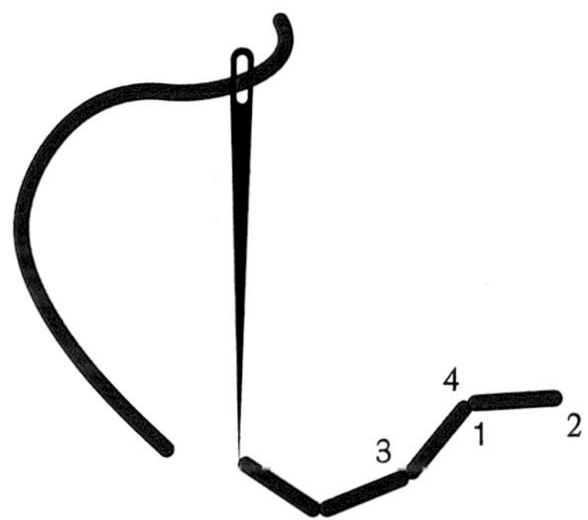

Backstitch Diagram

A French knot adds dimension to a cross-stitch piece and is often used to signify an eye, a flower center, or a textured surface. Bring the thread up where indicated on the chart by the large dot. Wrap the floss once around the needle and reinsert it close to where the thread came up. Hold the wrapping thread tightly, close to the surface of the fabric. Pull the needle through, letting the thread go just as the knot is formed; see the **French Knot Diagram.**

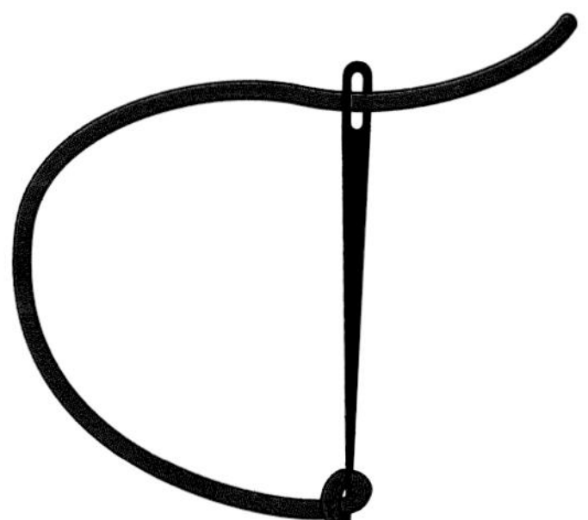

French Knot Diagram

Washing and Pressing: When you have finished stitching, wash your piece in lukewarm water with mild soap and rinse well. Do not scrub. Roll the embroidery in a clean towel to remove the excess moisture. Place the completed cross-stitch face down on a dry, clean terry cloth towel. Press it carefully until the piece is dry and smooth.

Needlepoint

Needlepoint is enjoying a resurgence among needlecrafters. For many years, the emphasis at bazaars was on quickie crafts, but shoppers have rediscovered the beauty of more intricate designs and are willing to pay more for quality projects to give as gifts or to decorate their homes.

Canvas: Needlepoint canvas comes in many varieties and counts. Check your local needlework store for advice on choosing appropriate canvases and yarns. Bind all raw edges of your needlepoint canvas with white artist's tape before you begin to stitch to prevent raveling.

Tapestry Wools, Yarns, and Needles: Most tapestry wools and needlepoint yarns come in plies; you can separate plies to achieve the best coverage for your chosen canvas. Cut strands into 18-inch lengths. When crafting projects for your bazaar, you can use up scrap skeins or small lengths of wools and yarns; just be sure that the yarn weights are identical or very close matches to give a uniform look to your work.

Blunt-end tapestry needles with long, open eyes are best to use. Needles range in size from fairly fine to large rug needles. Choose a needle with an eye large enough to accommodate the yarn, but not larger than needed.

Charted Designs: Needlepoint designs are worked from charts. Each square on a chart represents one stitch. Each chart also gives you the number of horizontal and vertical stitches in the design. The symbol in each square of the chart represents the tapestry wool or yarn color used. Each chart is accompanied by a Color Key that gives the tapestry wool's or yarn's color number. If a color name appears without a symbol, the color is only used for decorative stitches or is mentioned in the text because of a special usage.

Starting to Stitch: Unless otherwise directed, center your design on the canvas. Follow the arrows at the bottom and side of a charted design to find the center. Count the canvas threads or fold the canvas in quarters to find its center; mark the center with a straight pin.

Thread your tapestry needle with the number of strands indicated. Bring the threaded needle from the back of the canvas to the front of the canvas. Hold an inch of the tapestry wool's or yarn's end against the back, then anchor it with your first few stitches. To end the length or begin a new one, weave the wool or yarn through the backs of several stitches; do not knot it.

The Stitches: The basketweave, or diagonal, stitch is worked by bringing the needle out at the lower left of an intersection that has the horizontal thread of canvas on top, then in at the upper right of an intersection and out again two threads to the left, completing the first stitch and beginning a second one. Complete the second stitch, then work the third stitch down and to the right, as shown in the **Basketweave Stitch Diagrams,** completing a second row. Continue diagonally upward and work fourth, fifth, and sixth stitches for a third row. Work the fourth row diagonally downward. Continue working to the left in diagonal rows, alternating "up" rows with "down" rows. Make sure that all "up" row stitches cross canvas intersections with a horizontal thread on top and all "down" row stitches cross intersections with a vertical thread on top. Do not turn your work as you stitch.

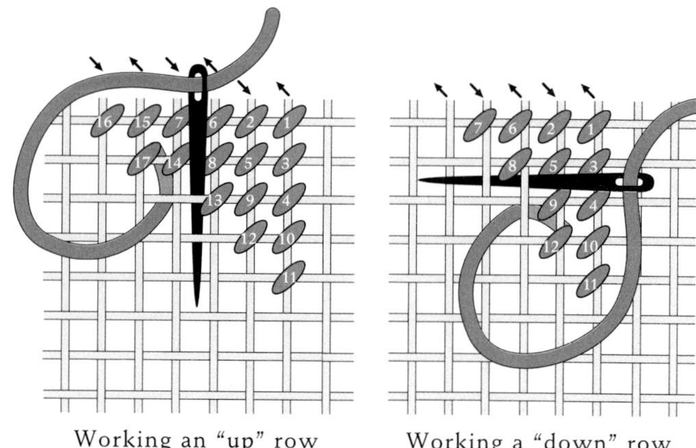

Basketweave Stitch Diagrams

The continental stitch is worked by bringing the needle from the back to the front at the lower left of a thread intersection, then in at the upper right of an intersection and out again two threads to the left and one down, completing the first stitch and beginning the second. Continue to the left in a straight line; see the **Continental Stitch Diagram.** At the end of the first row, turn the canvas (and chart) 180 degrees and work from the right to the left again for the second row. Be sure to turn your work after each row.

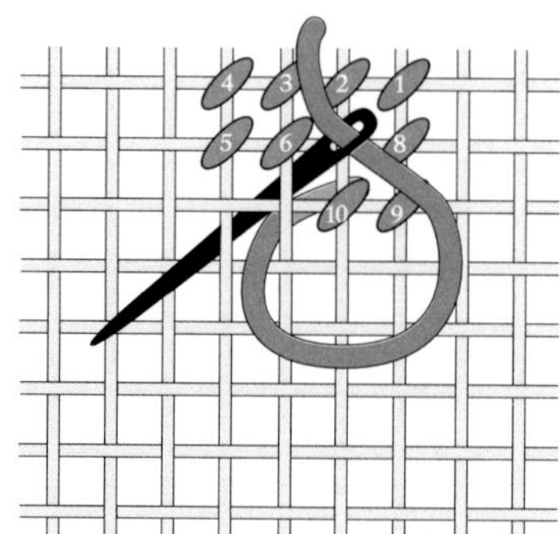

Continental Stitch Diagram

Blocking: To block the needlepoint when completed, mist the finished piece with cool water. Do not soak the canvas. Staple the piece to a blocking board, pulling the canvas taut and square as you go. Allow it to dry flat.

Stitch Details

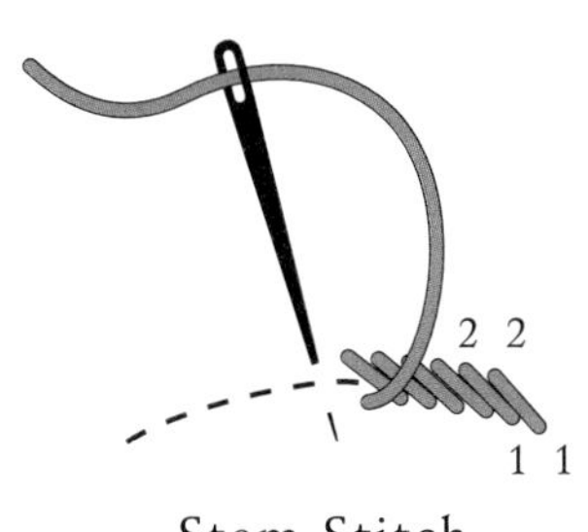

Stem Stitch

2
2
1
1

Outline Stitch

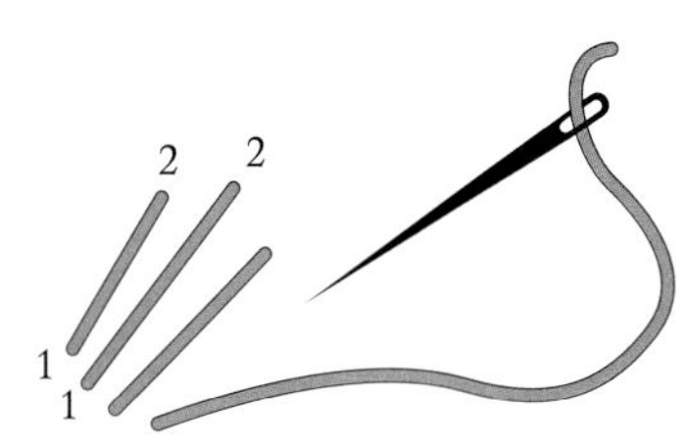

Straight Stitch

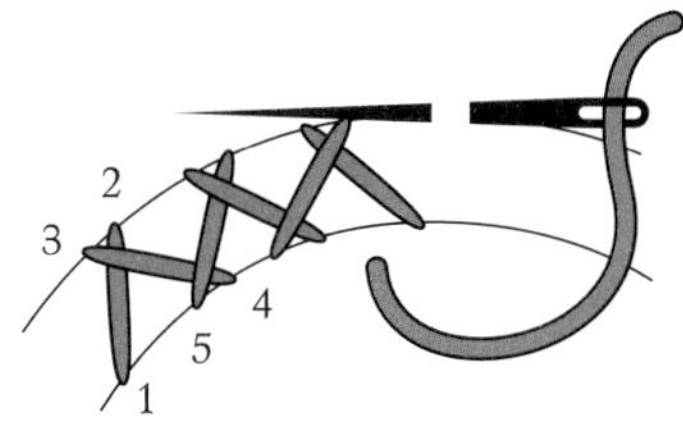

Herringbone Stitch

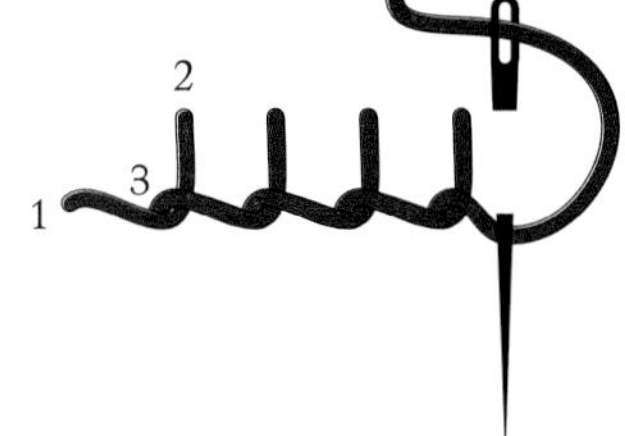

Blanket Stitch

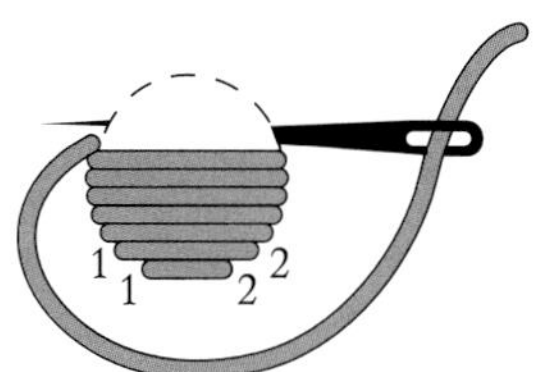

Satin Stitch

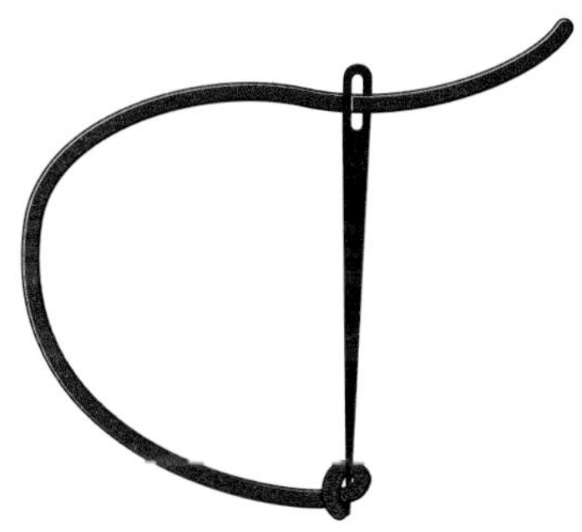
French Knot

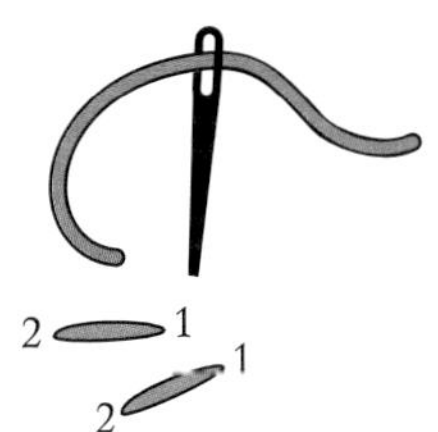

Long Stitch

Featherstitch

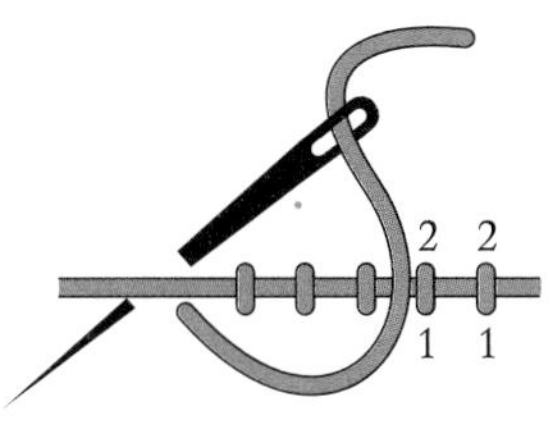

Couching Stitch

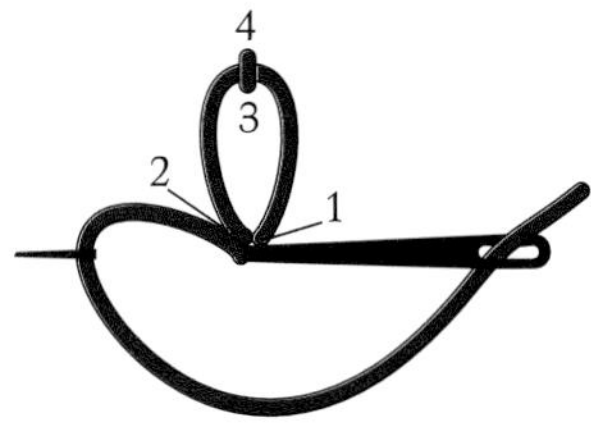

Lazy Daisy Stitch

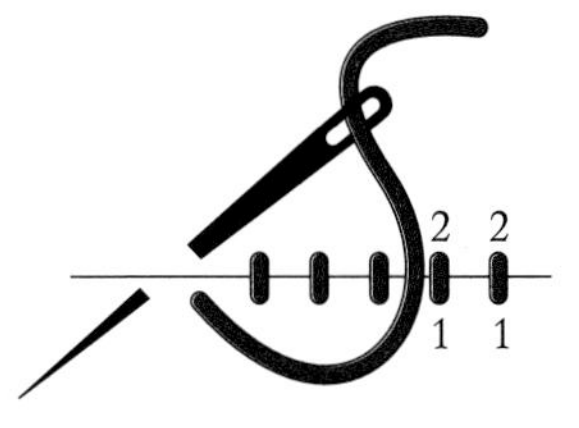

Slip-Stitch

Buyer's Guide

The following companies offer products that are featured within this book.

Anchor
C. J. Bates & Sons
P.O. Box E, Route 9A
Chester, CT 06412
Embroidery floss

Charles Craft, Inc.
P.O. Box 1049
Laurinburg, NC 28353
Prefinished accessories, including cross-stitch hand and fingertip towels

Coats & Clark
Consumer Service
P.O. Box 27067
Greenville, SC 29616
(800) 648-1479
Knitting yarns and crochet threads

Colonial Candles of Cape Cod
Hyannis, MA 02601
(800) 343-4534
Candles

Craft & Needlework Age
225 Gordons Corner Plaza
Box 420
Manalapan, NJ 07726
Craft & Needlework Age Annual Directory

Decart
Lamoille Industrial Park
Box 309
Morrisville, VT 05661
(802) 888-4217
Deka Translucent Waterbase Glass Paint

The DMC Corporation
Port Kearny Building #10
South Kearny, NJ 07032-0650
(201) 589-0606
Embroidery floss and needlepoint yarns

Duncan Enterprises
5673 East Shields Avenue
Fresno, CA 93727
(209) 291-4444
Quik-Crackle

Freudenberg Nonwovens
20 Industrial Avenue
Chelmsford, MA 01824
(508) 454-0461
Fusible webs and fleece

J. & P. Coats
Consumer Service
P.O. Box 27067
Greenville, SC 29616
(800) 648-1479
Embroidery floss and crochet threads

JHB International
1955 South Quince Street
Denver, CO 80231
(303) 751-8100
Buttons

Kate's Paperie
8 West 13th Street
New York, NY 10011
(212) 633-0570
Decorative oriental and colored papers

Kunin Felt
380 Lafayette Road
P.O. Box 5000
Hampton, NH 03842
(800) 292-7900
Felt fabric and squares

Modern Options, Inc.
2325 Third Street, Suite 339
San Francisco, CA 94107
(415) 243-0357
Patina Blue Liquid Finishing Solution

National Nonwovens
P.O. Box 150
Easthampton, MA 01027
(800) 234-1039
Felt fabric and squares

C. M. Offray & Son, Inc.
360 Route 24
Chester, NJ 07930-0601
(908) 879-4700
Decorative ribbons

Plaid Enterprises
1649 International Court
Box 7600
Norcross, GA 30091
(404) 923-8200
Mod Podge Acrylic Decoupage Medium

D. A. Rinedollar Blacksmith Shop
P.O. Box 348
Clarksville, MO 63336
Iron topiary tree

3M
Commercial Office Supply Division
St. Paul, MN 55144-1000
Spray-Mount Artist's Adhesive

Tulip Paint
A Division of Polymerics
24 Prime Park Way, 4th Floor
Natick, MA 01760
(508) 650-5400
Fabric and puff paints, including Colorpoint paint

Leo Uhlfelder Co.
Mount Vernon, NY 10553
Lucco Brand Quick-Drying Gold Sizing

Weston Bowl Mill
P.O. Box 218
Weston, VT 05161
(802) 824-6219
Wooden acorns, bowls, and trays

Woodworker's Store
21801 Industrial Boulevard
Rogers, MN 55374-9514
(800) 279-4441
Behlen Salad Bowl Finish

Zweigart Inc.
Weston Canal Plaza
2 Riverside Drive
Somerset, NJ 08873
(201) 271-1949
Cross-stitch fabrics and natural linens

Acknowledgments

I owe a great deal of gratitude to several people who worked closely with me during the writing of this book. First, I must mention my wife, Lynn, who put up with countless bags of craft supplies, piles of in-progress projects, and ceiling-high stacks of boxes scattered throughout our tiny apartment for oh-so-many months. Her support and advice, not to mention her stitching skills, have been very helpful and, for too often, silently appreciated.

I also owe many thanks to my dear friend and crafting cohort Abby Ruoff. Many's the idea we've tossed about, and many's the project that we've created in a fit of artistic frenzy. I appreciate her creative contributions to these pages, as well as her undying friendship and support.

Thanks to my mother, Betty, for coming to my aid to cross-stitch and knit several projects in this book. Her unselfish readiness to assist me is a pleasure, and her support and desire to back me in whatever I choose to do is greatly appreciated.

Margaret Sindelar, a seamstress extraordinaire, is responsible for sewing the Holiday Baby Bibs and St. Nicholas Place Mat, as well as the "Bringing in the Tree" Wallhanging from my sketches. I admire her ability to decipher my notes and to turn them into handsome finished pieces, and I am thankful that she could fit me into her busy sewing schedule.

The colorful photographs and golden lighting that show off the projects on these pages would not have been possible without photographer Michael Watson. I have greatly enjoyed working with him on this project and on others over the past few years. I know I can always count on him for an agreeable smile, pleasant attitude, and splendid work even though I'm constantly pressing and rushing so we can get another shot done.

Thanks, too, to all the people at Rodale Press for giving me this marvelous opportunity and for trusting and believing in my abilities. Marta Strait, whose thoughtful design enhances every project, and Karen Bolesta, my editor on this book, assisted in grueling photo shoot after grueling photo shoot of the projects. A special "Thank You" goes to Karen for her constant enthusiasm and continual encouragement, patience, and understanding during this project; she always made me feel like somebody special.

A note of appreciation to Joan Barry, Edward Lehrman, and Pastor Richard L. Bruckart of the Emmaus Moravian Church for their kindness and assistance on a snowy winter day.

Thank you to the New Hope–Solebury Home and School Association for sharing their crafts bazaar poster.

And last, but not least, my heartfelt gratitude to Ann E. Smith for her technical assistance and jolly disposition during a tight deadline.

Design Credits

Beaded Stars, "Junk" Jewelry Kissing Ball, and Decorator Flowerpots: Abby Ruoff

Crocheted Choirboy: Michael Cannarozzi for Coats & Clark

Warm Woolen Mittens: Elizabeth Williams

All others: Jim Williams

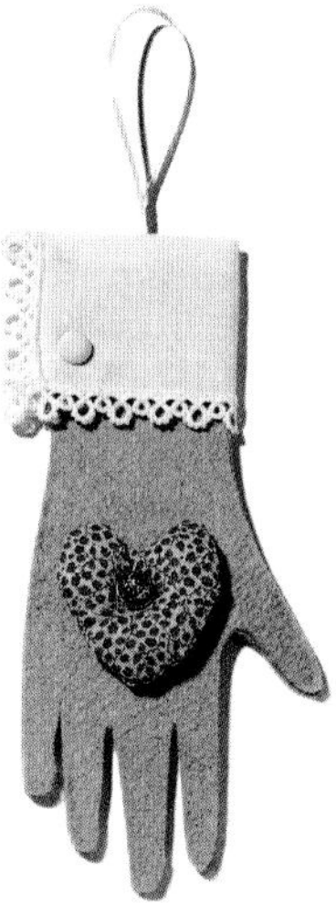